# THE LITTLE BIGHORN CAMPAIGN

*Lieutenant Colonel George A. Custer, April 1876. "If I were an Indian," wrote Custer, "I often think[,] I would greatly prefer to cast my lot among those of my people adhered to the free open plains rather than submit to the confined limits of a reservation, there to be the recipient of the blessed benefits of civilization, with its vices thrown in without stint or measure."*

# GREAT CAMPAIGNS SERIES

*The Atlanta Campaign*
*The Chancellorsville Campaign*
*The Gettysburg Campaign*
*The Little Bighorn Campaign*
*The Philadelphia Campaign*
*The Peninsula Campaign*
*The Wilderness Campaign*

GREAT CAMPAIGNS

# THE LITTLE BIGHORN CAMPAIGN

## *March–September 1876*

**Wayne Michael Sarf**

COMBINED
BOOKS

# PUBLISHER'S NOTE

Combined Books, Inc., is dedicated to publishing books of distinction in history and military history. We are proud of the quality of writing and the quantity of information found in our books. Our books are manufactured with style and durability and are printed on acid-free paper. We like to think of our books as soldiers: not infantry grunts, but well dressed and well equipped avant garde. Our logo reflects our commitment to the modern and yet historic art of bookmaking.

We call ourselves Combined Books because we view the publishing enterprise as a "combined" effort of authors, publishers and readers. And we promise to bridge the gap between us–a gap which is all too seldom closed in contemporary publishing.

We would like to hear from our readers and invite you to write to us at our offices in Pennsylvania with your reactions, queries, comments, even complaints. All of your correspondence will be answered directly by a member of the Editorial Board or by the author.

We encourage all of our readers to purchase our books from their local booksellers, and we hope that you let us know of booksellers in your area that might be interested in carrying our books. If you are unable to find a book in your area, please write to us.

For information, address:
COMBINED BOOKS, INC.
151 East 10th Avenue
Conshohocken, PA 19428

*Library of Congress Cataloging-in-Publication Data*
Sarf, Wayne Michael, 1957-
    The Little Bighorn campaign, March-September 1876/ Wayne Michael Sarf.—1st ed.
        p.    cm. — (Great campaigns)
    Includes bibliographical references and index.
    ISBN 0-938289-21-7
    1. Dakota Indians—Wars, 1876. 2. Little Bighorn, Battle of the, 1876.
3. Cheyenne Indians—Wars, 1876. I. Title. II. Series.
E83.876.S24 1993
973.8'2—dc20                                                         92-31839

First Edition      1  2  3  4  5
Printed in Hong Kong

Maps by Robert L. Pigeon, III

*To my parents—for being so patient*

# Acknowledgments

In addition to the vast legion of scholars and "buffs" whose writings and conversations have provided intellectual stimulation, the author would like to thank the following. That distinguished military historian, Dr. Albert A. Nofi, first suggested that I contribute to the "Great Campaigns" series. Joseph Fox supplied source materials, and Father Vincent A. Heier valuable "sidebar" suggestions. Kitty Belle Deernose, Museum Curator of the Little Bighorn Battlefield National Monument, energetically pursued illustrations with which to enhance the volume. Major General Hoyt S. Vandenberg, USAF (Ret.), lent his expertise in the field of Victorian weaponry, while W. Donald Horn offered an expert's comments on the Little Bighorn fight. Special thanks are due Gary B. Gouin, who graciously applied his erudition and analytical powers to the manuscript.

The photograph on page 227 is from the Western History Collections, University of Oklahoma Library. All other photographs appear with the kind courtesy of the Little Bighorn Battlefield National Monument.

# A Note on Nomenclature

One of the minor debates surrounding Custer's last battle concerns the proper spelling of its site's name. I have compromised by using the government-favored "Little Bighorn" in the main text and "Little Big Horn" (as well as the contemporary "Little Horn") when quoting accounts using these instead.

The U.S. Army's system of "brevet rank," under which officers could boast ranks higher than those in which they actually served, is decidedly confusing. Officers were frequently addressed by their highest rank not merely socially, but also in official situations and even official correspondence. Many had actually held such ranks in the great volunteer armies of the Civil War period; thus Lieutenant Colonel George Armstrong Custer not only held the rank of brevet major general and brevet major general of volunteers, but had actually served as a major general of volunteers while retaining his Regular Army rank of captain. However, his two brevets as major general came when he was still only a serving brigadier! Apart from the famous example of General Custer, I have routinely referred to officers by their active rank.

In 1876 cavalry troops were still officially known as "companies," and squadrons as "battalions." However, both "squadron" and "troop" were sometimes used unofficially, as well as by contemporaries writing later of the campaign. Times have been rendered on a 24-hour basis.

# Contents

## Maps

# Sidebars

# Preface to the Series

*J*onathan Swift termed war "that mad game the world so loves to play." He had a point. Universally condemned, it has nevertheless been almost as universally practiced. For good or ill, war has played a significant role in the shaping of history. Indeed, there is hardly a human institution which has not in some fashion been influenced and molded by war, even as it helped shaped and mold war in turn. Yet the study of war has been as remarkably neglected as its practice commonplace. With a few outstanding exceptions, the history of wars and of military operations has until quite recently been largely the province of the inspired patriot or the regimental polemist. Only in our times have serious, detailed and objective accounts come to be considered the norm in the treatment of military history and related matters.

Yet there still remains a gap in the literature, for there are two types of military history. One type is written from a very serious, highly technical, professional perspective and presupposes that the reader is deeply familiar with the background, technology, and general situation. The other is perhaps less dry, but merely lightly reviews the events with the intention of informing and entertaining the layman. The qualitative gap between the last two is vast. Moreover, there are professionals in both the military and academia whose credentials are limited to particular moments in the long, sad history of war, and there are laymen who have more than a passing understanding of the field; and then there is the concerned citizen, interested in understanding the phenomena in an age of unusual violence and unprecedented armaments. It is to bridge the gap between the two types of military history, and to reach the professional and the serious amateur and the concerned citizen alike, that this series, GREAT CAMPAIGNS, is designed. Each volume in GREAT CAMPAIGNS is thus not merely an account of a particular military operation, but it is a unique reference to the theory and practice of war in the period in question.

The GREAT CAMPAIGNS series is a distinctive contribution to the study of war and of military history, which will remain of value for many years to come.

# Introduction

"*T*he early morning was bright," recalled Captain Edward S. Godfrey, "as we ascended to the top of the highest point whence the whole field came into view, with the sun at our backs. 'What are those?' exclaimed several as they looked out upon what appeared to be white boulders. Nervously I took the field glasses and glanced at the objects; then almost dropped them, and laconically said, 'The dead!' Captain Weir who was sitting near on his horse, exclaimed, 'Oh, how white they look! How white!'...everything of value was taken away; arms, ammunition, equipment, and clothing. Occasionally, there was a body with a bloody undershirt or trousers or socks, but the name was invariably cut out. The naked mutilated bodies, with their bloody fatal wounds, were nearly unrecognizable...."

Such was the wreckage of Custer's immediate command after the battle of the Little Bighorn—the climax of the Sioux campaign of 1876. The campaign itself would prove the high point of Indian warfare on the Great Plains, and the greatest display of Sioux and Cheyenne prowess in solidarity against the white man, while the annihilation of five companies of the 7th Cavalry would prove to be the U.S. Army's greatest battlefield defeat at the hands of Western Indians.

Yet even the greatest Indian victory could only briefly postpone the inevitable. The military's casualties, however shocking and tragic, were a pinprick to a great industrializing nation. Under normal circumstances, such a failure might seem merely an embarrassment, to be quickly forgotten—

though in 1876 President Grant could reflect, if he so chose, that a mere 11 years after his acceptance of Lee's surrender as head of the world's mightiest fighting force, the U.S. Army had been thwarted by a few thousand nomadic hunters. But Custer's defeat would endure in legend.

True, military disasters are often better remembered than brilliant victories. Yet even by the standards of past Indian warfare, the Army's failures were neither unprecedented nor uniquely horrific. In the Ohio territory of 1791, U.S. forces under General Arthur St. Clair had suffered their greatest losses in Indian warfare at the hand of Little Turtle's Miamis, with over 600 slain. But "St. Clair's Defeat" is barely remembered at all.

Why then has this campaign inspired such a vast literature, and compelled such fascination over the last century? Perhaps the answer lies in a timely confluence of mystery, myth, and mass communication. Mighty warriors—Custer, Sitting Bull, Crazy Horse— rode directly from their contemporaries' consciousness into the mists of legend. Unlike the epic figures of earlier ages, however, they would remain recognizably historical figures. From Colonel Joseph J. Reynolds' precipitous retreat from his Powder River attack to the last sputtering gasps of the Army's vain pursuit, the campaign generated controversy, with even the elaborate distortions surrounding the Little Bighorn tragedy—what Colonel W.A. Graham termed "The Custer Myth"—rooted in the massive documentation of a literate, newspaper age.

If we believe, as did the poet Whitman, that Custer's fall was the renewal of an ancient legend, we can still credit Brian W. Dippie's comment that even in 1876, Custer's last stand was "an anachronism." Truly, as an ephemeral frontier melted away like a dream remembered, the day of cavalry combat against nomadic tribesmen was fast coming to an end. But the Great Sioux War would assure that it went out with a blaze of terrible glory.

# CHAPTER I

# Shadows of War

## January-March 1876

Whose was the right and wrong
Sing it, O funeral song
With a voice that is full of tears,
And say that our broken faith
Wrought all this ruin and scathe
In the Year of a Hundred Years.
>—Henry Wadsworth Longfellow,
>*The Revenge of Rain-in-the-Face*

White Americans believed, of course, that all of the Lakota Sioux, like other free-roaming, buffalo-hunting Plains Indians, would soon be confined to reservations. The Fort Laramie treaty of 1868 required that they do so as soon as the buffalo herds vanished from the unceded territories where the Sioux maintained the right to roam. And most of the Sioux were already in conformity with the policy of "concentration," surviving on government rations while occupying reservations in the Dakota Territory and Nebraska. In all, some 25,000 Indians were in some way associated with these agencies.

Under the "peace-policy" announced by General-in-Chief Ulysses S. Grant on the eve of his inauguration as President, the Indian was to be transformed from a hunter and warrior into a peaceful agriculturalist. What the Indians preferred was not relevant, and in this respect, as in many others, Grant's policy was not terribly different from the previous one. As he himself had warned, "Those who do not accept this policy will find the new administration ready for a sharp and severe war policy."

But though pressure from white settlement was increasing, the buffalo herds had not yet vanished. Many Sioux, with their allies among the Northern Cheyennes and Northern Arapahoes, still chose to roam the "unceded" Indian lands of Montana's Powder River country while pursing the congenial path of war against tribal enemies and, less frequently, white settlers sometimes located far from any claimed Sioux lands. Other Indians, nominally enrolled at agencies, divided their time between drawing government rations and joining the non-treaty bands in the free hunter's life of the Plains; wintering at the agencies, they remained the most disruptive element on the reservations. The summer roamers, complained Colonel David S. Stanley, "abuse the agents, threaten their lives, kill their cattle at night, and do anything they can

*Miners discovered Black Hills gold at Custer's Golden Valley camp in July 1874. Seventh Cavalry lieutenant James Calhoun thought it a "great pity that this rich country should remain in a wild state, uncultivated and uninhabited by civilized men."*

*The Peace Commission photographed at Fort Laramie in 1868 brought a treaty yielding to the demands of Red Cloud and abandoning three forts on the Bozeman Trail—even as white emigration and the railroad continued to hem in the Indian. Pictured, left to right, are Generals A.H. Terry, W.S. Harney, and W.T. Sherman, an unidentified Sioux woman, Indian Commissioner N.G. Taylor, Mr. S.F. Tappan, and General C.C. Augur.*

to oppose the civilizing process, but eat all the provisions they can get."

Unlike these quasi-agency Indians, the Hunkpapa Sioux medicine man Sitting Bull openly bid defiance to the whites, desired contact with them only for trading purposes, and had never signed a treaty. "You are fools," he told the so-called "Laramie Loafers" or "Hang-Around-the-Forts" clinging year-round to the agencies, "to make yourselves slaves to a piece of fat bacon, some hard-tack, and a little sugar and coffee." Such determination attracted such equally bold spirits as Crazy Horse of the Oglalas.

Meanwhile the whites continued to irritate the Sioux. In 1873 the Northern Pacific railway reached the Missouri River

# Sitting Bull

Born along the Grand River of what was to become South Dakota sometime between 1831 and 1834, the Oglala boy nicknamed "Slow" counted coup on his first Crow enemy at age 14. He thus won from his father the new name Tatanka Iyotake, Sitting Bull, more correctly "Buffalo Bull Sitting Down."

At the age of 20, he was invited to join the Brave or Strong Hearts, an *akicita* or warrior society which he came to dominate. Sitting Bull acquired his well-known limp in 1856 while killing a Crow chief hand-to-hand, a bullet striking his left foot. He waged war only against Indian enemies until 1862, the year Minnesota's Santee Sioux, angered by a government failure to provide needed food, rose up to massacre hundreds of settlers. When his Hunkpapas, migrating east of the Missouri to hunt, camped with Santee Sioux refugees from the Army's follow-up campaign, the combined camps were attacked. The following year General Alfred Sully marched against both the Santees and their Teton cousins.

Henceforth Sitting Bull's Hunkpapas considered themselves at war with the palefaces. Since their lands were not directly threatened, they took no part in Red Cloud's War. But Sitting Bull raided extensively in the Dakotas, reportedly saying in 1867: "I have killed, robbed, and injured too many white men to believe in a good peace. They are medicine, and I would eventually die a lingering death. I had rather die on the field of battle....Look at me; see if I am poor, or my people either. The whites may get me at last...but I will have good times until then." Sitting Bull could not be accused of breaking any treaties since, as one scholar pointed out, he never signed any.

"He had a big brain and a good one," recalled one old Lakota warrior, "a strong heart and a generous one." Paleface opinion, as might be expected, was sometimes mixed. In 1868, when his celebrity was still local, Colonel Philippe Régis de Trobriand considered him "one of the most dangerous and evil Indians in Dakota", adding: "His fierceness is masked by a good-natured manner and a conversation abounding in good humor. To judge by appearances one would believe him to be

and extended "the iron road" toward the Yellowstone Valley, promising an even faster influx of whites and destruction of Indian game. Grant's successor as commanding general, William Tecumseh Sherman, observed to General Philip H. Sheridan, commanding the Division of the Missouri, that the Army should support the railroad even though it would

the most harmless of the redskins. In reality, he is a ferocious beast who seems to be laughing when he is showing his teeth." Reporter John F. Finerty, seeing him in 1879, testified to his "strong personal magnetism," and "fine aboriginal countenance," adding that "once seen, he can never be forgotten. I heard his voice many times—deep, guttural, but at the same time melodious." With two hot skirmishes against Custer's cavalry on the Yellowstone in 1873, Sitting Bull gained increasing fame as the leader of the Indian resistance. Distinguishing him from a friendly Oglala chief, Custer himself observed: "You know there are two Sitting Bulls. This one (the Hunkpapa) has never been in an agency and is a dangerous character."

In May 1877, Sitting Bull avoided pressure from U.S. troops by leading his followers across the "Medicine Line" into Canada, where other bands joined him. But with the buffalo dwindling, even Sitting Bull finally had to submit; surrendering in 1881, he was unjustly sent with his small band to Fort Randall as a prisoner of war. By now Sitting Bull's fame was

such that an officer was assigned to translate his mail from the French and German.

Reunited with the Hunkpapas at the Standing Rock Agency in 1883, Sitting Bull commenced a battle of wills with agent James McLaughlin as leader of the so-called "nonprogressives." In 1885 he toured with Buffalo Bill Cody's Wild West exhibition, selling autographed photos, and giving his spare earnings to some of the many poor people he met in the streets of the white man's cities.

Fiercely opposing the 1889 reduction of the Great Sioux Reservation, Sitting Bull may have endorsed the subsequent Ghost Dance movement more as a rallying point of Sioux resistance than out of conviction. In any case, Agent McLaughlin ordered his arrest. On 15 December 1890, Sitting Bull refused to mount his horse when arrested by Indian policemen. A supporter, sparking a fight that would cost the lives of 14 Sioux on both sides, fatally shot Lieutenant Bull Head. Bull Head in turn shot Sitting Bull—and Sergeant Red Tomahawk fired another bullet into the back of the unarmed man's head.

---

prove troublesome, as "it will help bring the Indian problem to a final solution." Support consisted partly of military escorts for railroad surveying parties, and in 1873 the 7th U.S. Cavalry under Lieutenant Colonel (Brevet Major General) George Armstrong Custer, as part of Colonel Stanley's Yellowstone expedition, had several brisk fights with followers of Sitting Bull. In 1874 Custer's Black Hills expedition explored deep into that half-fabulous realm of the Dakotas, guaranteed to the Sioux not as temporarily "unceded" land, but as part of their permanent reservation.

General Sheridan had desired the reconnaissance largely to establish possible sites for a post deemed necessary to control the non-treaty Sioux. But the two "practical miners" with the expedition also discovered small amounts of gold. While Custer was officially cautious about further prospects, a second Army expedition in 1875 affirmed that the gold could be found in paying quantities. Lieutenant John G. Bourke, this column's engineer officer, noted that the Sioux non-occupants used the Hills only for gathering lodgepoles and expressed the widespread belief that "this magnificent country ought not, in justice to ourselves, be...sequestered from the national domain."

Custer himself recommended extinguishing Indian title "at the earliest moment practicable for military reasons," though also insisting that until that time the military would do its duty in repelling white trespassers. But the gold rush had already begun. Hundreds, then thousands, of well-armed miners boldly defied the Sioux and erected such far-flung mining camps as Custer City and the legendary Deadwood.

While the Army vainly tried to stem the inrush, the government attempted to purchase the Hills from the Sioux. In September, 1875, a special commission journeyed to a council ground between the camps of agency chiefs Red Cloud and Spotted Tail, hoping to get three-fourths of all adult male Sioux to assent. But even the reservation chiefs willing to consider selling the Hills thought the Great Father in Washington a miser for offering a mere $6,000,000 for outright sale, or $400,000 per year to lease. Younger men from the northern hunting bands would tolerate no cession whatsoever and openly threatened violence against potential signers. Crazy Horse's friend Little Big Man, mounted and armed and stripped for war, boldly told the frock-coated commissioners: "My heart is bad. I have come to kill a white man." In the Hills themselves, scattered interlopers were killed. But

*Sitting Bull in 1881. "I am no chief," he told a journalist. But the Hunkpapa medicine man was the leading spirit among the "nontreaty" Indians who scorned the white man's reservations.*

*The Oglala Sioux war chief Low Dog counted his first coup when he went on the warpath at 14: "I went against the will of my parents and those having authority over me." In this 1881 portrait by D.F. Barry, he seems to embody the very essence of the Plains Indian warrior.*

overall Sioux reaction was consistent with their concept of war as a largely individualistic activity in which long-term planning need play no part; angrily denouncing the invasion, they did almost nothing to stop it, though Sitting Bull's warriors could have made the Hills temporarily untenable for miners.

Then Grant, bowing to the inevitable (much as well-behaved Indians were supposed to do), ordered a change in policy following a November conference at the White House to discuss the "Indian question." Under the premise that settlers would no longer be barred from the unceded Indian territory to the west of the Sioux reservation boundary, miners ostensibly headed there could travel free of interference—"and if some go over the Boundary into the Black Hills," as General Sherman explained, both President and Interior Department would "wink at it for the moment." Furthermore, despite the treaty provision for Sioux use of the Powder and Big Horn river areas, on 6 December 1875 the Commissioner of Indian Affairs issued a fateful ultimatum to "non-treaty" Sioux and all others roaming free: if they did not report to their respective agencies by 31 January 1876, they would be considered "hostile." The deadline was short and the weather bad for traveling, and the free-roamers in any case disinclined to come in. With no discernible response to his message, the Secretary of the Interior, having ordered the ultimatum and thus made the Indian Bureau officially responsible for initiating military action, referred these Indians to the Secretary of War.

Officially, the unsold Black Hills did not influence the decision to abrogate that portion of the treaty permitting the Sioux to roam outside the reservation. Instead, the administration argued that by raiding in the vicinity of the unceded lands, against both whites and friendly Indians such as the Crows, the Sioux had themselves nullified the treaty. But such scattered raids hardly justified the government's illegal actions. Aside from frustration over failing to buy the Black Hills, perhaps those in authority also felt an impatience over the mere fact that powerful bands of armed, warlike Sioux still roamed free, seemingly unhindered by any diminishment of game or advancing line of settlement. In any case, the United States would not wait for the railroad or the irresistible tide of immigration to settle the "Indian problem"

The stage was set. "Unless they are caught before early spring," warned General Sheridan, "they cannot be caught at all." So despite the short deadline given the "hostiles," Sheridan—faced with pursuing warriors over vast stretches of Montana, Wyoming, and the Dakotas—would have preferred launching a winter campaign without even waiting to see if the Sioux would come in. He had first employed this strategy in the winter of 1868-69 against tribes on the Southern Plains, using three columns of troops. Two of them had succeeded in destroying Indian villages, Major Andrew W. Evans' mixed cavalry-infantry force striking the Comanches and Custer's cavalry a Cheyenne village on the Washita River in what is now Oklahoma. Striking when snow immobilized the Indians' villages and left ponies weakened by lack of grass, troopers mounted on grain-fed horses could overcome the warriors' greatest advantage—their mobility. "If a single one of these large villages could be surprised and destroyed in the depth of winter," wrote Bourke hopefully, "the resulting loss of property would be so great that the enemy would suffer for years." But now it seemed too late.

Lacking winter as an ally, Sheridan could still use the strategy of converging columns he had employed both in 1868 and in the Red River War of 1874-75. In the latter campaign against Comanches, Kiowas, Cheyennes, and Arapahoes raiding in Texas and Kansas, no fewer than five columns had marched from north, south, east, and west, forcing thousands of warriors back to their reservations by the spring of 1875—after which "ringleaders" and prominent raiders were exiled to Florida.

In both campaigns, Sheridan had been willing to push the Indians to the limit of their resources with relentless pursuit and the destruction of property; thus, following his battle on the Washita against Chief Black Kettle's snowbound Cheyennes, Custer slaughtered almost 800 ponies and destroyed

Indian lodges, food, and other property. But while Army casualties were light in both campaigns, the other costs of such a strategy had been quite high. During the Washita campaign, the inability to stockpile enough forage and punishing marches had killed horses by the hundreds, with Custer's men reduced almost to a starving condition as they doggedly pursued fugitive bands of Indians into the spring of 1869.

The Red River campaign, though launched in summer, likewise witnessed operations teetering on the edge of logistical disaster. At one point, men under Colonel Nelson A. Miles, marching far from any water, opened the veins in their arms and wet their lips with their own blood. But such persistence did succeed in thoroughly demoralizing the foe.

In order to trap the Sioux, two columns were to set out from the Department of Dakota, commanded from St. Paul by Brigadier General Alfred H. Terry, and a third from the Department of the Platte, headquartered at Omaha under Brigadier General George Crook. The columns were not expected to act in precise concert—nor, given the vast area to be covered and the lack of easy communication between columns, could such tidy cooperation be expected. But a column failing to encounter Indians might still serve in the role of beater, driving warriors in toward one or both of the others.

Each column was presumed capable of handling any number of Indians it might encounter, largely because no truly impressive village could long cohere; the available fuel, game, and grass at any one site became depleted too quickly. In 1874, Sheridan had assured a congressional committee that even if the Sioux had three or four thousand warriors in the field, the Army "cannot have any war with Indians because they cannot maintain five hundred men together for three days; they cannot feed them." In any case, experience showed that the Plains warriors generally disdained the sort of stand-up battle craved by the "soldier-chiefs." The Indian Bureau downplayed the number of potential foes, one official insisting that a single regiment of cavalry would suffice.

*A Plains Indian village was a completely portable community, but highly vulnerable to attack in the winter.*

Had the Army struck in deepest winter, it might in fact have found only the 500-800 warriors assumed by the Indian Bureau to be living year round in the unceded territory, sheltered in various scattered camps. But no one knew the total number of agency Indians who might swell this number when good weather came. Many would ultimately leave the agencies due to poor conditions, including inadequate rations.

Sheridan was unable to signal the advance to his department commanders until 8 February, and General Terry received his official orders two days later, delaying the consolidation of the dispersed companies of his most powerful force, the 7th Cavalry. Hoping to begin his march early in April, Terry mused to Sheridan on the 21st: "I think my only plan will be to give Custer a secure base well up on the Yellowstone from which he can operate, at which he can find supplies, and to which he can retire at any time the Indians gather in too great numbers for the small force he will have." But Terry also ordered Colonel John Gibbon to move eastward with all available troops gathered from posts in Montana, hoping to keep any "hostiles" from crossing over to the north bank of the Yellowstone either to hunt or to escape other troops.

Only Crook's column succeeded in leaving its base at Fort Fetterman on the North Platte River before the potentially useful bad weather had lifted, General Crook having prepared his men so carefully for the anticipated cold that his aide, Lieutenant Bourke, devoted six pages of his diary to the special winter clothing issued. Carrying with him 200,000 pounds of fodder, Crook was hopeful that his cavalry mounts could outlast grass-starved Indian ponies. His total strength of 662 enlisted men and 30 officers included his staff, 5 troops each from the 2nd and 3rd Cavalry Regiments, and 2 companies of the 4th Infantry. Besides 86 mule-drawn wagons, 3 or 4 ambulances, and ambulatory beef in the form of 45 head of cattle, Crook had also prepared a mule train. Manned by 62 packers, it featured 5 divisions of 80 mules, 1 division to each 2 companies.

The 31 civilian scouts under Paymaster Major Thaddeus H. Stanton were a colorful collection of white frontiersmen and "mixed-bloods," including such notables as Ben Clark, the "half-breeds" Baptiste "Big Bat" Pourier and Baptiste "Little Bat" Garnier, and even a half-Tahitian named Frank Grouard. Known to the Lakota as "the Grabber," Grouard had spent years among Sitting Bull's Sioux. Major Stanton himself doubled as correspondent for the New York *Tribune*, and Robert A. Strahorn of the Denver *Rocky Mountain News* also accompanied the troops leaving Fort Fetterman. While Crook evidently took an active part in supervising the "Wyoming column," the troops were under the immediate command of 3rd Infantry colonel Joseph J. Reynolds as they drove north on the Bozeman trail.

Crook defined his object as "to move, during the inclement season, by forced marches, carrying by pack animals the most meager supplies, secretly and expeditiously, surprise the hostile bands and, if possible chastise them before spring fairly opened and they could receive re-enforcements from the Agencies...." But he also implied an intent to reconnoitre in force, informing Terry that he planned "to get some idea of the country and difficulties to be overcome in a summer campaign"—and hoped to return to base before "so using up" his livestock as to make them unfit for summer employment. The column marched out on 1 March.

On 2 March, some enterprising Lakotas shot a herder through the lung and stampeded the command's entire beef herd—a serious loss.

The soldiers pushed on under leaden skies, their few bits of uniform dress generally concealed by their outer wrappings. On the evening of 5 March, a small band of Sioux made a harassing attack on the bivouacked troops, a "brisk inter-change of leaden compliments" leaving a corporal slightly wounded.

The next day, the command passed through the pitiful ruins of old Fort Reno, one of the Army posts abandoned after Red Cloud's War in 1867. Lieutenant Bourke noted the graveyard's "half dozen or a dozen broken, dilapidated head-boards to mark the last resting-places of brave soldiers who had fallen in desperate war...that civilization might extend her boundaries." Camping on the Crazy Woman's Fork of the Powder River that evening, Crook sent his wagons and infantry back to the ruins, where a base camp was improvised. Henceforth he would travel fast and light, with an all-mounted force—and no tents.

About 1900 on the night of 7 March, the column began a moonlit march, ending at 0500 the next morning after 35 grueling miles. On the Clear Fork of the Powder, the troops settled down for a rest—and four hours later a "norther" began. The blowing snow lasted for two more days, the temperature dropping to six degrees below zero. Bourke wrote that the soldiers' mustaches and beards appeared "coated with pendent icicles several inches long, which with their raiment of furs and hides" made "this Expedition of cavalry look like a long column of Santa Clauses on their way to the Polar regions."

Pushing his horsemen through the snow, Crook passed the burned remains of abandoned Fort Phil Kearny. Nearby was the site of the Fetterman massacre of 1866, where a mixed force of 80 infantry and cavalrymen under Captain William Judd Fetterman had been annihilated by Red Cloud's warriors. Scouting Rosebud Creek and the upper waters of the Tongue River, Crook turned southeast toward the Powder, having been informed by an Arapaho named Black Coal that the hostiles were encamped on the Little Powder, a mere 150 miles from Fort Fetterman.

From the 11th to the 17th the temperature never went above 23 degrees below zero. Tentless, shivering men chopped their breakfast bacon with an ax—and sometimes the ax suffered more damage. The temperature plummeted several times to 39 below, mercury congealing in thermometers. Utensils and bits were run through hot water or ashes, to keep the skin of men's and horses' tongues from being torn away.

On 15 March, about 30 miles from the Powder, the command halted at the site of an old Sioux camp and found an Indian's partly decomposed arm; missing two fingers and pierced with five buckshot, it was believed to be that of a Crow warrior. Scout Grouard argued that the Indians sought were not camping to the east and south on the Little Bighorn River, as Crook had thought, but could be found at their usual wintering spots on the Tongue River.

The next morning, 16 March, scouts reported spotting two Sioux hunters on a ridge near the valley of Otter Creek, a tributary of the Tongue—and since the terrible cold had discouraged the Sioux from shadowing the troops, their appearance suggested a village close by. With a surprise attack his ideal, Crook hoped to deceive the Indians into thinking that he was headed down the Yellowstone, with no intention of following them. Accordingly, he first ordered his men into camp near the creek's mouth, then sent Colonel Reynolds to follow the Indians' trail. With Reynolds were six troops of cavalry (E, I, and K of the 2nd and E, F, and M of the 3rd) in three squadrons, roughly half the scouts under Major Stanton, and one day's rations. Since the Powder offered the only likely source of water for any nearby village, its probable location was obvious.

Crook was to stay back with two squadrons and the remaining scouts. Apparently he had asked Reynolds if he would like to lead the attacking troops, a choice honor for a subordinate in a frontier army with so few chances for combat laurels. Crook's stated purpose was to avoid the appearance of a division in command. But perhaps he was also giving the elderly Brevet Major General Reynolds a chance to reburnish a name tarnished by accusations of corruption during his command of the Department of Texas.

A more important question involved Crook's battle orders. He had apparently told Reynolds to attack and hold the village until the rest of the troops under Crook could join him. If he found no village, the two forces were to link up at a predesignated point near the mouth of Lodgepole Creek to the south. Crook claimed that he had specifically ordered Reynolds to destroy the village, slay as many warriors as possible, capture their ponies, and carry off any food he might find. But Reynolds claimed that he had received no such precise instructions—having instead been vaguely told to attack, do the maximum amount of damage, and then withdraw.

That afternoon, at roughly 1730, Reynolds and about 300 cavalrymen set out on the hunters' trail, Frank Grouard sometimes crawling on hands and knees to find their "sign" in the darkness or when snow flurries obscured the trail. The scouts detected a hunting party estimated at 30 to 40 warriors, and the soldiers followed until they saw smoke—issuing naturally from burning coal fissures. But very soon after this false alarm, Grouard warned that the village stood in the valley just beneath them, beside the Powder River.

Consisting of perhaps 110 lodges with between 500 and 700 inhabitants, including possibly as many as 250 fighters including older boys, the village was believed at the time to be that of Crazy Horse. But other evidence suggests a camp of Northern Cheyennes under Old Bear, with Little Wolf and Two Moon the other Cheyenne leading men, plus a few visiting Miniconjou and Oglalas under He Dog. An Indian woman captured by the soldiers was to supposedly state that it was Crazy Horse's village, with 40 new lodges of agency-supplied canvas belonging to recent Cheyenne arrivals from

Red Cloud Agency and two lodges of Sioux from the same place. But she may simply have claimed herself and some others to be of Crazy Horse's following. After a night march over ground slippery as glass and heavily cut up by ravines and gullies, the shivering soldiers, forbidden even to stamp their feet, concealed themselves in a ravine, waiting while Grouard and two other scouts reconnoitered.

At about 0600 Grouard returned to report a fresh, heavy trail leading down to the river, and the soldiers prepared for an early morning, though not a dawn, attack. But as the rising sun burned off the morning mist, the hazy smoke of campfires obscured the location of the village. Thinking that it lay along a creek bottom at the eastern base of the mountain where the command now stood positioned, the scouts recommended that Reynolds attack the camp simultaneously from opposite sides, one detachment marching down the mountain's north side, the second going down the southern side onto the valley floor. Detachment commanders would need good judgement, since the descent to the bottomland would require crossing broken and unfamiliar country.

Captain William Noyes' battalion of 3rd Cavalrymen was to descend the southern side of the mountain to the river, then move to the right before striking; Captain James "Teddy" Egan's Company K was to charge northward into the village firing revolvers among the tipis, but wheeling about and charging back if unable to storm the camp. Meanwhile Noyes' Company I would cut out the hostile pony herd, driving it upstream. Captain Anson Mills's two 3rd Cavalry troops, E and M, would descend into the valley from Reynolds' center and ride in from the west behind Noyes' battalions, following Egan's charge. Taking possession of the village and the plum thicket surrounding it, the soldiers would destroy the tipis and their contents. Captain Alexander Moore's two companies, E of the 2nd and F of the 3rd, would descend by the left and occupy the bluffs immediately to the northwest of the village. From there the dismounted troopers could cut down any fleeing warriors, protecting Egan's men from hostile fire by preventing the Indians from taking up positions on the

bluffs or in the underbrush. All would stay carefully hidden—until the Irish-born Egan opened the ball this St. Patrick's Day.

They moved out, Noyes' men in the lead, descending into
the ravine with difficulty. Unfortunately, the village, nestled
in a growth of cottonwoods and thick underbrush, was a mile
to the east of its supposed site, and half a mile farther
north—with another mountain in between.

Even after Indians could be clearly seen awake, if not alert,
the soldiers had not yet gotten into position. It was 0900
before Noyes' battalion reached its jumping-off point on the
river bottom. Captain Moore's men were still not in position
on the bluffs. Yet the soldiers went unseen, even in broad
daylight.

They also seemed to go unheard, even though cavalrymen
were a noisy, jingly lot when moving. Egan's 47 men (including reporter Strahorn) headed toward the flat land south of
the village, and as Noyes' company split off to attend to the
horses, Egan wheeled his men neatly into line. The men were
even colder now, though not necessarily chilled with anticipation; they had stripped off their heavier garments and
overshoes for ease in fighting. They advanced at a fast walk;
at the command of "Charge!" they were to quicken only to a
trot, due to the weakened condition of their mounts. At the
edge of the camp they came upon a ravine at least 10 feet deep
and 50 feet wide. Their winter-wasted horses climbed out of
it—to suddenly confront a Cheyenne pony-tender. Bourke
recalled him as a young boy about 15 years old:

> He was not ten feet off. The youngster wrapped his blanket
> about him and stood like a statue of bronze, waiting for the fatal
> bullet; his features were as immobile as if cut in stone. The
> American Indian knows how to die with as much stoicism as the
> East Indian. I levelled my pistol. "Don't shoot," said Egan, "we
> must make no noise." We were up on the bench upon which the
> village stood, and the war-whoop of the youngster was ringing
> wildly in the winter air, awakening the echoes of the bald-faced
> bluffs.

The troopers rode on, and even after a woman raised the
door of her lodge and cried out at the sight of the enemy, no

*The Powder River fight. Wooden Leg's 1930 pictograph, done for his friend Dr. Thomas Marquis, depicts the Cheyenne warrior rescuing two children from the soldiers, whose flashing carbines can be seen at the upper right. The stippled marks at the lower left represent soldiers' bullets, while the penciled caption is by Ben Shoulderblade, a school-educated Cheyenne.*

shot was fired. No village sentries had been posted, other than the youthful horse-tender, even though the Indians knew there were troops in the area. The Cheyenne warrior Wooden Leg later recalled an old man who had gone that morning to pray on a nearby knoll, only to rush shouting toward the camp: "The soldiers are right here! The soldiers are right here!" But already the white invaders were between the warriors and their horses.

Bourke wrote that Egan's line had emerged from the clump of cottonwoods and the thick undergrowth alongside the nearest tipis "when the report of the first Winchester and the zipp of the first bullet notified us that the fun had begun." Wooden Leg recalled: "Women screamed. Children cried for their mothers. Old people tottered and hobbled away to get out of the reach of the bullets singing among the lodges. Braves seized whatever weapons they had and tried to meet the attack." Some warriors lacked either guns or ammunition for them; Wooden Leg himself had no bullets for his muzzle-

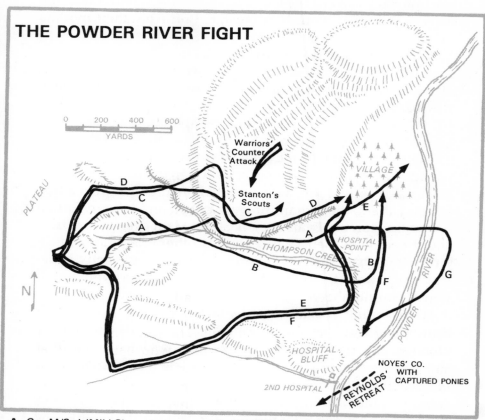

# THE POWDER RIVER FIGHT

Warriors' Counter Attack

Stanton's Scouts

VILLAGE

PLATEAU

THOMPSON CREEK

HOSPITAL POINT

POWDER RIVER

N

HOSPITAL BLUFF

2ND HOSPITAL

NOYES' CO. WITH CAPTURED PONIES

REYNOLDS' RETREAT

0  200  400  600
YARDS

A. Co. M/3rd (MILLS)
B. Co. E/3rd (LT. J. B. JOHNSON)
C. Co. E/2nd (LT. W. C. RAWOLLE)
D. Co. F/3rd (MOORE)
E. Co. K/2nd (EGAN'S GRAY-HORSE TROOP)
F. Co. I/2nd (NOYES)
G. Co. I/2nd (DETACHMENT UNDER LT. HALL)

loading rifle and had lent his cap-and-ball revolver to another, receiving in return a bow and arrows. Wooden Leg grabbed and mounted the first horse he could find before starting back toward his lodge to secure his shield, medicine objects and other items. But most, cut off from their mounts by the charge, remained afoot.

As Egan's gray-horse troop rode in amongst the tipis, unable to see much to shoot at, the warriors deliberately fired at the horses, falling back as the cottonwoods and underbrush slowed the bluecoats' charge. Some women joined in the firing. Men slit open their tipis to escape out the back rather than emerge from eastward-facing doors into plain sight.

The warriors at first retreated slowly on foot to shield their noncombatants and old people and get them to a place of safety. But with Moore's dismounted men not yet in position to harry them, the Indians bravely rallied and poured forth a heavy fire, forcing Egan's small band to halt even before they could complete their charge through the village. Reynolds' strike force had enjoyed superior numbers and vastly superior firepower. But now it was Captain Egan who found himself outnumbered.

Dismounting, the 47 formed a line to return fire with their Springfield carbines. For an estimated 25 minutes, they were alone against the warriors—for nothing had been heard from the other units, even as the Indians tried to outflank and encircle them. A Private Schneider was killed and three men were wounded, while nine horse were killed or injured; since the horses shot were not those of the wounded men, by now one-fourth of Egan's mounted strength was disabled.

Having already driven off the main pony herd, Captain Noyes might have led his company in echelon on Egan's left and swept the village. But he contented himself with obeying his instructions, securing the Indian mounts with the aid of the scouts—and allowing his men to dismount, unsaddle, and boil coffee. It was Colonel Stanton and Lieutenant Frederick W. Sibley who—without orders—led a small group of scouts in opening a hot fire on Egan's left and later fended off an Indian counterattack from the north.

With Moore still not heard from, the Indians had retired to the rocks on the other side of their tipis, and when Moore's men did show up, unable to see their potential targets and in the wrong place, they fired dangerously close to their comrades in the village. Finally Mills, advancing on foot, pushed past Egan's left —and pushed out the warriors still lingering in the village and holding the heavy undergrowth on its far side. Mills then detailed part of his force to destroy the village. Positioning his men on the right, Egan also assigned a party to help in the work of destruction.

Gradually their comrades, including Moore's men, joined the beleaguered troopers in the village. But now the dispossessed Indians held the high ground to the north, firing down into their own camp. Three concealed Cheyenne warriors concentrated their attention on a single soldier. Ritually passing his hand up and down parallel to his rifle's barrel, Chief Two Moon announced: "My medicine is good; watch me kill that soldier." But Two Moon missed, while a bullet from Bear Walks on a Ridge's muzzleloader struck the back of the soldier's head. The third warrior, Wooden Leg, remembered: "We rushed upon the man and beat and stabbed him to death. Another Cheyenne joined us to help in the killing. He took the soldier's rifle. I stripped off the blue coat and kept it."

Now in complete possession of the village, Reynolds intended to leave nothing valuable for its inhabitants. Into the fires went hide valises, warbonnets, ornamented elk hides, and some 150 saddles. But Reynolds, having "determined to destroy everything that we could lay our hands on," left little or nothing for his own suffering cavalrymen; in three or four lodges no less than a thousand pounds of dried and fresh meat were found— and destroyed. "Much bad management was displayed about this time," wrote Bourke—and "with a command undergoing every hardship, suffering from intense cold and hunger, tons of first class meat and provisions were destroyed and many things of positive necessity to the men wantonly burned up." Warm furs, quillworked robes, and precious food—all went up as the tipis burned. Some literally exploded as the fires ignited gunpowder in kegs and canisters, sending long, wrist-thick lodgepole fragments sailing up into the air to descend with smashing force among the troopers, but injuring none seriously. The Indians watched, aghast, as their homes and material culture vanished before their eyes. All except some of the warriors had been set afoot.

But they were far from being either cowed or helpless, and drove Moore's and Egan's men backward with their gunfire, leaving Mills' flanks uncovered. Boldly they pressed back into their village, allegedly entering it from one side as the soldiers departed from the other—for Colonel Reynolds had ordered a withdrawal. Just why he did so has never been adequately explained. Perhaps he feared that a counterattack in force might overwhelm him—an unlikely possibility, considering the losses that his breechloading carbines could have inflicted and the possibility of hunkering down and asking Crook for reinforcements. It was the white soldier, after all, who was presumed capable of overawing superior numbers with his ardor and discipline, and there was something decidedly unseemly about some 375 well-armed cavalrymen retreating from little more than half their number of warriors.

This sudden departure, after roughly five hours of fighting, began somewhere between 1330 and 1400. Not only were the bodies of several dead soldiers left in Indian hands, but, most damnably, the wounded Private Lorenzo Ayers, Company M, 3rd Cavalry, was apparently abandoned and subsequently carved limb from limb. The Sioux warrior Iron Shield later told his friend White Bull that a party of hungry Cheyenne had roasted and begun eating the soldier—or at least told Iron Shield so after watching him consume some of their meat. Four men were killed and five soldiers and one officer wounded.

The Cheyennes put their losses at one warrior slain and one wounded. One old blind woman was missing. But when some mounted warriors returned to the smoldering camp, they found one lodge still standing; the missing blind woman and her tipi had been left entirely unharmed. "We talked about this matter," said Wooden Leg, "all agreeing that the act showed the soldiers had good hearts." It was this woman who had served as the soldiers' informant as to the Indians' identity.

The villagers were in bad shape. Many were dismounted, only a few had buffalo robes to shelter them against the cold, and there was little food. While some warriors managed to boldly steal horses from the captured herd—even trying to get their own favorite mounts if they could—they could not retrieve them all, or seize any of the whites' mounts. Several half-clad women and children froze to death. On the fourth day of their bitter trek to shelter, apparently led by the Sioux among them, they found the camp of Crazy Horse's Oglalas far up a creek east of the Powder River.

Reynolds' men at least had horses. But they had virtually no food and suffered from the cold, partly because clothing and furs among the loot had been so imprudently destroyed. Having already ridden nearly 55 miles since the previous morning, they now marched 20 more miles up the Powder, stopping about 10 miles from the mouth of Lodge Pole Creek to bivouac and await the agreed-upon junction with Crook.

If, as he later argued, Reynolds had not been informed of Crook's intention to use the captured camp as a base for further operations, or been given precise instructions as to the disposition of property, his conduct in destroying all was understandable, if not particularly farsighted. Less easily excused was his hasty withdrawal, abandonment of the dead—and the fact that he had not sent for help from Crook, who was within supporting distance.

Furthermore, the Indians' recapture of some 550 of their ponies was made possible by the exhausted troops' failure to post guards over the herd. Apparently because his men were so tired and, perhaps, demoralized, Reynolds resisted any suggestion that an attempt be made to pursue and overtake the herd—as though he had no idea of just how important dismounting his enemy really was. It was in suddenly meeting Crook's forces that the Indians again lost some of their ponies, the general personally shooting a feather-bonneted warrior from the saddle. Crook drove in some 50 head as he linked up with Reynolds at midday. Then the united command marched eight miles to camp in another snow storm.

Still suffering from cold and short rations, encumbered by the wounded and cold-crippled, without beef herd or supplies, and now facing an alerted foe, the column found itself continually harassed due to the several hundred coveted ponies still in its possession. Though he had planned to use some in remounting his command, Crook finally ordered all remaining ponies killed, simply to remove the Indians' incentive to stay in the area. Some had their heads knocked in with axes or their throats cut, forcing the soldiers to hear the pathetic trumpeting as dying breath gushed from severed windpipes. Another 50 were shot before sundown; with a yell of defiance and a parting volley, the frustrated Indians withdrew. Fewer than 100 ponies were left to distribute to the scouts in partial payment for their efforts. Rejoining the infantry and wagons at Fort Reno, Crook began the weary march back to Fetterman.

Originally pleased to hear of the village's destruction, Crook noted that Reynolds had failed to attack vigorously with his entire force, some elements failing to support the initial assault. Furthermore, he had failed to secure vital provisions or prevent the pony herd's recapture. On 26 March, the very day he arrived at Fort Fetterman, an angry Crook initiated court-martial proceedings against Reynolds and, for their failure to properly engage the enemy, Captain Moore (who had been heard to boast that he would get a "bucketful of blood") and Lieutenant Noyes. Convicted of neglect of duty, Moore was suspended from command and confined to the limits of his post for six months, while Noyes, for conduct prejudicial to good order and military discipline, was to be "reprimanded by the Department Commander." Reynolds himself was convicted on several counts despite his contention that Crook sought a scapegoat. He was suspended from rank and command for one year and, though his old West Point classmate Ulysses S. Grant remitted the sentence, retired due to disability on 25 June 1877. But even Sheridan, not noted for tolerating timid officers, cited the weather as a mitigating factor in the Powder River failure, while Reynolds complained to Sherman that "winter campaigns in these latitudes should be prohibited..."

General Crook scattered his troops to the various posts from which they had come, and returned to his Omaha headquarters. It was an inauspicious beginning, and one which could only encourage the Indians in their feeling that the whites were their inferiors as fighters. Only a full-scale Indian war—how big, no man could say—would be likely to decide the issues. But Crook's winter expedition had never been intended to strike a decisive blow, for as early as February, he, Terry, and even Sheridan had come to believe that a summer's campaign would be necessary. The hapless Reynolds' reputation was only the first to suffer as a result of the Great Sioux War.

# Who Owned What?

They called themselves *Lakota*, but to white Americans they were known as the Teton Sioux— "Sioux," dismissed by the historian Parkman as an "unmeaning French term," being a corruption of a Chippewa word signifying snake or adder. Other branches of the Sioux, the Santee, and Yankton, called themselves Dakota or Nakota; but whites also used the first term to describe the Lakota, who made up over half of the total Sioux population. For future generations, the word "Sioux" would conjure up images of tipi-dwelling nomadic horsemen, with lives centered about warfare and the hunt.

Like most Indian inhabitants of the Great Plains, the Sioux were fairly recent arrivals. While a French chronicler of 1640 found them in Wisconsin and around the headwaters of the Mississippi in northern Minnesota—essentially a forest people, without horses or firearms—the Teton branch had been driven westward by pressure from other Indians. Migrating from the Great Lakes region and crossing the Missouri, they moved out onto the Plains—and, having adopted the white man's horses, would come to symbolize the Plains horse culture.

During the 19th century the Teton Sioux continued their push westward, expelling other Indians and claiming the lands for themselves. As their own population grew, their expansion was aided by the horrible inroads of diseases against tribes with more frequent contact with whites, especially such corn-growing, semi-sedentary groups as the Mandans, Arikaras, and Hidatsas east of the Missouri River. In 1851 the great treaty signed at Fort Laramie, Wyoming, set boundaries to confirm Sioux land claims, but ignored the fact that much of this land had recently been wrested from other tribes. A Sioux chief, objecting, "You have split my lands and I don't like it," clarified the moral climate by explaining, "These lands once belonged to the Kiowas and Crows, but we whipped these nations out of them, and in this we did what the white men do when they want the lands of the Indians."

But the Sioux had taken possession of the Black Hills of the Dakotas long before. Apparently reaching the Black Hills around the year 1775, the Sioux found the Cheyenne Indians, who on moving into the area themselves had found Kiowas and Comanches. The Crows were also pushed away from the Black Hills. Apparently no tribe actually spent much time dwelling in the buffalo-poor Hills, and despite later claims, they seem to have had no unique religious significance for the Lakota.

Still, the Sioux claim to *Pa Sapa* was good enough for an expansionist U.S. government—at least at first. The Fort Laramie treaty of 1868 following "Red Cloud's War" granted the Sioux all of present-day western South Dakota from the Missouri westward to the Wyoming border, including the Black Hills. But as Cheyenne historian John Stands-in-Timber observed: "The Cheyennes understood very little of what was signed at the treaty...the Sioux were given rights to the Black Hills and other country that the Northern Cheyennes claimed."

After the white man's Civil War, the pressure of a Sioux alliance estimated at 5,000 warriors—including Tetons, Yanktons, Cheyennes, and Arapahoes—continued to squeeze other Indians on the Northern Plains. Asked in 1866 why the Cheyenne and Sioux laid claim to Crow land, a Cheyenne chief replied: "We stole the hunting grounds of the Crows because they were the best....We fight the Crows because they will not take half and give us peace with the other half." The 1868 treaty did more than define for the Sioux a permanent reservation; it also, as historian Don Russell observed, permitted them hunting rights in the Powder River country, including areas claimed by the Crows, "mainly because they were there and there was no practical manner of getting them out—appeasement, if you will, or certainly *status quo ante bellum*." At the same time some Sioux bands, like those of Sitting Bull, persisted in trespassing on lands set aside for the Crows, outside even the "unceded"

Sioux hunting grounds defined by treaty. Thus the greatest battle of the Sioux War of 1876 took place on land surrounded by the Crow reservation.

Despite the fact that this solemn treaty guaranteed Sioux possession of the Black Hills, the whites and their government decided all too soon that it was yet another area which the Indians would be better off without. General George Crook solemnly reported that the white invasion of the Hills "had nothing to do" with the hostilities begun in 1876 and other factors could be (and were) cited as causes of the Great Sioux War. These included Sioux raids against whites (mainly intruders into the Black Hills) and friendly Indians, and even the Crows' complaint, as relayed by their agent, that much of their reservation "is permanently occupied by their enemies." But the November 1875 White House meeting where President Grant decided to subdue the non-reservation bands—a meeting including Generals Sherman, Sheridan, and Crook, the commissioner of Indian Affairs, and the Secretaries of War and the Interior— reportedly covered not merely Indian matters in general, but the Black Hills "in particular." Perhaps Crook, and other officials, did protest too much.

# The Sioux Divided

One seeming anomaly of the Great Sioux War was that the greater portion of Sioux warriors took no active part in it. But it was rare for an entire tribe of Plains Indians to consider itself at war with the whites, and the loose confederation of bands known as the Teton Sioux was no exception. During the 19th century the two major divisions migrating to the Plains, the Brules or Burnt Thighs, and the Oglala, had expanded into five additional tribes, the Hunkpapas, Miniconjou, Sans Arcs, Two Kettles, and the Lakota Blackfoot—the so-called Seven Council Fires of the Sioux. As Don Russell put it, "Their council fires were rarely lighted at the same time for any common purpose...." Yet as early as 1851, the U.S. had officially recognized the Brule leader Brave Bear (killed three years later in a needless fight with soldiers) as chief of all the Sioux.

Though this "Sioux Nation" had no central government, and its leaders lacked the power either to compel a unified policy or prevent dissidents from splitting off into their own bands, white soldiers and officials yearned for powerful Indian chiefs who could simultaneously speak for their tribes, control their followers' behavior, and submit to whatever the government desired. But even in their absence, one could always find chiefs willing to sign whatever treaty was handy.

Thus in 1866, signing a treaty with the chiefs of the so-called "Hang Around the Forts" or Laramie Loafers (largely dependent on government rations), the United States had secured permission to open the Bozeman Trail to the Montana goldfields—and theoretically ended armed conflict with the Tetons begun during the Civil War. But war leaders such as the Oglala Red Cloud, leader of the Bad Faces camp, rejected the treaty, and fought "Red Cloud's War," which climaxed in the annihilation of 80 men from Wyoming's Fort Phil Kearny under Captain William Fetterman.

The factionalism among tribes, bands, clans, and camps had long made it difficult for the military to distinguish between hostile and friendly Indians, especially for the purpose of attacking the former. In 1868, following the battle of the Washita, General Custer was criticized because in attacking a Cheyenne village, his troops had slain Black Kettle, a notable "peace chief." Yet many of his young men had been less peaceable, raiding Kansas settlements and slaying Army dispatch riders. In 1876, at least, troops in the field would find the distinction simple: those Sioux off the reservations were arbitrarily declared hostile, and thus legitimate targets. But of course members of one party could become members of the other quite quickly—and in the end all would suffer.

By 1876 the great majority of Lakotas were living at least part of the year on reservations. But they had not meekly succumbed to military conquest and removal. In "touching the pen" to the treaty of 1868, Red Cloud seemed the victor of his war, since the U.S. agreed to abandon the Bozeman Trail forts. In 1870 a delegation led by Red Cloud visited Washington to discuss settlement on a reservation. Like Spotted Tail of the Brules before them, they saw the amazing power and numbers of the white man.

With the government desiring to clear the Sioux from the Platte and settle them along the Missouri River, Red Cloud pressed for an agency near Fort Laramie where he could trade and draw rations. In 1873 the government compromised by building Red Cloud Agency for the Oglalas and Spotted Tail Agency for the Brules in northwestern Nebraska, just outside the reservation's boundaries. Throughout, Red Cloud and Spotted Tail attempted to win benefits for the Sioux (and retard the "civilizing" process) without alienating followers wary of too much compliance with the government. Other Sioux were served by various agencies along the Missouri, bordered to the east by the reservation. Some Cheyennes and Arapahoes also reported to the Red Cloud Agency, but the northern divisions of these tribes remained outside the system. Combined, the agencies could count perhaps as many as 25,000 full or part-time Indian residents,

though the Indians had an aversion to being counted at all.

But while such non-treaty chiefs as Sitting Bull and their followings (termed at Red Cloud the "northern Indians") preferred to have nothing to do with the agencies, they appear to have been outnumbered by warriors who divided their time between reservation and the old free life. Drawing blankets, rations, and tobacco from government stores, they might suddenly appear armed and painted for war to demand additional allotments, or threaten their agent with death for attempting to take a census, or even launch raids from the reservation itself.

With the war of 1876, archenemies Spotted Tail and Red Cloud, whose influence depended largely upon their ability to wring concessions from the whites, remained at peace. But Red Cloud gave, if not his blessing, then at least his engraved Winchester rifle (a gift from President Grant) to his son Jack Red Cloud, who joined the roamers in April. And if even the more peacefully inclined Spotted Tail failed to dissuade a substantial minority of Brules from the warpath, this was typical of a society more likely to fragment than to reach a consensus. Some Indians would chose resistance, others accommodation, and still others waiver between the two extremes. But there would be enough for a grand war.

# Warriors of the Plains

"War is the breath of their nostrils," wrote Francis Parkman of the Lakota in 1846. His judgement of these "wild democrats of the prairie" could apply equally well to other nomadic, buffalo-hunting tribes. To this day the 19th century Plains warrior, preferably in the full glory of ceremonial paint and feathered warbonnet, remains the personification of the American Indian. Later sympathizers might portray him as a near-pacifist, the better to admire him without guilt. But it was as a fighter that he was admired in his own day, even by whites who disparaged his culture and way of life. In war, the tribesman was in his element and his glory, and young boys yearned for the day when they too could join a war party.

While whites typically saw warfare as an unpleasant interruption of peaceful "normality," aimed at a specific purpose (whether self-defense, saving the Union, or simply gobbling up more aboriginal land), the Plains tribes rarely fought distinct wars, and never made a peace with all their neighbors at once. Though enemies and allies might change, warfare was virtually the only means by which the average man could gain status. Society *required* war, and a permanent peace would have uprooted it. The more sedentary tribes of the region shared this philosophy; when in 1806 explorer William Clark counseled the Hidatsa to give up tribal warfare, only the older men, already established in war, seemed in-terested. A young man objected that their chiefs "were now old and must shortly die" and that their nation could not exist without chiefs—for save through the medium of warlike achievements, they knew no method of "making" leaders. Understandably, whites often confused leaders of war parties with men holding formal rank as chiefs.

The re-introduction of the horse to America by Europeans not only permitted such peoples as the Arapaho, Blackfoot, and Sioux to expand onto the Plains and embrace a new hunting culture, but gave a new impetus to war. Horses became a measure of wealth and status, and much of Plains warfare revolved around their theft—or, as the Indians would consider it, capture. Two basic types of war parties were revenge raids and horse-stealing expeditions in which killing was incidental to successful theft. Whether he sought horses or battle, the warrior's usual objective, save when acting in immediate defense of his people or village, was personal honor. Each tribe had its system for "counting coup" (from the French word for "blow"), grading such deeds as capturing a horse or gun, or rescuing a fallen comrade's body. Most coups literally required touching an enemy or prize, perhaps with a bow, gun muzzle or special "coup stick." Thus a Cheyenne warrior who shot and killed an enemy only gained credit if he were among the first three men who touched the body, the greatest honor going to the first. Coups were sometimes interpreted so rigidly as to bear no relation to the valor actually displayed. But the highest coup, because riskiest and rarest, was touching an armed foe without harming him.

Acts such as galloping across an enemy's firing line, however brave, had no strictly military purpose. The Plains "war complex" produced magnificent warriors. But it did not produce soldiers. Emphasis on individual distinction discouraged strategic and even tactical thinking. A Blackfoot song expressed a common Plains sentiment: "It is bad to live to be old/Better to die young/Fighting bravely in battle." In practice, reluctance to suffer casualties often kept victories from becoming what the whites might term "decisive." Lieutenant William P. Clark believed that canards of Indian cowardice could be attributed simply to their unspoken maxim of war: "Greatest amount of damage to the enemy with the least amount to one's self." But the Plains Indians went well beyond this. Generally speaking, a war party suffering even one fatality was deemed a failure—no matter how much damage was done the enemy. By contrast, a party which rode out on a long journey, to return months later with a single scalp and no losses, was considered worth the trouble.

While rigid discipline could be enforced on the communal buffalo hunts vital for group survival, war leaders usually had to rely on force of personality and a record of past successes. Certainly no chief could expect his braves to immolate themselves, Zulu-like, against lines of flaming rifles. The method behind General Grant's futile Cold Harbor attack, with 7,000 men lost in just 30 minutes—like the concept of "sacrificing" men to win an objective— was neither possible nor desirable. Determined charges by mounted warriors, such as those of Roman Nose's Cheyennes at the Beecher's Island fight of 1868, were memorable for their very rarity. Investigating several sites where small bands of whites held off vastly superior numbers of Indians, Robert J. Ege claimed that "500-600 yards separated the forces during these engagements," with Indians sometimes charging from 700 yards away to perhaps 500 before falling back.

A lack of authority also contributed to the failure to post village sentries—and an inattention to the principle of security which one writer on primitive warfare termed "frankly incomprehensible" in men who themselves relied upon stealth and surprise for success in war. Even the common ploy of luring enemies into ambushes often failed when young men eager for distinction sprang traps prematurely.

But while the U.S. Army enjoyed superior organization and sometimes firepower, the Indian, taught the warlike arts from childhood, was man for man greatly the soldier's superior at scouting, tracking, living off the land, and fighting as an individual. A superb horseman, he might average 50 miles a day while being pursued, using several horses (some perhaps stolen en route). Clark wrote of how, accustomed "from their earliest youth to take advantage of every knoll, rock, tree, tuft of grass and every aid the topography of the country affords to secure game," each warrior "becomes an adept in their way of fighting, needing no orders to promptly seize, push and hold any opportunity for success, or in retreating protect themselves from harm."

But spiritual power—what the whites termed "medicine"—was also deemed vital to success in war, and reliance on personal medicine "bundles," clothing, paint or rituals co-existed with a high level of individual combat skill. While a vision might inspire a war party, a bad omen might encourage it to turn back, while defeat suggested the inadequacy of a leader's power.

For the Sioux and Cheyenne, fighting the whites was an interruption of more pleasurable efforts directed against other Indians, and raids between tribes continued even after confinement to reservations. Finally this too was suppressed. "Nothing happened after that," insisted the aged chief Two Leggings, concluding his tale of leading the last revenge raid by Crow warriors in 1888. "We just lived. There were no more war parties, no capturing of horses from the Piegans and the Sioux, no buffalo to hunt. There is nothing more to tell." But for whites privileged to hear the tales of such an old warrior, as Stanley Vestal did in recording the life of Miniconjou chief White Bull, the heroic style of Indian warfare could prove a pleasant contrast to the anonymous mass slaughter of the 20th century. "To me, at least," wrote Vestal in 1934, "it is no small thing to have known and talked with a man straight out of Homer."

# CHAPTER II

# Three Columns

## May-June 1876

*T*hat conscientious soldier General Alfred Terry would ultimately manage to get both of his department's two columns into the field before Crook's refitted Wyoming force could resume its pursuit of the hostiles. However, Terry was still behind schedule, his plans to launch his "Dakota column" delayed not merely by terrible weather, but by political considerations as well.

As early as 27 February, Terry had ordered the 7th Infantry's Colonel John Gibbon, a hard-bitten veteran of 34 years' Regular Army service, to prepare for field duty all available troops from the various Montana garrisons under Gibbon's overall command. Gibbon was then to move eastward against the Sioux and Cheyenne. But, largely due to unexpectedly bad weather, Gibbon could not begin even his preliminary movements until 14 March.

That day Captain Walter Clifford's Company E, 7th Infantry, marched out of Camp Baker, struggling through deep snowdrifts and finally arriving at Fort Ellis, 120 miles away, on the 22nd. There Clifford took charge of a train consisting of 28 contract wagons and 100,000 pounds of supplies before heading for the Crow Agency on the Stillwater River to establish a new supply depot for Gibbon. At 1000 on Saint Patrick's Day, while Reynolds' men battled to maintain possession of the Indian village on the Powder River, 5 more 7th

Infantry companies, with 10 contract wagons and 10 days' rations, left Fort Shaw for the 180-mile march to Fort Ellis. That very day Major James Brisbin's four 2nd Cavalry companies arrived after a possibly unnecessary evacuation of "Fort Pease," a trappers' and traders' post on the mouth of the Bighorn River.

En route to Ellis, the 200 infantrymen struggled against rough roads and rough weather, snow yielding to slush and mud. Snowblindness incapacitated column commander Captain Rawn, who returned to the fort after leaving Captain H.B. Freeman in charge. It also temporarily overcame 7th Infantry Lieutenant James Bradley, who commanded a detachment of 12 mounted infantry scouts, and whose eyes, unable to bear the light, seemed "to roll in liquid fire with a grating feeling as though in contact with particles of sand."

When the roads again became dry and hard, they proved painfully so to weary foot soldiers on the 22nd, Gibbon overtaking the column as Freeman camped some four miles from the territorial capital at Helena. Dry roads yielded again to mud on the 23rd, one officer describing the day's march as "eighteen miles long and six inches deep all the way."

But such rigors at least helped acclimate the troops to the greater trials ahead, and on the 25th they managed to march 25 miles without noticeable ill effects. They finally arrived at the town of Bozeman and then Fort Ellis on the 28th, with a few officers and men disabled by snowblindness, having made 180 miles in 11 days. More good training, as a military philosopher might view it, was provided when mud and dirty water continually poured down the slope where the wretched infantrymen had pitched camp. Spending a day in preparation, Gibbon resumed his march toward the Yellowstone River on the 30th, shortly after learning of the Reynolds fight almost two weeks before. The initial reaction, here as elsewhere in Army circles, was to view it as a splendid and certainly encouraging victory.

Montana, established as a territory just 12 years before, already had a white population of 15,000. But most of this population was concentrated in its western portion. Gibbon's

*General Alfred Terry. After President Grant forbade the more ener-getic Custer to lead the Dakota column, this department com-mander was obliged to take the field himself.*

soldiers would now proceed into the domain of the Indians, where a few scattered whites lived at their own risk. Gibbon himself would remain at Fort Ellis for the moment and later catch up in the company of Brisbin's cavalry battalion, which was not yet ready to march.

Besides getting his first news of Reynolds' attack, Gibbon had been disconcerted to learn that General Crook had not only veered east toward the Powder River, but had actually withdrawn from the field entirely. Gibbon promptly sent a wire to Terry, asking:

In view of the information from General Crook, am I not

# Philip H. Sheridan

Delayed by a year's suspension after he threatened an upperclassman with a bayonet, Sheridan (1831-1888) was graduated from West Point in 1853. As a young infantry officer in the Northwest, he was commended in General Orders signed by General Winfield Scott for distinguished service in the Yakima War of 1855, and subsequently helped guard reservation Indians in western Oregon.

A 30-year-old captain when the Civil War came, Sheridan was promoted to brigadier general of volunteers by September 1862, winning a second star at Stones River—and General Grant's attention at Missionary Ridge. When Grant went east as supreme Union commander in March 1864, he brought Sheridan along to command the Army of the Potomac's cavalry. Given an independent command in Virginia's Shenandoah Valley, he made the famous "Sheridan's Ride" from Winchester to rally his troops and crush Jubal Early's rebels at Cedar Creek, then launched a notorious scorched-earth campaign to render the Valley inhospitable to rebel troops. Sheridan drew a useful lesson from the experience: that war was "far worse" than a mere duel between lines of combatants, and that "reduction to poverty brings prayers for peace more surely and more quickly than does the destruction of human life." Sheridan's troops blocked Lee's retreat at Appomattox, and he ended the war with the Regular rank of major general.

operating in a wrong line by going south of the Yellowstone, instead of north of it? Brisbin reports a large fresh lodgepole trail leading north from the mouth of the Rosebud. He thinks Sitting Bull is on the Big Dry Fork, toward which this trail leads. Must I limit my offensive operations to Indian reservation lines, or may I strike Sitting Bull wherever I can find him?

Terry wired his response on the 31st. Until the department commander learned what General Crook's further movements might be, and until Custer started out, he thought that Gibbon should avoid going south of the Yellowstone, instead attempting to keep the Indians from "getting away" to the north. Doubting that Sitting Bull was on Dry Fork, Terry believed that his present location was somewhere on the Powder. "I think that if you move to the mouth of the Big Horn, by the time that you reach it I shall be able to send you information of the movements of Crook and Custer, upon which you will be able to determine your course." If, how-

Reassigned to head the Department of Missouri when he proved overzealous in "reconstructing" Texas and Louisiana, he was promoted to lieutenant general in March 1869 and made commander of the vast Division of the Missouri in March 1869. Embracing the Departments of the Missouri, the Platte, Dakota, and Texas, as well as most of the Indians living in the U.S., it extended from Chicago westward to the far borders of New Mexico, Utah, Wyoming, and Montana, and from Canada south to the Rio Grande.

Blunt, and ruthless against those he viewed as enemies, Sheridan allegedly replied to a self-proclaimed "good Indian" that "The only good Indians I ever saw were dead." Yet he denied expressing this (hardly original) sentiment, and insisted that "I have the interest of the Indian at heart as much as anyone, and sympathize with his fading out race." Noting that the Indians' dispossession made some fighting inevitable, he laid much of the blame for strife on the government's failure to adequately feed and clothe its "wards." Unlike many white reformers, Sheridan believed that to "civilize and Christianize the wild Indian" required stern military control, and advocated total-war methods reminiscent of those used in the Shenandoah if the Indian resisted.

In 1883 Sheridan replaced Sherman as commanding general, a position with few vital responsibilities, since the adjutant general acted as *de facto* commander under the Secretary of War. Shortly before his death, Congress voted Sheridan his fourth star.

---

ever, Gibbon was able to strike a hostile band anywhere, he was to do it "without regard to reservations;" but even in doing so he must take care not to neglect "the great object" of keeping between the Indians and the Missouri River. Such instructions reflected the essence of Terry's and Sheridan's dilemma: attempting to coordinate three columns toward a common goal when immense distances and imperfect communication made this impossible.

On 1 April, "Grasshopper Jim" Brisbin left for Fort Ellis with companies F, G, H, and L of his 2nd Cavalry, having insisted on leading in person despite rheumatism which made it impossible to mount a horse or even walk without crutches. Moving at a slow pace due to poor roads and snow, with Brisbin initially riding in an ambulance, the battalion joined Gibbon's waiting infantrymen on 8 April, opposite the mouth of the Stillwater River and roughly 15 miles from the

*General Philip H. Sheridan during the Rebellion, where he honed his philosophy of total war. "We took away their country and their means of support," he wrote of the Indians in 1878, "broke up their modes of living, their habits of life, introduced disease and decay among them, and it was for this and against this they made war. Could anyone expect less?"*

B-4496

Crow Agency. Since Terry's revised plan required setting up a new supply depot on the north side of the Yellowstone (which would in a few weeks have been impassible due to the spring melting of the snows), they here established "Camp Supply."

Gibbon had originally intended to march his Montana column directly toward the ruins of Fort C.F. Smith by way of the old Bozeman trail, then cross the Big Horn River and move directly eastward, striking and destroying any camps in the region "watered by the Little Big Horn, Tongue, and Rosebud"—that is, in the valleys of these three rivers. But Terry's assessment of the situation had changed. He now believed that the free-roaming warriors were fewer than previously estimated, and that these fighters would choose to flee north when Crook resumed operations against them, afterwards crossing to the north bank of the Yellowstone—if not that of the Missouri.

Gibbon would have to block such a crossing if even one of the two other columns was to strike successfully. And he

*Half-French, half-Sioux, and an adopted Crow, Mitch Boyer normally dressed as a white man, but chose tribal dress for this photograph. Wrote Gibbon: "He was the protege and pupil of Jim Bridger; was the best guide in this section of the country, and the only half-breed I ever met who could give the distances to be passed over with any accuracy in miles."*

would have to act quickly. It was known that the Indians' preferred crossing places at this time of year were located just above and just below the mouth of Rosebud Creek, and it was therefore necessary, as Gibbon explained, that the Montana column push forward down the Yellowstone "as rapidly as possible, for the Indians, if moving north, would succeed in getting across that stream before the yearly spring rise, and before either the eastern or western column could interfere."

At Gibbon's new camp on the Yellowstone his quartermaster, who had already hired two civilian guides, added two more: H.M. "Muggins" Taylor and Michel "Mitch" Boyer (or Bouyer), the former a white man, the latter the son of a French trader and a Sioux woman, who lived as an adopted Crow and whose skill and reliability as a guide were considered unparalleled. As Gibbon sat in his tent, "a man with the face of an Indian and the dress of a white man approached the

# John Gibbon (1827-1896)

The "proud possessor of a Wellington nose—a kind of proboscis which...all ambitious soldiers try to cultivate," Gibbon was born in North Carolina. Graduated from West Point at age 20, he saw action against Mexicans and Seminoles, and as a West Point artillery instructor in 1860 published the well-respected *Artillerist's Manual*. Unlike three Rebel brothers, Captain Gibbon chose for the Union and in 1862 formed Wisconsin and Indiana volunteers into a stalwart unit which became the Army of the Potomac's legendary Iron Brigade. That May he was promoted to brigadier general. Twice, at Fredericksburg and as a divisional commander temporarily leading the *II Corps* at Gettysburg, serious wounds forced him from the field for months. Briefly commanding the *XVIII* and *XXIV Corps* as a major general of volunteers, with peace "Fighting Johnny" served first as colonel of the 36th Infantry and then of the 7th Infantry while commanding the District of Montana.

A well-liked commander who en-

door, and almost without saying anything seated himself on the ground, and it was some moments before I understood that my visitor was the expected guide. He was a diffident, low-spoken man, who uttered his words in a hesitating way, as if uncertain what he was going to say."

From Boyer Gibbon learned that the Mountain band of Crows were waiting to see him, and he immediately rode to the agency through an 18-mile snowstorm. In the council oration which followed, Gibbon told the Crows that he wanted men to act as his "eyes," that the Sioux were their common enemies, and that he was marching to punish them for making war upon the white men: "If the Crows want to make war upon the Sioux now is their time. If they want to drive them from their country and prevent them from sending war parties into their country to murder their men, now is the time. If they want to get revenge for Crows that have fallen, to get revenge for the killing of such men as the gallant soldier, Long Horse, now is their time."

The Crow chiefs were mighty men of valor, with nothing against either war or revenge. But while willing enough to voice various complaints against the government and de-

couraged regimental spirit even while the 7th Infantry's companies were widely dispersed at frontier posts, Gibbon was known to the Crows as "No Hip-Bone" or "The One Who Limps" due to his old Civil War wound. Sensitive to critics who indulged "in sarcastic calculations as to how many millions of dollars are required to kill one Indian," he wrote that "in Indian wars the labor performed is far greater than in so called *civilized* wars (as if war in any shape could be called civilized!), whilst the troops engaged have not even the poor consolation of being credited with 'glory', a term which, upon the frontier, has long since been defined to signify being 'shot by an Indian from behind a rock, and having your name wrongly spelled in the newspapers!' Hence, if the American people do not wish to spend money they should not go to war."

And war could be best avoided by reforming an Indian policy which Gibbon termed a "foul blot" on the American people and "a disgrace to the age and the country." But, pursuant to his duty, he caught a bullet in the thigh while fighting, rifle in hand, at the Big Hole fight during the 1877 Nez Perce war. Gibbon retired a major general in 1891.

*Colonel John Gibbon, 7th Infantry, in 1875. The conduct of this gallant veteran during the Sioux campaign would prove strangely unaggressive—and at times simply enigmatic.*

nounce their agent, they seemed reluctant to furnish the scouts requested. Though they appreciated a chance to strike at the Sioux and recover their Powder River hunting grounds, they were not entirely impressed with their white brothers' sluggish, heavy-handed methods of war-making.

Besides, these older men had already established their warlike reputations. Younger Crows, however, proved more willing. As Gibbon put it, "as soon as 'Young America' had a chance to be heard in the camps our chance for obtaining scouts improved, and the next morning the whole number required came forward into the United States service." Wishing to bind them to an enlistment of three months, the white officers were informed of the Crow method of taking an oath. Accordingly, the new recruits were paraded, "and an officer presented to each in succession a hunting knife, on the point of which each one gravely placed the tip of his forefinger and the deed was one." The ceremony over, one of the Crows solemnly presented the knife's point to Gibbon, explaining that he wished to bind the officer to do what *they* said. However, Lieutenant Bradley, who would act as their commander, "offered to swear that he would see they got all the pay, rations, etc., they were entitled to, and as all they wanted apparently was some kind of a mutual obligation, they readily consented to this, and the officer solemnly touched the point of the knife." The scouts numbered 23 in all, most young, but with 2 of middle age and 2 others over 60. To prevent the ignorant whites from mistaking them for Sioux, each would wear a piece of red cloth on the left arm above the elbow. Enlisted with the Crows were two white men, Bernard "Barney" Bravo and Thomas H. LeForge, who lived with the tribe and would act as interpreters.

With the addition of the Crows and 4 quartermaster guides, the Montana column officially numbered 477 men, including six companies of the 7th Infantry (13 officers and 210 men), 4 troops of the 2nd Cavalry (10 officers and 185 men), contract surgeon Dr. Holmes O. Paulding, and 20 civilian employees manning 24 government and 12 contract wagons. Gibbon's heaviest firepower came in the form of a muzzleloading Napoleon 12-pound gun-howitzer and two rapid-fire Gatling guns manned by a 7th Infantry detail under Lieutenant Charles A. Woodruff.

Leaving Captain William Logan to guard Camp Supply with the 7th's Company A and one Gatling, Gibbon started down the Yellowstone on 13 April, Bradley's Crows in the van combing the countryside for Sioux or Cheyenne. A week later the soldiers pitched camp 200 miles from their starting point at Fort Ellis, opposite the mouth of the Big Horn River—considered the westernmost limit for Sioux villages, if not war parties.

Receiving dispatches from Terry dated the 15th, a dismayed Gibbon, well into hostile country, learned that since General Crook was not expected to take the field again until mid-May, and Terry's column would not begin its march out until even later, Gibbon's force—the smallest of the three—would for a time remain the only column in the field. Nor did the enemy force seem as small as previously thought. (One of the campaign's more embarrassing features was the way in which military opinion swung wildly between belittling and grossly inflating Indian numbers and prowess.) Confided Bradley to his journal: "General Crook's victory was not so decisive as we have regarded it, while the fighting seems to have demonstrated that there are heavier forces of warriors to encounter than had been counted on. General Terry fears that the Indians may combine and get the better of us." Gibbon was not to proceed farther than the mouth of the Big Horn, "unless," he himself wrote later, "sure of striking a successful blow," leaving his men condemned to three weeks of inactivity and "what to a soldier is the hardest of all duties—*waiting*." Gibbon moved his camp two miles downstream and camped outside the walls of Fort Pease, where, he confidently informed Terry, "I am strong enough to defy the whole Sioux nation, should they feel inclined to come this way." Gibbon assured his superior that he would keep his scouts "busy every day in various directions" and hoped that "we shall be able to definitely settle this Sitting Bull matter..."

Gibbon failed, however, to move boldly in settling it. Though condemned to play a waiting game, he was still the only commander in the field, and therefore in the best position to gather intelligence on Sioux movements. But the intelligence his scouts actually gathered was not forwarded to those who could benefit from it, and his dispatches were sometimes misleading. Thus, while assuring Terry on the 21st that he was that day sending scouts "to the *north* of us where some sign was seen yesterday," Gibbon failed to note that scout leader Bradley had already dismissed this Indian "sign" as a couple of "wild horses in the neighborhood; so no Sioux yet." He also failed to probe north afterward, while dispatching scouts in other directions. However, at times Gibbon himself did not receive the intelligence possessed by others. On 23 April Captain Freeman's Company H, with Boyer guiding, left with the empty contract wagons. While on their way back to Gibbon with Logan's infantry company and wagons freshly loaded with stores, they met a Crow war party and learned that its members had ridden nearly to the Powder River in search of Sioux to raid—but had found none even that far down. Apparently Gibbon was not even informed of this meeting, which at least hinted at where the Sioux were *not*, when Freeman's party rejoined his command on 8 May.

Initially, Gibbon's own scouts also had trouble finding Sioux. One party setting out on 24 April under Captain Edward Ball, and consisting of two 2nd Cavalry companies as well as white and Crow guides, rode up the west bank of the Little Bighorn River as far as the Fort C.F. Smith site, then proceeded southeast along the Bozeman. On 29 April, at a deserted Sun Dance camp used by the Sioux the previous summer, strangely close to the future site of the Little Bighorn fight, Crow warrior Jack Rabbit Bull found a discarded breadbox and covered it with charcoal markings to inform the Sioux that the Crows and soldiers would clean them out—sticking green grass in its cracks to show that it would happen that summer. Crossing the Wolf Mountains and camping that night on a dry tributary of Tullock's Creek, Ball's men rode down the rugged valley of that stream the next day. They returned 1 May without seeing a single hostile Indian. However, the seven-day scout was not without significance, as we shall see.

Six Crows dispatched by Lieutenant Bradley on 27 April journeyed as far as Rosebud Creek, but also returned on 1 May after seeing nothing. "Where are they?" Bradley asked his journal, recording on 2 May the command's general, and wholly erroneous, impression that, having learned "the extensive preparations making for waging war on them, they have become frightened and resorted to the agencies..."

If with hindsight this seems absurdly optimistic, it conformed with the military's faith in the possibility of overawing the Sioux with a mere display of strength—a faith which had somehow survived even the suspicion that "heavier forces of warriors" might have gathered. In fact, the relatively few hostile warriors in Montana, though drifting toward the west, were simply farther east than anyone had expected, in the valleys of the Powder and Tongue. Many of the warriors, far from returning to the agencies, had instead just begun their journey to join the non-treaty bands under Sitting Bull. Still others were too close for comfort. On the morning of 3 May, the Crow scouts found that a band of 50 bold raiders had stolen all 35 of their mounts from the riverine island where they had herded them. Gibbon, noting that they had assembled in camp and "cried like children whose toys had been broken," commented:

> There is nothing unnatural in a crying child, and the manly grief of a broken heart excites one's sympathy but to see a parcel of great big Indians standing together and blubbering like babies with great tears streaming down their swarthy faces because they had lost their horses, struck everyone as supremely ridiculous.

Tom LeForge, who better knew his Crow brethren, later argued that this was "not merely an effeminate yielding to emotions....They themselves claimed high proficiency in the art of horse-stealing, and to be beaten so badly in this game, with white men observing their defeat, was hurtful to their pride."

The vengeful Crows pursued afoot, but were driven back at a point eight miles downstream by gunfire from the raiders— a band of enterprising Northern Cheyennes under Two Moon. This disaster left the Crows completely dismounted and thus neutralized. However, Jack Rabbit Bull and Half Yellow Face, with borrowed mounts, set out on 6 May to redeem Crow honor; some 15 miles down the north bank, they boldly charged a trio of Sioux and recovered three mounts. Convinced by this that a war party of respectable size lay in that direction, Bradley requested permission to do additional scouting, Captain Clifford predicting glumly that Bradley's scouts were "very likely to be scooped up by an overwhelming force of Sioux."

On 7 May Bradley left camp with a small force of Crows, Tom LeForge, guide Henry Bostwick, and the mounted infantry detachment. Perhaps a mile beyond the spot where the two Crows had snatched back the ponies, the party found three freshly abandoned lodges, and farther downstream another campsite capable of accommodating all 50 raiders. Later scouting missions also discovered hostile "sign"—and on 15 May, some 15 to 18 miles above the mouth of the Tongue, Bradley's men found a large Indian village and managed to fix its location accurately despite observation from a great distance. The Crows persuaded Bradley not to risk discovery by getting any closer; instead, they insisted that they could estimate a village of no fewer than 2,000 to 3,000 lodges simply by examining the rising smoke. Reluctantly, Bradley returned on May 17. But he could now report a target lying barely 35 miles from Gibbon's command.

Gibbon issued rations for three days and ordered a forced night march to reach the village in time for the traditional dawn attack. He had every reason to be confident. Even after leaving the 7th Infantry's Company K to guard his camp, he would still have 33 officers and some 325 enlisted men, plus the Crows, to pit against the Sioux. While sheer numbers were against them, Bradley's scout had already solved what most soldiers of the day would have seen as Gibbon's main problem. He had found the enemy, and it remained only to fight them. Over 300 disciplined regulars, armed with modern breechloading rifles and carbines, would presumably be more than a match for a horde of warlike but unmilitary Sioux, so long as they stood steady and held their nerve.

On the morning of 17 May, a flotilla of small riverboats, secured from Fort Pease and manned by infantry volunteers, began ferrying Brisbin's cavalrymen across the Yellowstone;

*If it wished to compete in mobility with a Plains Indian village, the Regular Army's only hope lay with the humble, if often cantankerous, mule.*

four horses being led behind the boats drowned during the tedious business. Then Gibbon called a halt. While the Crows expressed disgust at the white man's inability to make a simple river crossing, Lieutenant Bradley, among others, was simply puzzled. "What the trouble is," he wrote, "I did not then understand, and I don't know now, and I have never seen anybody that did." Gibbon himself hyperbolically ascribed the halt to the Yellowstone's status as "a raging torrent." But the band of Sioux observed watching the soldiers' activities that morning may also have given him second thoughts. These warriors might well ride to alert the camp before Gibbon could possibly strike it. A surprise attack at dawn was one thing; a blind lunge by a largely unmounted force against rapidly fleeing Indians, or into a well-prepared ambush like that which had destroyed Fetterman's men in 1866, was quite another.

Incredibly, Gibbon did not report to Terry Bradley's discovery of a large village, let alone his own abortive attempt to reach it. However, reconnaissance did continue. Captain Lewis Thompson went on a three-day patrol downriver to the mouth of the Tongue on the 18th, while Bradley took a detachment of mounted infantry and Crows up the Yellowstone. Four unassigned Crows also struck out on their own, simply swimming over to the south bank of the Yellowstone and heading for the village on foot to steal horses. Two days later they returned, to report hundreds of warriors approaching the scouts' Wolf Mountain vantage point from the direction of Tongue River and heading for the mouth of the Rosebud.

Fearing that Captain Thompson's detachment might be attacked, Gibbon hurried to the rescue in a driving rain, leaving one infantry company to guard his wagons. Finding nothing, he went into camp two miles below the Rosebud's mouth, and on 21 May ordered the wagon train to join him and help form a new base camp. Thompson's men rode in that afternoon, reporting 40 to 50 warriors seen on the river's opposite bank. But Gibbon took no action, and was to remain in camp for two weeks.

Glimpses of Indian activity suggested that the camp was under constant scrutiny. On Monday, 22 May, Sioux fired on three soldiers hunting near camp, and the next day killed two cavalrymen and a teamster similarly engaged. Silent warriors watched their funeral from across the bluffs. On 24 May a lone Sioux was seen almost inside the camp before escaping in a Plains-style act of derring-do. Then the warriors were seen no more; the Crows surmised that they had left to dance over the single scalp they had taken.

On 27 May another scouting party under Bradley, crossing to the Rosebud's south bank a mile below its mouth, rode up a concealing ravine before reaching the Crows' old lookout point. From here they could see Indian lodges and a huge pony herd grazing some 8 or 10 miles south up the valley of the Rosebud—and now perhaps a bare 18 miles from Gibbon's encampment. Bradley at first attempted to have all his infantrymen inspect the view to confirm the presence of so mighty a gathering, then discretely retreated. By noon, the zealous young officer was reporting to his commander.

This was what Gibbon had been waiting for—or at any rate *should* have been waiting for. At the mouth of the Rosebud, the Yellowstone could have been easily forded with horses, or the cavalry's mounts left behind. The troops themselves might have been ferried across in relays, then marched by night to reach the village by morning. If Gibbon meant to strike at any point, or at any time, this was his chance.

Yet he did nothing. The sarcastic Dr. Paulding wondered in his journal "whether Gibbon's instructions or disposition will allow us to go for them...I suppose we will wait for Crook and Terry, hoping our untutored friends across the river will await their arrival. In the meantime Bradley can go over and take a look every day or so to see that they are still there. His party will be accommodated in a small grave 30 x 8 x 4 some day." Bradley himself could only wonder why no attack had been ordered and assume that "the General probably had good reasons."

What they might have been remains a mystery. Theoretically, caution might have justified Gibbon in not taking on the Sioux alone. But his behavior went beyond even the excessively cautious to the downright bizarre. Soon after receiving Bradley's report, he wrote to Terry: "No camps have been seen, but war parties of from twenty to fifty have been seen to the south of the river and a few on the north side." Stating that he intended to keep scouting parties out to watch for any northward movement, and to march farther down the Yellowstone when supplies from Fort Ellis reached him, he merely added in a postscript: "A camp some distance up the Rosebud was reported this morning by our scouts. If this proves true, I may not start down the Yellowstone so soon."

What could Gibbon have been thinking? Twice a village had been discovered, and twice he had failed to report it—and since Bradley had accompanied the scouts, any skepticism on Gibbon's part could not be laid to doubts about the Crows' liability. As if this were not enough, in his later published account (and annual report) Gibbon made no reference to discovering the village on the Rosebud. Whatever his motives, he would leave Terry in the dark.

On 28 May Gibbon received Terry's orders to march along the Yellowstone's north bank toward a point above the mouth of Glendive Creek, where Terry had suspected a gathering of warriors. Gibbon would then cross the river and cooperate with Terry's Dakota column. But Gibbon may have agreed with Bradley's suspicion that the Indians were working their way in the other direction, and this might account for an

*Fort Abraham Lincoln, Dakota Territory, bordering the Missouri River and, like most frontier posts of the period, virtually unfortified. Sioux war-parties occasionally harassed the garrison and ran off stock, but a full-scale assault by Indians was considered highly unlikely.*

indolence in marching down the river officially attributed to bad weather and roads. On 1 June, a blizzard struck, so reducing the flow of water to the Yellowstone that the river dropped three feet, making it easier for any Sioux to cross over, had any been so inclined. Gibbon's men, after holding a 0200 alert to guard against surprise, huddled about their campfires, shivering in their overcoats and blankets as the snow fell. And there let us leave them for a time.

Terry's "Dakota column" was also slow in getting started. But the reasons were not entirely similar. To the usual harsh weather and logistical troubles were added political intrigues directly affecting the course of the campaign. The immediate victim was a man who had managed to anger the President of the United States—George Armstrong Custer, lieutenant colonel commanding the 7th U.S. Cavalry. And it was the wrath of President Grant which had prevented Terry's Dakota column from being Custer's Dakota column. Custer had been Sheridan's first choice to command the expedition to move out of Fort Abraham Lincoln—and a logical enough choice, if only military factors were considered. A favorite of Sheridan, he had not only compiled a brilliant Civil War record, but had since enjoyed relative success at Indian warfare and diplomacy, displaying awesome tenacity during

Sheridan's first winter campaign. Placing him in command would ensure an aggressive pursuit. "There is no use of asking who will go in command of any troops or expedition sent against the Indians in Dakota," Sheridan's aide Colonel James W. Forsyth had written, "for if Custer is available *he is certain to have the command.*"

In any case, his regiment, headquartered at Lincoln, would make up the column's most powerful (and mobile) element. Terry's early proposal to "give Custer a secure base" on the Yellowstone, if adopted, would probably have left the available infantry to guard supply dumps and provide logistical support while the 7th Cavalry rode down the Sioux—a simple but logical strategy summed up by historian Robert M. Utley as "turn Custer loose." Terry and Custer had begun preparations in mid-February at departmental headquarters in St. Paul, with the tentative date for departure from Fort Lincoln set at 6 April. Neither could have foreseen that their commander-in-chief's petty spite would endanger both Custer's role and the success of the campaign. But on 15 March, General Custer was summoned by telegraph to testify at the hearings of the House Committee on Expenditures in the War Department, investigating Secretary of War William Belknap's role in "selling" Army post traderships in the Indian country. Custer was well aware of abuses suffered by Indians and soldiers at the hands of traders and Indian Bureau officials and had made no secret of his disgust with the prevailing system. But, while busy preparing for the upcoming campaign, he proved reluctant to heed the summons to come Washington. He withdrew a request to submit his testimony telegraphically only because he feared that it might "be construed into a desire to avoid testifying."

Custer's actual testimony on 29 March and 4 April, much of it hearsay, produced little hard evidence that could be used against Belknap, who had already resigned. But his word portrait of collusion between traders and Indian agents was suitably appalling, and he did not neglect the role of Orvil Grant, the President's self-confessedly corrupt brother, in franchising post traderships. Finally securing his release on

# Alfred Howe Terry

Fascinated by the military arts, the Hartford-born Terry (1827-1890) learned German and French to peruse original accounts of military campaigns, struggling along as a trial lawyer, city clerk, and court clerk before an inheritance enabled him to study European battle sites firsthand. Long active in the Connecticut militia, he assumed command of a volunteer regiment in 1861 and commanded a corps as a brevet major general of volunteers. On 15 January 1865 Terry personally led the storming of Fort Fisher, commanding the sea approaches to Wilmington, N.C. Congress tendered its thanks and awarded him a brigadier's commission in the Regular Army.

Heading the Department of Virginia from June 1865 to August 1866, Terry secured command of the Department of Dakota at his own request. Serving on the 1867-68 Indian Peace Commission, he was briefly recalled from Dakota duty in 1869 to head the Department of the South, and also served on the commission negotiating for the sale of the Black Hills.

Following the 1876 campaign, Terry disarmed reservation Sioux at Standing Rock and, the next autumn, met Sitting Bull in Canada with a vain offer of amnesty. His primary objective as department commander became the consolidation of superfluous posts. In April 1886 the Army made Terry major general commanding the Division of the Missouri, but retired him due to poor health in 1888.

20 April, he paused to inspect the wonders of the Centennial Exposition in Philadelphia, and proceeded to New York. It was there, on 24 April, that he received a summons back to Washington from the senate managers of the Belknap impeachment—though it might have been engineered by pro-Belknap forces or the President for purposes of harassment. When on 28 April Belknap's successor Alonzo Taft, who had been importuned by General Sherman, mentioned to President Grant his intention of writing a letter appealing for Custer's release, Grant forbade this. Taft was instead to designate another officer to command the Dakota column.

A shocked Custer secured his own release from the impeachment managers, but delayed his departure at General Sherman's suggestion so that he could plead his case at the White House the following Monday, 1 May. But when Custer showed up, Grant simply refused to see him, and when he left the capital, had General Sherman order his arrest in Chicago on the quite specious grounds that before departing he had seen neither Sherman (then in New York City) or the President! To disgrace Custer further, Grant ordered that he be denied any role in the upcoming campaign. Terry, at General Sheridan's suggestion, had already agreed to lead the Dakota column himself. But now Custer could not even command his own regiment, no matter what the preferences of Sheridan or Sherman.

Terry also desired Custer's participation. Their relationship had suffered various strains in the three years following the transfer of Custer's regiment to Terry's department; the younger man had at times shown a tendency to act without proper regard for military channels, to exceed his own authority, and to test his superior's tolerance. But Terry, who had not exercised a field command since the Civil War, recognized his useful qualities, as well his own lack of experience in Indian campaigning. Agreeing to Custer's request for intercession, he endorsed the fiery cavalryman's telegraphed entreaty to Grant—allegedly composing it as well, though it has the ring of Custer rhetoric. With no hope of commanding the expedition, Custer requested that he at least be permitted "to serve with my regiment in the field. I appeal to you as a soldier to spare me the humiliation of seeing my regiment march to meet the enemy and I not share its dangers."

Whether influenced by military considerations or public criticism of his vindictiveness, or both, Grant relented. Leaving Saint Paul as soon as possible, Terry and Custer arrived at Fort Abraham Lincoln, near Bismarck, D.T., on 10 May, while the Bismarck *Tribune* melodramatically publicized news of "hostiles 1500 lodges strong in camp on the forks of the Little Missouri, waiting anxiously for the long-haired chief." If so, they would have to wait a bit longer, for heavy rains delayed the column's move. Terry finally determined upon a departure date of 17 May, rain or shine.

On 15 May he revealed his awareness that Indians previously wintering at agencies had left to join non-treaty bands, writing to Sheridan that:

> Information from several sources seems to establish the fact
> that the Sioux are collected in camps on the Little Missouri and
> between that and the Powder River....It is represented that they
> have 1500 lodges, are confident, and intend to make a stand.
> Should they do so, and should the three columns be able to act
> simultaneously, I should expect great success...

At a conservative estimate of 2 fighting men per lodge, this would have given the hostiles some 3,000 warriors. Ironically, Terry seems to have exaggerated the number then out, for the summer roamers had yet to join Sitting Bull in strength. But the Army would indeed find more warriors than the Indian Bureau had predicted.

Terry's observations to Sheridan reflected several dubious assumptions. Not only did he assume that even 1,500 lodges of "confident" warriors would prove no match for his troops, but actually thought that their willingness to "make a stand" worked in his favor. Nor did Terry, whatever his hopes of having three columns act "simultaneously," feel that his Dakota force lacked the strength to go it alone, assuring Sheridan on the 16th that he had "no doubt of the ability of my column to whip all the Sioux whom we can find." Terry suggested that Crook move immediately, "with the idea that if he moved up he would force them toward us and enable us to get at them more easily." Expressing equal confidence in Terry's column, but less optimism concerning possible coordination, Sheridan warned: "I will hurry up Crook, but you must rely on the ability of your own column for your best success. I believe it to be fully equal to all the Sioux which can be brought against it, and only hope they will hold fast to meet it....You know the impossibility of any large number of Indians keeping together as a hostile body for even one week."

Despite rains that might have dampened lesser spirits, Custer prepared for the big day with characteristic energy. Mark Kellogg, a *Bismark Tribune* reporter whose dispatches would also appear in the *New York Herald*, saw him in action on 14 April, at the tent city two miles below Fort Lincoln where the 7th Cavalry lay encamped, its stray companies brought to Fort Lincoln at Terry's behest.

Gen. George A. Custer, dressed in a dashing suit of buckskin, is prominent everywhere. Here, there, flitting to and fro, in his quick eager way, taking in everything connected with his command, as well as generally, with a keen incisive manner for which he is so well known. The General is full of perfect readiness for a fray with the hostile red devils, and woe to the body of scalp-lifters that comes within reach of himself and brave companions in arms.

On 17 May, the Dakota column began its march. It was a rarity in frontier warfare for an entire regiment to fight as a unit. But now, for the first time, all 12 companies of the 7th Cavalry marched together—32 officers and 718 enlisted men, including the famed gray-mounted band which had blared "Garry Owen" across the snowy Washita valley eight years before. Two officers and 40 men of Company B, 6th U.S. Infantry Regiment, served as part of Terry's headquarters, along with 3 enlisted men, and a staff of 9 officers. Captain Louis H. Sanger's battalion of companies C and G, 17th Infantry, numbered 7 officers and 89 men, while Lieutenant William H. Low's 20th Infantry detachment of 2 officers and 29 men served 3 multi-barrelled, crank-operated Gatling guns. Quartermaster-hired civilian guides and employees included the taciturn "Lonesome Charley" Reynolds, forage master Boston Custer (brother to the general) and nearly 200 packers, teamsters, and herders; among the latter was Custer's 18-year-old nephew, Armstrong "Autie" Reed. Logistical support included over 150 supply wagons (114 of them 6-mule government types carrying about 2 tons' freight, the rest 2-horse contractors' wagons carrying less than a ton each), an inadequate and amateurish mule train, and a beef herd to supplement the staples of salt pork and bricklike hardtack.

Custer's chief of scouts, Lieutenant Charles A. Varnum, commanded some 39 Indian scouts. Among the 35 Arikara Indians rode Custer's favorite, the half-Sioux Bloody Knife— held in such high regard by his white brother that he was hired as a civilian for $50 a month, rather than enlisted into the Army's scout force at $13. Other Indian scouts included four Sioux and the part-Blackfoot Jackson brothers, Robert

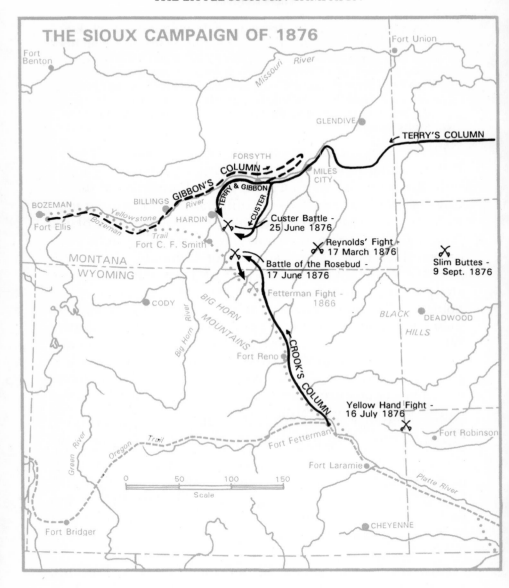

*This 1874 photograph of Custer's wagon train on the Dakota Plains suggests the massive logistical "tail" needed to sustain a conventional military force.*

and William. Interpreting for the Arikaras or "Rees" was white frontiersman Fred Girard; Custer's Sioux interpreter, Isaiah Dorman, was a black man who had lived among the Santee Sioux. In all, Terry's force numbered 52 officers (including 4 contract surgeons and a veterinary surgeon) and 870 men.

Here indeed seemed a force able to "whip all the Sioux" it could find. As Private Charles Windolph, destined to be the last survivor of those who fought with Custer, remembered seven decades later: "You felt like you were somebody when you were on a good horse, with a carbine dangling from its small leather ring socket on your McClellan saddle, and a Colt army revolver strapped on your hip....You were a part of a proud outfit that had a fighting reputation, and you were ready for a fight or a frolic."

The leave-taking at Lincoln was a spectacle and, for many, an occasion for foreboding. "The morning for the start," wrote

Custer's beautiful wife Elizabeth, "came only too soon." Apparently Terry had ordered the command to parade partly to reassure the post's women of his column's strength. For the same reason, Custer had the Rees sing their war songs. At the head of the column rode Custer himself, his wife, and his sister Margaret, married to the 7th's Lieutenant James Calhoun. The buckskinned cavalryman known to the Indians as "Long Hair" now wore his reddish-gold locks cut short.

Mrs. Custer's description remains a classic of American literature. The command passed the quarters of the Arikara scouts, where keening Indian women crouched upon the ground, burdened with a foreboding that needed no translator, or restrained children who sought to follow their chanting fathers; then "Laundresses' Row," where the families of soldiers lined the road, tearful mothers holding their children while they beheld their husbands for perhaps the last time, and where toddlers, "unnoticed by their elders, had made a mimic column of their own. With their handkerchiefs tied to sticks in lieu of flags, and beating old tin pans for drums, they strode lustily back and forth in imitation of the advancing soldiers." At the parade ground the column halted so that married officers could embrace wives and children before swinging back into the saddle. Then, when the 7th's band struck up "The Girl I Left Behind Me," the "most despairing hour seemed to have come," as officers' wives, forcing themselves to their doors to wave a stoic farewell, retreated in anguish at its first notes "to fight out alone their trouble, and seek to place their hands in that of their Heavenly Father...."

From Officers' Row the column moved to join the wagon train, Custer still in the lead, accompanied by a troop of the 7th's advance battalion. The three Gatling guns rumbled behind; then the wagons four abreast, with infantrymen marching between the files. Along one flank of the train ambled the beef herd; on the other, the herd of horses and extra mules. Two battalions of cavalry rode the column's flanks, and the fourth served as rear guard and for the "general assistance" purpose of aiding stalled wagons.

Libbie Custer remembered:

From the hour of breaking camp, before the sun was up, a mist had enveloped everything. Soon the bright sun began to penetrate this veil and dispel the haze, and a scene of wonder and beauty appeared. The cavalry and infantry in the order named, the scouts, pack-mules and artillery, and behind all the long line of white-covered wagons, made a column altogether some two miles in length. As the sun broke through the mist a mirage appeared, which took up about half of the line of cavalry, and thenceforth for a little distance it marched, equally plain to the sight on the earth and in the sky.

The future of the heroic band, whose days were even then numbered, seemed to be revealed, and already there seemed a premonition in the supernatural translation as their forms were reflected from the opaque mist of the early dawn.

The sun, mounting higher and higher as we advanced, took every little bit of burnished steel on the arms and equipments along the line of horsemen, and turned them into glittering flashes of radiating light. The yellow, indicative of cavalry, out-

*Members of the 3rd Infantry at Fort Meade, South Dakota, in 1890—more neatly and more closely arrayed than they were likely to appear "in the field." Their long Springfield rifles inspired respect among Indian foes.*

lined the accoutrements, the trappings of the saddle, and some-times a narrow thread of that effective tint followed the outlines even up to the head-stall of the bridle. At every bend of the road, as the column wound its way round and round the low hills, my husband glanced back to admire his men, and could not refrain from constantly calling my attention to their grand appearance.

On this day of Terry's departure, a company each of cavalry and infantry under Captain Egan, sent by General Crook to patrol the Cheyenne-Black Hills trail, rescued a wagon train in the Hills from Indian raiders. But Crook himself had yet to take the field. Returning to his base in the aftermath of the Reynolds debacle, he had determined to await the new spring grass necessary to sustain his cavalry. But while the grass arrived in late April, Crook was to fall two weeks behind even his tentative departure date of 15 May.

Stripping his department of garrison troops, Crook, a great proponent of using Indians against Indians, also went in search of warrior allies. Leaving his Omaha headquarters, Crook journeyed to Fort Robinson at the Red Cloud Agency, hoping to secure at least 300 Sioux willing to take the war-path against their fellow Lakotas. But not a single Oglala would volunteer, while the agency's hay scales were shortly set afire and the beef herds at both Red Cloud and Spotted Tail run off. When Crook left empty-handed on 16 May, a small party of agency Sioux waited to ambush him. Finding him too well escorted, they instead killed mail-carrier Char-ley Clark as he rode toward the agency.

Desperate for scouts, Crook telegraphed to Camp Brown, on the Shoshone reservation in western Wyoming, and to Fort Ellis, plausibly near the Crows' Montana agency. He re-quested that each tribe send several hundred auxiliaries to join him on the Bozeman Trail crossing of the Powder River, at the Fort Reno site. But while some Shoshones did volun-teer, they would not leave until 4 June.

On 17 May part of Crook's cavalry, under saber-scarred Lieutenant Colonel William B. Royall, set forth from Fort D.A. Russell, two miles from Cheyenne, toward Fort Fetterman. Two more companies followed on the 19th, accompanied by Irish-born *Chicago Times* correspondent John F. Finerty, who characterized the cavalrymen as "for the most part, young, but well seasoned, and in their blue shirts, broad felt hats, cavalry boots, and blue or buckskin pantaloons—for on an Indian campaign, little attention is paid to uniform—looked both athletic and warlike. Their arms were as bright as hard rubbing could make them, and around the waist of every stalwart trooper was a belt filled with sixty rounds of fixed ammunition for the Springfield carbine....The sabers had been left behind at the different posts as useless encumbrances." Some, of course, preferred not to play the game, no fewer than 69 cavalrymen deserting on the night of 19 May as Royall's men rested before resuming their march to Fetterman.

The troops were soon reminded of just how far-ranging their opponents could be. On 21 May, a nine-man 2nd Cavalry patrol guided by Frank Grouard, sent to explore possible stream crossings between Fetterman and Fort Reno, narrowly eluded a night ambush by Sioux. Leaving dummies made from blankets, the men sneaked out of camp and rode along the Bozeman til dawn before hiding out the next day. On the 23rd the patrol headed toward the Dry Fork of the Powder, hoping to find Crook's Crow allies before their Sioux enemies did.

At times the troops proceeded in the apparent belief that the Sioux would not show up where they were not wanted, and would refrain from attacking at inconvenient times. They could waver in this belief, however. Marching east of the North Platte River, through what Finerty called "a perfect labyrinth" of twisting gorges, some pondered the likelihood of an attack from the bluffs on troops with little cover or chance to withdraw. The reporter noted elevations so steep that the men had to dismount and lead horses in ascending or descending, commenting: "It was up hill and down dale for eight long miles, and had Col. Royall been opposed by a capable foe, his part of Crook's expedition would never have reached the rendezvous." In fact, "'Sitting Bull' lost a fine opportunity for clipping Crook's wings, and nearly all the officers recognized the fact." On 25 May, Major Andrew "Beans" Evans, with five companies of cavalry and one of infantry, arrived at Fetterman from Medicine Bow, Wyoming, warriors watching from the ridges north and west of the post.

The command spent the 26th transferring men, wagons, horses, and supplies from the south to the north bank of the North Platte, swollen by the spring thaw. Using massed muscle power, they hauled by rope a crude ferryboat guided by a block-and-tackle system fastened to both banks. A teamster was swept away by the current while attempting to retrieve a snapped rope, and two 2nd Cavalry troopers and a sergeant drowned with their mounts while swimming the horses across. But nearly every mule and horse ultimately had to be ferried, for they refused to approach the rapid current. In this, felt Bourke, they "showed more sense than the men in charge of them." The first day 60,000 pounds of stores were ferried across, and 100,000 the next, besides "soldiers by solid companies." On the 27th, Crook was informed that a hundred more young warriors from Red Cloud Agency had gone north to join Sitting Bull, and anxiously dispatched two companies of cavalry to Fort Reno to learn whether the Crows had arrived.

Finally marching out on 29 May, Crook's Wyoming column, formally the "Big Horn and Yellowstone Expedition," was largest of the three. His mounted forces were impressive: 10 companies of the 3rd Cavalry (A-G, I, L, and M) and five companies of the 2nd (A, B, E-G) under the command of Brevet Colonel Royall, totalling about 900 effectives. Some 300 infantry under Major Alexander Chambers included Companies D and F of the 4th Infantry and C, G, and H of the 9th. Crook's staff included Captain George M. Randall as chief of scouts, plus a chief engineer officer, a chief quartermaster, chief commissary officer, medical director Assistant Surgeon Albert Hartsuff (a civilian contract surgeon), and two aides-de-camp, one of them Lieutenant Bourke. In all, 51 officers and 1,000 fighting men would march against the Sioux. No fewer than five reporters accompanied the column. But, whether through Crook's optimism concerning the availability of Indian allies or false economy, or both, only three civilian guides or interpreters rode with him: Frank Grouard,

Louis Richard, and Baptiste Pourier. The pack train included 81 men and 250 mules; the wagon train 116 men and 106 wagons.

They started at about noon, the unsavory denizens and *demi-monde* of a nearby "hog ranch" waving farewell to the four-mile long column. The cavalry preceded the infantry, followed in turn by wagons and the beef herd. Packers and mules rode in single file to the soldiers' right. With the infantry setting an average pace of two and a half miles per hour, Crook made only 10 miles the first day, heading north and slightly west along the old Bozeman trail to Sage Creek.

Though he seems not to have suspected it, Crook would need everything he had. He could certainly not expect more. Summing up his estimate of the situation to General Sherman on the day of Crook's departure, Phil Sheridan pointed out that he now had in the field some 2,200 troops, which new Secretary of War J.D. Cameron asserted were as many as the Army could spare, or maintain in such country. As "no very accurate information can be obtained as to the location of the hostile Indians, and as there would be no telling how long they would stay at any one place, if it were known," he explained that he had

> given no instructions to Generals Crook or Terry, preferring that they should do the best they can under the circumstances and under what they may develop, as I think it would be unwise to make any combinations in such country as they will have to operate in. As hostile Indians in any great numbers can not keep the field as a body for a week, or at most ten days, I therefore consider—and so do Terry and Crook—that each column will be able to take care of itself and of chastising the Indians should it have the opportunity.

Sheridan believed that General Terry would probably drive the Indians toward the Big Horn Valley, General Crook drive them back toward Terry, and Gibbon move down on the Yellowstone to intercept those attempting to go north of the Missouri. Yet he suspected that his unfolding campaign might accomplish little. The troops' movements *might* inspire many braves to head back to their reservations—simply to leave again after the troops had returned to garrison in the fall. Sheridan thus renewed his previous recommendation that Congress authorize the construction of two forts on the Yellowstone River—and that the Sioux agencies be placed under military control to prevent such comings and goings.

"I hope that good results may be obtained by the troops in the field," wrote Sheridan sadly, "but am not at all sanguine, unless what I have above suggested be carried out. We might just as well settle the Sioux question now; it will be better for all concerned." The next day, his pessimistic mood unbroken, he expressed the fear that "all the agency Indians capable of taking the field" were either already on the warpath or eventually would be. Sheridan would receive his two forts only in the wake of disaster, and Army control would come too late to stop the flow of warriors from the agencies. But he did what he could, on 2 June ordering eight companies of the 5th Cavalry transferred from Kansas to posts near the Red Cloud and Spotted Tail agencies.

Meanwhile, Crook's movements were under observation; after 31 May, the command noticed smoke signals daily. On 1 June the troops awoke to the same norther tormenting Gibbon's men, but marched on through snow and sleet, the mule-mounted Crook at their head. On 2 June they reached a camp near the burnt-out Fort Reno, where Captain van Vliet returned with his battalion of cavalry from a mission to find the Crows at their appointed rendezvous. He bore disquieting news: no Indian allies had appeared.

Choosing the least unpleasant of his options, Crook left himself bare of scouts by having his three civilians sneak out that night and head for the Crow Agency to fetch the auxiliaries, while he headed toward Goose Creek at the site of the present Sheridan, Wyoming. There he could set up a secure camp fairly close to known Sioux haunts. But going scoutless had its price. On 6 June, after reaching the ruined Fort Phil Kearny and passing the Fetterman Massacre site, Crook, expecting to reach Goose Creek early that afternoon, lost the dimming trail. Prematurely turning north, he ended up on the same trail Reynolds had used that winter, finally camping roughly six miles east of his real objective.

For some reason, Crook decided to march the next day down Prairie Dog Creek toward Tongue River, though he must have known that this would make him miss any rendezvous with the expected auxiliaries. With no guides, he was going deeper into hostile country, with his foes far more likely to discover Crook than he them.

This is precisely what happened. A party of Cheyenne hunters, observing the column, shadowed it for a day before hastening toward their camp with the news, while the soldiers settled down on the west side of Prairie Dog Creek in an angle formed by its confluence with the Tongue. There, in a narrow bottom dominated by high bluffs, they set up what they suspected might be a permanent base of operations, though Crook still gave no hint of his plans. On 8 June couriers gave Crook the reassuring news that 180 Shoshone warriors were on their way.

But on 9 June a band of Northern Cheyennes showed up instead, led by Little Hawk, who hoped to stampede the white men's horses. With the troops at mess, puffs of white smoke appeared on the bluffs across the river as slugs ripped through the largely unoccupied tents. Civilian employees returned a fire more vigorous than accurate, while four 3rd Cavalry companies under Captain Anson Mills saddled up, crossed the Tongue and dismounted. One Indian seemingly wearing a hat of tin topped by a plume rode rhythmically back and forth atop the bluffs in full view of the whites below. High-spirited packers jokingly ran back and forth to match his movements, as though trying to catch him.

Detaching every fourth man as a horse-holder, Mills advanced up the bluff in skirmish formation, pursuing the Indian riflemen over several ridges in succession. Though some imagined that hundreds of warriors had been driven before them, they had displaced a mere handful of snipers. The 2nd Cavalry skirmished briefly on the left when a few Indians forded the river, and a small attack from the south was also repelled. Several companies of infantry advanced to occupy the bluffs, ultimately to huddle shelterless and soaked by rain. The Indians withdrew without a fatality, but two soldiers were slightly wounded by spent balls, while three horses and a mule had to be destroyed.

Crook finally broke camp on 11 June and retreated 11 miles back up Prairie Dog Creek before marching southwest seven miles through the rain to set up camp at the planned Goose Creek location, where his men hunkered down to hunt, fish and wait. Perhaps Crook simply wanted to correct his original mistake. But that taciturn chief confided his plans, if indeed he had any, to no one. While artillery lieutenant Louis Capron found Crook "quite weary and nervous," the 3rd Cavalry's Lieutenant James Foster praised "a faculty for silence that is absolutely astonishing. There is one thing very certain: none of the General's plans will ever be discussed until after they are executed—a precious quality in a commanding officer. Grant is loquacious when compared to him." But perhaps Crook simply failed to express his own uncertainty. His scouts had not returned, his Indian allies had not shown up, and he was consuming his supplies without advance or result.

On the afternoon of 14 June guides Grouard and Richard galloped into camp with Crow chief Old Crow and the assurance that Big Bat and 175 friendly warriors, under chiefs Medicine Crow and Good Heart, were only 10 miles away. Crook's scouts had encountered the Crows on the Bighorn below the Fort Smith site, then spent four days persuading and cajoling them—as well as taunting them that they would be women if they did not come. The other Crows had hung back from entering Crook's camp only because, having spotted his 7 June camp on Prairie Dog Creek, they had found him later on the Tongue and so suspected him of retreating from the Sioux. A relieved Crook gave them a warm welcome. Soon after the Crows mock-charged into camp, 86 Shoshone warriors, riding in neat ranks, appeared under their chief Washakie, though the rest of the 130 had turned back after leaving the reservation. Crook formed his rugged, ragged command into a regimental front nearly a mile in length, Regular Army pomp meeting the tribal splendor of warbonnet and feathered lance.

That evening Crook ordered that most of his men be ready by the morning of 16 June to march as a highly mobile force. In best Crook style, no wagons would be taken, and the men would carry only the clothing on their backs, 1 blanket each, 4 days' rations, and 100 rounds of ammunition. Only 20 packers would accompany the abbreviated pack train, which included one mule bearing medical supplies and another laden with pioneering tools.

All were to be mounted—even the infantry. Thus 15 June witnessed the amusing spectacle of some 175 doughboys attempting to break in their wagon-mule mounts. A stockade of wagons would be formed on a small island in the creek. Leaving behind a guard of 100 soldiers plus the remaining civilians, Crook would go on with roughly 1,325 men, to find the Sioux and Cheyenne.

Unless, of course, they decided to find him first.

# An Army on the March

Compared to a Plains Indian war party, or even to a village of tipis on pony-borne travois, a column of Regulars was a cumbersome and slow-moving thing. While cavalry was considered the arm most likely to finally close with an Indian force, a column including infantry was not considered seriously handicapped on an extended campaign; men could survive hardships better than horses, and over long periods the foot soldiers could outmarch the mounted men at a respectable average rate of 20 miles per hour. A bigger handicap in attempting to bring large forces against Indians was the sheer difficulty of keeping them adequately supplied. Travelling light and fast, as General Crook preferred to do, was a strictly short-term measure, and an officer in 1891 compared the usual expedition to a chained dog—"within the length of the chain irresistible, beyond it powerless. The chain was its wagon train and supplies."

Troops could, of course, be moved by railroads—where railroads existed. Steamers could move supplies to the nearest point accessible to troops, but only where and when major rivers were navigable. Normally wagon trains or river steamers, usually owned by civilian firms under contract, stockpiled supplies. Wagons then shuttled between depots and field forces.

The supplies consumed were impressive. A soldier's normal daily ration included a pound of rock-like hardtack, three-fourths pound of bacon or salt pork, one-sixth pound of beans and one-fourth pound of coffee and sugar, amounting to five pounds per man with normal packing. Horses required 12 pounds of grain daily, usually corn. Reserve carbine ammunition weighed 105 pounds per 1,000-round box. Terry's column alone required daily some eight tons of supplies—and though it was to carry only enough to last until resupply by steamboat, its train consisted of 1,694 horses and mules, and even with wagons rolling four abreast, stretched out over close to half a mile.

While each infantry company needed the equivalent of at least one six-mule wagon, each cavalry troop required that of three due to forage needs—for "American" horses could not exist on grass even when there *was* grass. Wagons were more "fuel-efficient" than pack mules; while a 6-mule wagon carried a practical load of roughly a ton, the same 6 mules bore only 1,200 pounds when used with packs. Since a pack mule was supposed to get 10 pounds of grain a day, each could eat all he carried in 20 days.

But Indians might well go where wagons could not, and only by using pack mules could the Army hope to follow them. Their greatest proponent was Apache warfare veteran George Crook, who preferred using wagons to support his initial march and to provision his supply base camp, then pack mules for the final phase. Crook organized his trains into self-sufficient units of 14 men to each 50 mules, including a packmaster, his assistant (*carcadore*), a blacksmith, and cook. Trained to graze within earshot of their bell-horse, such mules did not need to carry their own fodder, and could bear an average 250 pounds each at 5 miles per hour.

But such a professional train had to be maintained in active service, and only Crook's column had one. General Terry later complained that as none had ever been organized in his department he was "necessarily dependent upon wagons," though he took some 250 pack saddles along to be placed on his 95 pack mules, and presumably those from the wagons, as required. Once separated from Terry, Custer took with his 7th Cavalry at least six packers, one of whom would die at the Little Bighorn. But these were the only professionals in a train of some 175 mules, 90 of them wagon mules—including 12 per company, 12 to carry extra ammunition, 4 for the headquarters staff, 2 for medical officers, 2 to carry tools, and camp gear and 11 for scouts, packers, and civilians. They straggled so badly that Custer finally assigned 126 men, or 1 NCO and 6 soldiers from each company, to expedite their progress.

Even with mules, the Army could scarcely hope to outpace its enemies. But it might be able to employ superior resources and persistence in wearing them down, and ultimately running them to earth.

# Frontier Army

There was Sergeant John McCaffery
and Captain Donahue,
They made us march and toe the mark,
in gallant Company "Q"

Oh the drums would roll upon my soul,
This is the style we'd go,
Forty miles a day on beans and hay,
In the Regular Army O.

So sang two irreverent New York vaudevillians in 1875, either inventing or popularizing a song to which the Regulars themselves would add topical verses. But often public irreverence was a less pleasant affair. With the ending of the Civil War, the beloved Boys in Blue had become again despised, mercenary "regulars"—an army dismissed by the *New York Sun* as "composed of bummers, loafers, and foreign paupers."

The Regular soldier of 1876 was paid $13 a month, with deductions, plus a clothing allowance. Like roughly half his comrades, he might be an immigrant, most likely Irish or German—or perhaps an unemployed laborer, a Union or Confederate veteran, or (in four black units officered by whites) an ex-slave. He might well have enlisted under an alias, and there were good reasons for doing so. Reporter John F. Finerty regretfully reported that "the American enlisted soldier is socially ostracized, except by laundresses and camp followers....It is not the discipline within the army,

but the disdain outside of it, that oppresses the American soldier." New 7th Cavalry recruit William Slaper, destined to survive the Little Bighorn fight, admitted: "Being in my own home town, and well known, I felt somewhat ashamed of being seen in my uniform."

Typically receiving rudimentary drill (and his basic uniform of dark blue woolen blouse, képi-like "forage cap", and sky-blue trousers) at a recruit depot, the frontier soldier arrived at his post, where he shared a straw-filled mattress with his "bunkie." He would serve three years as a foot soldier, five years as a cavalryman—unless, of course, like about one-third of those enlisted between 1867 and 1891, he deserted, perhaps having joined simply to get transport west. If he stayed, he faced isolation, wretched food, shoddy clothing, and sometimes ferocious discipline. Entertainment might include bad whiskey and fornication with laundresses, Indian women or prostitutes.

The soldier's best hope of overcoming the Plains Indian's superiority as a fighter lay in steadiness and discipline. But training in marksmanship, horsemanship, and other combat skills was often neglected, sometimes because soldiers were kept busy at manual labor to build or sustain their posts, the would-be hero forced to serve as a "brevet architect" despite the civilian chant of: "Soldier, soldier, will you work? No indeed, I'll sell my shirt."

A cavalry regiment consisted of 12 companies, an infantry regiment of 10. But since a regiment's companies were rarely concentrated at one post, training in large-unit tactics was often impossible. During the winter of 1876 Colonel Nelson A. Miles took advantage of his 5th Infantry's consolidation in the field to drill it despite the harsh weather; its training in skirmishing would help Miles to defeat Crazy Horse at Tongue River early in 1877. The soldier might never see a hostile Indian, but was often outnumbered when he did; Congress had limited paper recruiting strength to 25,000 in 1874 and the Army usually numbered under 19,000 enlisted men, including 10 regiments of cavalry (4 established in 1866), 25 of infantry, and 5 of artillery, plus 4 regiments of the Veteran Reserve Corps (formerly the Invalid Corps of disabled servicemen). Much of this force was still reserved for Reconstruction duty in the South. A German immigrant confessed himself "wonderstruck" by the work of his fellow soldiers. "The handsome, finely organized cavalries of Europe know nothing of real hard cavalry work.

For the work I have seen a squadron of United States Cavalry performing on the plains, Germany would send two regiments, and deem it hard service...."

On the other hand, tiny bands of Indians might tie down several hundred Regulars; during California's Modoc War of 1872-73, a force never exceeding 60 warriors inflicted several embarrassing defeats. Congress provided no moral support for these wars which were not wars; in 1877, barely a year after Custer's defeat, an appropriations dispute left officers and men payless from June until late November, even as some died fighting the Nez Perce War.

In garrison, neatness counted, and full-dress uniforms included gorgeous horsehair-plumed helmets for cavalry and artillery. But in the field the soldier might wear a shoddy black campaign hat or privately purchased "slouch," as well as other items of civilian clothing. If there was romance, it was of a decidedly rugged sort, captured perhaps by a *New York Times* reporter describing 5th Cavalry troopers in July of 1876:

> To a fastidious eye...there was something quite shocking in the disregard of regulation uniform, and the mud-bespattered appearance of the men; but it was a pleasure to see how full of vim, of spirit, and emphatically of fight, the fellows looked.... About the only things in their dress which marked them as soldiers were their striped pants and knee boots,

both well bespattered with mud. Their blue Navy shirts, broad brimmed hats, belts stuffed with cartridges and loose handkerchiefs knotted about the neck, gave them a wild, bushwhacker appearance, which was in amusing contrast with their polished and gentlemanly manners.

If the soldier proved valorous, he might receive the nation's only military decoration, the Medal of Honor; established since 1874, the Certificate of Merit was awarded more rarely, perhaps because money was tight and recipients were paid two extra dollars a month. From 1865 to 1898 there were some 938 Indian engagements involving Regulars, with 59 officers and 860 enlisted men killed, 65 and 960 wounded.

Characterized as a brute persecuting innocent Indians by eastern reformers, he might well sympathize with their plight, or marry an Indian woman if he stayed in the West after service. If he lived until 1905, he could wear an Indian campaign medal, marking him as a soldier of a vanished frontier which would soon seem almost impossibly remote.

# How to Fight Indians

One of the problems with Indian warfare was that everyone (except the Indians) knew that it would soon blow over. In 1876, General Winfield Scott Hancock told a congressional committee that the Army's Indian service was "entitled to no weight" in determining its strength or composition; it was "of secondary importance," comparatively "temporary," and furnished "only incidental duty" for a portion of the Army. Such duty could include protecting settlers from Indians (or Indians from settlers), waging elaborate punitive campaigns, dying under a rain of arrows, or acting as a glorified policeman. Soldiers might also find themselves exploring the West, assisting civil authorities, or chasing Southern "Ku Kluxers"—all unseemly distractions from the task of preparing for the next scrap with a "civilized" foe. But an obsession with Civil War glories also discouraged reform; when changes in staff bureaus were suggested in 1873, General Sheridan replied: "It answered well during the war, and we ought to be contented with it in time of peace." The wars marring this peace would soon be over anyway. So why bother with a "doctrine" of Indian warfare? Insofar as the Army had a policy beyond reacting to each outbreak as it occurred, it was to build sufficient forts to control the tribes or react quickly to strife, marking time while settlement and new railways did the quiet work of hemming in the Indian and eating away his hunting grounds. Unfortunately, the Army lacked the money to build the posts desired, General Sherman warning in 1872 "that for every post we establish an old one must be given up." Nor were there enough men to police the estimated quarter-million western Indians, though most were already concentrated on reservations.

Overtaking and punishing Plains raiders was almost impossible given the Indians' speed and custom of scattering into small parties while fleeing. Widely dispersed troops could be drawn together for offensive operations, but their only natural target was the village of tipis, portable dwellings moved by means of a travois or wooden drag frame. Such mobile communities were hard to overtake. But if they succeeded in capturing them and seizing the Indians' ponies, the soldiers could reduce the warriors and non-combatants alike to utter poverty—lacking shelter, foodstores, clothing, and transportation.

Indeed, destruction of Indian resources was the easiest way to victory, and government officials looked kindly upon white hide-hunters who nearly annihilated the Plains buffalo herds. Sheridan's campaign strategy of total war, preferably in winter, seemed the best way to exploit both the Indians' logistical weaknesses and the Army's superior organization, tenacity, and ability to supply forces over long distances. Converging columns could keep the Indians harried and demoralized simply by keeping them on the move, as in the Red River War of 1874-75.

But even in employing Sheridan's relatively new strategy, the Indian-fighting army remained a resolutely conventional force faced with a decidedly unconventional foe. Westerners often jeered at the Regulars' awkwardness in finding and fighting Indians. Though the few experiments with units of frontiersmen in Army service ended in disbandment, as late as 1883 a former cavalry officer advocated that the War Department "play Indian" by organizing a regiment of buckskin-clad scouts living "entirely in the field." With the Army obliged to rely on white frontiersmen, "mixed-bloods" or friendly Indians as guides and scouts, a surgeon with Gibbon's column asserted that cavalrymen were generally "about as well fitted to travel through a hostile country as puling infants, and go mooning around at the mercy of any Indian who happens to catch sight and takes the trouble to lay for them behind the first convenient ridge."

When he did close with the foe, the soldier was expected to act as part of a unit; individualism might be limited to taking cover behind the tree of his choice, or picking a target when allowed to fire at will. In small-unit fighting this had both drawbacks and advantages; a Pawnee Indian scout observed:

"The group formations of the army made a bigger target, but army marksmanship was better and steadier." While a skirmish line firing volleys on command might seem more useful against a "conventional" foe, it could prove effective in repelling mounted warriors. And to survive against fluid Indian tactics, the bluecoats had to maintain cohesion, especially while in retreat.

When attacking, cavalry could charge in one or two lines (with the two possibly merging in the course of the charge), in column of fours, or at extended skirmisher intervals. Since Indians would not meet such charges and could outride the troopers, the latter might regroup after a few hundred yards' charge, perhaps charging again when the Indians drew up. Few on either side were likely to be killed in such fighting. Even when the soldiers attacked from several directions, or used a holding force to engage the Indians while other detachments struck from flank or rear, the warriors could slip away like quicksilver through the fingers. Cavalry, most likely to actually engage Plains Indians, often acted simply as mounted infantry, dismounting to fire effectively. But in a defensive situation, it was the infantry—the "walking soldiers"—that the Indians most respected. As a Cheyenne army scout told artist Frederic Remington in 1890: "Dese walk-a-heap soldiers dey dig hole—get in—shoot heap— Injun can't do nothin' wid 'em— can't kill 'em—can't do nothin' but jes go 'way."

# CHAPTER III

# The Battle of the Rosebud

## 17 June 1876

*A*nd what of these elusive warriors? Having spent most of the winter dispersed in numerous small camps among the Powder River country's valleys, the easternmost in or touching upon the Black Hills, they had drifted to the Powder itself and its eastern tributaries by the time of the Reynolds campaign. After the refugees from the 17 March attack moved to the Little Powder's east fork to find succor with Crazy Horse's Oglalas, they found that his people had little enough to spare, and trekked on a further 60 miles to the north. Here camped Sitting Bull—and it was toward Sitting Bull that the more warlike Sioux gravitated as they realized the government's intentions.

With travel eased by the pony-fattening spring grass, and left in peace by Crook's withdrawal from the field, they made their leisurely way from the Powder to the lower Tongue. It was from this camp that the 50 bold Cheyennes rode to rustle the Crows' horses after a small hunting party discovered Gibbon's men on the Yellowstone, and as the soldiers marched downriver, small bands contented themselves with prudent attempts to pick off strays or gobble up isolated parties. By the time Crook made his late return to the field, the Indians the Army sought may have numbered from 400 to 500 lodges, with a safe minimum of 2 fighting men per tipi. Perhaps any one of Sheridan's three columns could have

# Crazy Horse

He was the warlike hero of a warlike people. Probably born between 1841 and 1844, Crazy Horse, first known as Curly or the Light-Haired Boy until his father bestowed his own name of Tashunca-uitco, achieved distinction in Red Cloud's War. As one of the Iteshica, or Bad Faces, of Red Cloud's Oglala band, he apparently led the decoy party which in December of 1866 lured Fetterman's 80 men into an annihilating ambush by perhaps two thousand Sioux and Cheyennes and a few Arapahoes.

Never a formal "chief" but renowned as a "shirt-wearer" or leading warrior, Crazy Horse earned a reputation for courage and generosity, allowing none to pass him in battle and keeping no booty for himself save weapons of war. Taciturn, termed by the Oglalas "Our Strange Man," he was in 1876 a youthful-looking individual with unusually light skin, waist-length brown hair, and a scar under his nose from a jealous husband's bullet.

His vision told him to rub dirt unearthed by gophers over parts of his horse in lines and streaks, wear a redbacked hawk in his hair and a brown pebble behind his ear, and avoid tying up his pony's tail or wearing a warbonnet. Later, as a member of the Thunder Cult, he fought stripped to his breechcloth, a lightning streak down his face, a splattering of hailmarks on his and his horse's body.

Crazy Horse apparently realized that fighting the whites required different methods, aimed at damaging the enemy rather than winning honor. But this die-hard traditionalist could only change so much, continuing to vary his forays against the whites with raids against Crows and Shoshones. Even stalking intruders into the Black Hills single-handed, Crazy Horse never tried leading a large force to drive them out.

His precise movements are sometimes difficult to pin down; his absence at the Reynolds fight was disputed by historian George E. Hyde, and his actions at the Rosebud remain obscure. Relying upon Sioux informants, Lieutenant W.P. Clark reported that the Custer fight brought him "more prominently before all the Indians than any one else. He rode with the greatest daring up and down in front of Col[.]

prevailed against such numbers, if not quite with the expected ease. But in early June, while camped on Rosebud Creek, the Indians learned that a great victory was at hand.

It was the time for the Sun Dance, the central communal rite of Sioux religion. The Hunkpapa holy man Sitting Bull, the very spirit of resistance to the white man and all his works,

Reno[']s skirmish line, and as soon as these troops were driven across the river, he went at once to Genl[.] Custer['] s front and there became the leading spirit."

After his surrender in 1877, Crazy Horse, according to Bourke—who "never heard an Indian mention his name save in terms of respect"—behaved "with stolidity, like a man who realized he had to give in to Fate, but would do so as sullenly as possible." Suspected of planning a breakout from the reservation, he was finally arrested. At Fort Robinson, Nebraska, he drew two knives before he could be put in the guardhouse and was fatally bayoneted—or, perhaps, accidentally stabbed by his friend Little Big Man with his own knife as he grappled with Crazy Horse. After watching him die, Sans Arc chief Touching-the-Clouds remarked: "It is good: he has looked for death, and it has come."

Other, less defiant Sioux chiefs were more influential, and, it is argued, did more to benefit their people; George Hyde, deriding what he termed the "cult" of Crazy Horse, termed it "an amazing thing." But if Crazy Horse has become to many the greatest of Indian heroes, it is because his refusal to compromise, to accept the verdict of history in the face of overwhelming odds, is the essence of the romantic. Lieutenant Bourke felt a mixture of relief that the United States would never again face "an aborigine who is a match in the field for the whole miserable skeleton called its army" and sorrowful admiration for "the gallant savage" who had "resisted with so much science and daring the forces sent against him." He sensed, perhaps, how the white man's histories would remember the spirit of such heroic resistance:

> "Crazy Horse" was one of the great soldiers of his day and generation; he never could be the friend of the whites, because he was too bold and warlike in his nature...As the grave of Custer marked the high-water mark of Sioux supremacy in the trans-Missouri region, so the grave of "Crazy Horse," a plain fence of pine slabs, marked the ebb.

Later, the body was moved from its scaffold and secretly reburied, so that no man might ever know the grave of Crazy Horse.

---

used an awl point to lift up 50 bits of flesh from each arm as a knife sliced them away in sacrifice. Dancing around a pole connected to skewers passed through his chest, staring at the sun, Sitting Bull finally tore free and collapsed. Awaking from his prophetic trance, he told of a vision of many soldiers—falling upside-down into the Sioux camp. The whites would have scorned such an omen had they known of it. But if his warriors believed, Sitting Bull's vision could become a self-fulfilling prophecy.

The Indians' growing numbers also ensured confidence. With spring, the so-called summer roamers had begun their exodus from the agencies to join the non-treaty bands. These were joined by an undetermined number of agency Indians—drawn not merely by the prospect of hunting, but also by resentment of the government's pressure to sell the Black Hills and its arbitrary denial of their right to roam their own lands. Both groups would swell the number of available warriors—perhaps into the thousands. By 14 June the assembled Indians had turned west and traveled down to the valley of the Little Bighorn, camping at the forks of the present Reno Creek.

It was a massive village, extending for two miles and including camp circles of the Cheyenne and of five Sioux bands: Hunkpapas, Oglalas, Sans Arc, Blackfeet and Miniconjou. There were also a few Santee Sioux, Brules, and Arapahoes—and, according to Cheyenne historian John Stands in Timber, a smaller camp of Cheyennes on nearby Trail Creek. The number of warriors is disputed, and while Crazy Horse's own reported estimate of 1,400 Sioux and 100 Cheyenne seems reasonable, a modern scholar has suggested an estimate of barely 750 fighters.

Due to problems of sanitation and the rapid exhaustion of any campsite's game, wood and grass, Sheridan had been quite right to claim that so many warriors could not camp together for long. But what if they were encountered before the camp broke up? Crook was apparently untroubled by the possibility. As Bourke wrote: "No one now doubts that we shall be victorious; the only discrepancy of opinion is in regard to the numbers we may find." Crook was more concerned about finding them in the first place. He had set out on 15 June with no reliable knowledge of their whereabouts, though told by scout Grouard that the Sioux might be camped on the Rosebud—presumably somewhere above the area viewed on his own return from the Crows' village. That, in fact, is where they still were—a mere 52 miles from his own camp. While the Crows assured the white chief they called "Three-stars" that he could still surprise the village, Crook thought that roaming Sioux hunters made this unlikely. But he was ready to try. On 16 June, without bugle commands, the day's march north began at 0600. The cavalry led, followed by the mounted infantry, with Indian allies on flanks and front. Crook's force of roughly 1,325 men forded Big Goose Creek and the Tongue River, the Big Horn Mountains receding as the column paralleled a dried-up branch of the Tongue, northwest to the divide between the Tongue and Rosebud valleys.

When the command came suddenly upon an immense buffalo herd, Crook's Indians belied the image of the silently cunning red man by wantonly shooting down over 100 animals—arguing when upbraided that it was "better kill buffalo than have him feed the Sioux." Any lingering hope that the quarry would be surprised was dashed when Indian hunters exchanged insults with Grouard and the Crow warrior Plenty-coups, fleeing in a direction suggesting a camp on the Rosebud.

In fact, a party of Cheyennes, led by Little Hawk of the Elks warrior society, had already informed the village; narrowly escaping detection before observing the large force of soldiers and Indians, they howled like wolves four times before entering camp to tell what they had seen. A council of chiefs advised the young men to hold off fighting until the soldiers attacked—only to be shouted down. It is said that when Crazy Horse spoke in council, the normally taciturn Oglala advised his brothers to fight not simply for honors, but to kill efficiently, as the whites did.

Soon men began saddling their favorite war-ponies. They donned warbonnets, painted faces and bodies, dressed in their best clothing in expectation of battle and possible death, and performed the necessary medicine rituals. They would not seek safety in flight. Instead they would do what the bluecoat soldier-chiefs, if asked, might have wished them to do—give open battle against the men of the Regular Army.

Crossing the divide that night, Crook made camp on the source of the Rosebud's south fork, in a valley commanded by bluffs on all sides. Sensing that the enemy might be close, he forbade fires; the men ate their rations cold, then slept on their weapons. A few of the Indian auxiliaries accompanied Grouard and Tom Cosgrove on a night scout of the region to their front. Captain Sutorious of Company E, 3rd Cavalry, head pillowed on his saddle, predicted: "We will have a fight tomorrow, mark my words—I feel it in the air."

Obligingly, most of the Sioux and Cheyenne were already on their way, feathers fluttering from lances, shields hung from backs, and ponies' tails tied up for war. Leaving a small force under the older chiefs to guard the noncombatants, the departing warriors took various routes. Some Cheyennes went east and slightly southward across the divide to the Rosebud under Two Moon, his nephew Young Two Moon and the most eminent Cheyenne chief present, Spotted Wolf, pausing to rest and prepare themselves ceremonially 11 miles north of the Rosebud's big bend. Others, less patient, had started up the south fork of Reno Creek and through Sioux Pass. Still others, including the Hunkpapas, would come in as reinforcements during the ongoing fight. But most, riding that night, would be there by morning.

On 17 June, with reveille at 0300, the march began at 0600, mule-mounted infantry leading the way only to be overtaken by the cavalry as they picked their way over rough country. Following the Rosebud, Crook proceeded eastward a few miles, then paralleled the turn of the south fork a mile and a half to a bend where the north fork joined it. Almost three miles to the east, the Rosebud again turned north to its big bend. At 0800 the van of the column, marching east, reached a point between the bend and the creek's north and south forks, Crook ordering a brief halt to rest men and animals. When Crow scouts reported Sioux sign and advised caution, he threw out pickets to the north.

He would bivouac in a natural amphitheater flanked by lines of bluffs paralleling the stream to the north and south— the northern bluffs from 200 to 600 yards from the stream, the southern bluffs a half-mile away. Beyond the low bluffs, to the north, was an irregular ridge about a mile from Rosebud Creek, extending westward from the Rosebud's big bend. Below a high promontory now called Andrews Point, this ridge was joined by another stretching down to the southeast. Between the two ridges was dry Kollmar Creek, running southeasterly from Andrews Point to the Rosebud, to the east of its forks.

The column had marched on both sides of the Rosebud, and straddled it in making bivouac. On the north side was a battalion of five 2nd Cavalry companies under Captain Henry Noyes, to the east of Captain Frederick Van Vliet's battalion of two from the 3rd Cavalry. Next came five companies of infantry, and further back, toward the west and Crook's future left flank, the packers and most of the Indian allies. On the south side were Captain Anson Mills' and Captain Guy V. Henry's battalions of the 3rd Cavalry.

Crook's considerable Indian-fighting experience had not involved the Plains tribes, and he gave no apparent thought to the possibility that he might be attacked in force. Mills later recalled that despite information available from guides and scouts, "from conversations with him I felt he did not realize the prowess of the Sioux...."

The men relaxed and unsaddled their mounts, many sprawling on the grass in the hot sun. Crows raced their ponies against those of the Shoshones. Crook and some of his officers broke out playing cards, while men from the long, strung-out column continued to come in.

At 0830 they heard shots echoing to the northeast, beyond the ridge, growing louder. "They are shooting buffalo over there," suggested Sutorious. Then, appearing on the northern crests and galloping madly down the slope, came the Crow scouts, one severely wounded. They had collided with enemy scouts, and now yelled their blood-freezing news:

"*Lakota! Lakota!*"

"Heap Sioux! heap Sioux!"

The warning was almost too late. Already a mass of Sioux, rushing up the valley upon hearing the first exchange of

# George Crook

Like the more famous Custer, Crook (1828-1890) was Ohio-born, did not drink or smoke, and was an undistinguished student at West Point before his 1852 graduation. As a lieutenant in the 4th U.S. Infantry, Crook served in various Indian campaigns on the Pacific Coast, suffering a severe arrow wound to his right hip in 1857 while fighting the Rogue River and Pitt River tribes.

In 1861, Captain Crook accepted an infantry colonelcy and subsequently served as brigadier general leading a cavalry division in both western and eastern theaters of the Civil War. Commanding the Department of West Virginia in 1864, and the Army of West Virginia during Sheridan's Shenandoah campaign, Crook was captured early in 1865. Exchanged a month later, he ended the war as major general of volunteers commanding the Army of the Potomac's cavalry.

Retaining his brevet rank of major general while reverting to his Regular rank of captain, Crook became lieutenant colonel of the 23rd Infantry in 1866. Heading the District of Boise, Idaho Territory, he fought Paiutes, Klamaths, and others before assuming temporary command of the Department of the Columbia, headquartered in Portland. In 1871 President Grant ordered Crook to Arizona. Using surrendering Apaches to track their unconquered brethren, he brought a temporary peace to the department and won his brigadier's star in 1873.

Gifted with an impressive physique, six-foot-plus height and intense blue-gray eyes, the taciturn Crook cultivated folksy eccentricities; these came to include braiding and tying back his parted blonde whiskers, preferring canvas brown overalls and moccasins to uniforms (Captain Charles King first saw Crook properly uniformed when in his coffin), and campaigning on muleback. But such self-effacing mannerisms concealed a keen ambition, an appreciation of a good press—and a sometimes caustic, even petty, critic of fellow officers.

Reassigned to command the Department of the Platte in 1875, Crook participated in the Great Sioux War and supervised the agency Sioux at Red Cloud and Spotted Tail. Recalled to Arizona in 1882, he effectively subdued the Chiricahau Apaches. But in 1885

shots, had charged upon Crook's pickets from the bluffs, driving them in. Then mounted warriors in all their fierce glory appeared along the ridge to the north, or galloped down from the small hills to the west in human streams.

Bullets began whizzing above the soldiers' heads. Captain Azor H. Nickerson, an aide to Crook, drank in the sight before

Crook's differences with Phil Sheridan over his pursuit of a handful of warriors under Geronimo—especially Crook's heavy reliance on Apache scouts—led to final estrangement from his former friend and his reassignment to the Platte. In 1888 he became major general commanding the Division of the Missouri.

Like most of his brother officers,

Crook at once sympathized with the Indians' plight and believed that salvation lay in de-Indianizing them. Unlike most, he became a vocal advocate of reform measures and a prominent member of the Indian Rights Association. Told of his death, old Red Cloud sadly noted that "he, at least, had never lied to us."

*General George Crook, 1876. The Sioux campaign of that year proved a low point in the career of this distinguished Indian fighter.*

him—"those justly celebrated Sioux and Cheyenne warriors," some in warbonnets, others in "half masks of the heads of wild animals with the ears and sometimes the horns, still protruding, giving them the appearance of devils from the nether world, or uncouth demons from the hills of Brocken." The painted, magnificently mounted braves "dashed here, there, everywhere; up and down in ceaseless activity; their

gaudy decorations, waving plumes and glittering arms, forming a panoramic view of barbaric splendor." First to respond
were the Crows and Shoshones. Led by Major Randall, they
galloped from the rear toward their charging foes, in a line
facing west and slightly to the north.

For perhaps 20 long minutes, Indian battled Indian, the
warring tribesmen swirling and mingling so that white on-
lookers could not tell hostile from friendly. Warriors on both
sides made "bravery runs," drawing fire to prove their
courage; Frank Grouard saw one of them, a Crow named Bull
Snake, watching the battle after his horse had been killed,
periodically yelling like a madman: "He seemed to be so
interested in the fight that he had entirely forgotten his
wound." A bullet had shattered his knee.

The soldiers stood by or girded for battle. "Why the devil
don't they order us to charge?" demanded Lieutenant Von
Leuttwitz. Sutorious asked reporter Finerty how he felt:

> "It is the anniversary of Bunker Hill," was my answer. "The
> day is of good omen." "By Jove, I never thought of that," cried
> Sutorious, and (loud enough for the soldiers to hear) "It is the
> anniversary of Bunker Hill, we're in luck." The men waved their
> carbines, which were right shouldered, but true to the parade
> etiquette of the American army did not cheer, although they
> forgot all about the etiquette later on.

Just then Lieutenant Henry Lemly, the 3rd Cavalry's regimental adjutant, galloped up on a foaming horse, sent by
Crook as the Indian auxiliaries held the Sioux at bay. "The
commanding officer's compliments, Colonel Mills!" he cried.
"Your battalion will charge those bluffs on the center." Mills
swung his four companies by the right into line, preparing for
the charge. What followed can be reconstructed with some
difficulty, though not without inviting dispute over the
precise time or sequence of events in the confusion of a
sprawling battle.

After dispatching Lemly, Crook had proceeded north to a
high vantage point to obtain a clear view of the field, leaving
Major Evans to deploy for a hastily organized defense. Evans
sent Captain Van Vliet and two cavalry companies to guard
Crook's rear by seizing the bluffs to the south, while Compa-

*"Indian Charge," by Frederic Remington. Though his braves convey an appropriate sense of spirited individualism, they seem to have lined up in improbably neat fashion before launching their attack.*

nies G and H, 9th Infantry, were sent to hold the low bluffs to the north. As he topped the crest, Van Vliet repelled a force of warriors riding from the east.

Evans sent four 2nd Cavalry companies to provide support in a dismounted skirmish line, Captain Thomas B. Dewees' Company A guarding their mounts in the valley and negating the need to detach every fourth man as a horseholder. Finding cover behind a small ridge, they turned back the attacking Indians with hot carbine fire as the braves charged down a large ravine from a gap in the ridge to the north. To the right, Company C of the 9th Infantry joined D and F of the 4th in a skirmish line. Advancing to the plateau's crest, they saw

Indians covering the hills, with more pouring from ravines and vales.

On the right flank, Mills rose in his stirrups and cried: "Charge!" The Indian allies were still in the forefront as Mills' men advanced in a column of companies—some horses tumbling down unwounded due to the sheer roughness of the ground. Finerty rode with them: "We went like a storm, and the Indians waited for us until we were within fifty paces. We were going too rapidly to use our carbines, but several of the men fired their revolvers, with what effect I could neither then, nor afterward, determine, for all passed like a flash of lightning, or a dream....I remember how well our troops kept their formation, and how gallantly they sat their horses as they galloped fiercely up the rough ascent...our men broke into a mad cheer...."

As Indians fired at the advancing whites from behind piles of rocks north of the crest, the Cheyenne chief Comes in Sight repeatedly drew fire with a series of charges. He rode in a southeasterly direction toward the bluecoats and Indian allies, obliquely crossing their front. Just as an equally bold warrior passed him galloping in the opposite direction, Comes in Sight's pony was shot from under him a few hundred yards in front of the enemy. He landed on his feet and began to run zigzag. Then his sister, Buffalo Calf Road Woman—a female warrior—rode up to save him; he leaped onto her horse's back and both galloped off. After that day, the Cheyennes would know the battle as the fight "Where the Girl Saved Her Brother."

The Sioux easily gave way as Mills charged at and through them, driving them to the top of the ridge. But Mills was obviously impressed, commenting that these Plains warriors "proved then and there that they were the best cavalry soldiers on earth. In charging up towards us they exposed little of their person, hanging on with one arm around the neck and one leg over the horse, firing and lancing from underneath the horses' necks, so that there was no part of the Indian at which we could aim."

Since the Sioux and Cheyenne regarded such familiar acts

*Shot from his horse and rescued by friends, the mortally wounded Black Sun is led away by Wooden Leg, the to-and-fro horsetrack patterns suggesting the confused rhythm of the Rosebud fighting. Since the Cheyennes had time to prepare, Black Sun's horse has his pony's tail tied up for war, and Wooden Leg wears his best war clothing. While going almost "naked," Black Sun had carefully covered his body with yellow "medicine painting," wrapping a blanket around his loins and placing upon his head the stuffed skin of a weasel.*

as scarcely worthy of mention, we must turn to their enemies' accounts to appreciate their fantastic skills. Correspondent Strahorn told his readers how:

> Some of the most reckless feats of equestrianism imaginable were performed by them within range of the broadsides of an entire company. In numerous instances one or two warriors dashed out from behind their cover of rocks, hugged close to the neck of the pony and half bounded, half tumbled down the nearly vertical banks after a bold Crow, Snake or white skirmisher, delivered a shot or two and like a flash disappeared in spite of volleys sent after them.
> Up hill or down, over rocks, through canyons and in every conceivable dangerous condition of affairs their breakneck devil-may-care riding was accomplished. One reckless brave got badly pressed by the cavalry, at a certain point in the field, and jerking out his bowie knife he slashed apart his saddle girt[h], slipped it with all of its trappings from under him while his pony was at full speed, and thus unencumbered made his escape. So closely did the Indians approach our skirmishers at times that

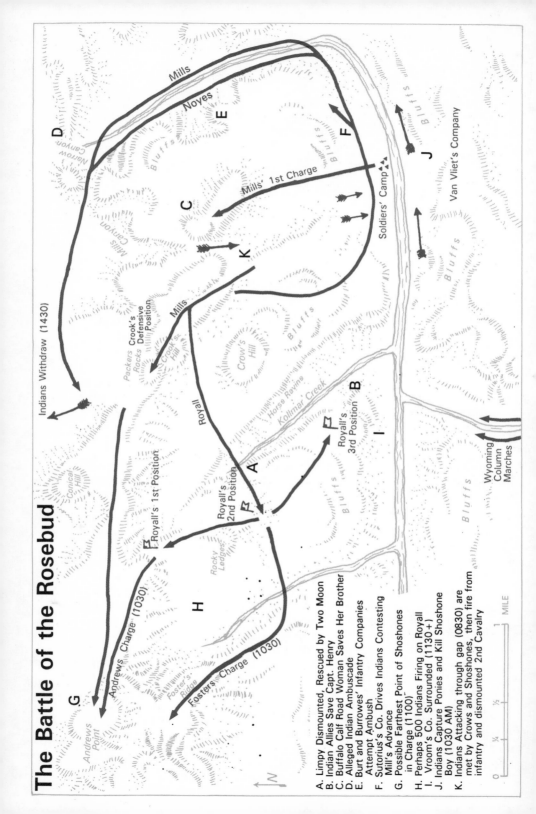

# The Battle of the Rosebud

Mills

Noyes

D

E

F

J

Narrow Canyon

Bluffs

Bluffs

Mills' 1st Charge

Soldiers' Camp

Van Vliet's Company

C

K

Mills Canyon

Packer's Rocks Crook's Defensive Position

Mills

Crook's Hill

Bluffs

Indians Withdraw (1430)

Royall

Crow's Hill

Horse Ravine

Kollmar Creek

B

Royall's 3rd Position

I

Wyoming Column Marches

Conical Hill

Royall's 1st Position

Royall's 2nd Position

A

Bluffs

Andrews Charge (1030)

Rocky Ledges

G

H

Foster's Ridge

Andrews Point

Foster's Charge (1030)

N

A. Limpy Dismounted, Rescued by Two Moon
B. Indian Allies Save Capt. Henry
C. Buffalo Calf Road Woman Saves Her Brother
D. Alleged Indian Ambuscade
E. Burt and Burrowes' Infantry Companies
   Attempt Ambush
F. Sutorius's Co. Drives Indians Contesting
   Mill's Advance
G. Possible Farthest Point of Shoshones
   in Charge (1100)
H. Perhaps 500 Indians Firing on Royall
I. Vroom's Co. Surrounded (1130+)
J. Indians Capture Ponies and Kill Shoshone
   Boy (1030 AM)
K. Indians Attacking through gap (0830) are
   met by Crows and Shoshones, then fire from
   infantry and dismounted 2nd Cavalry

0      ¼      ½      1
MILE

they inflicted several wounds from battle-axes, lances and arrows, and in one or two instances they closed in upon a brave soldier and got his scalp before comrades could rush forward to the rescue. They repeatedly courted death by endeavoring to secure the bodies of their own dead....

As Mills reached the ridge, the dismounted 2nd Cavalry troopers captured the ridge and gap to his left. Mills found that the Indians' whooping and appearance terrorized his horses, rendering them "almost uncontrollable" before he dismounted and sent them with horseholders behind the available rocks. But his men stood steady: "The Indians came not in a line but in flocks or herds like the buffalo, and they piled upon us until I think there must have been one thousand or fifteen hundred on our immediate front, but they refused to fight when they found us secured behind the rocks, and bore off to our left." As the Sioux and Cheyenne retreated to the west, across his front, Mills took stock. He found Andrews' company missing, it having been appropriated by Royall as he moved to the left with Henry's squadron. Having rallied on the second line of heights, warriors rode back and forth, wheeling in circles, slapping their rumps mockingly at Mills' soldiers as they beckoned them to attack.

To the west, on Crook's left, the three skirmishing companies of infantrymen had advanced to the rear of the friendly Indians, who may well have saved the day for the Army. Recalled the Crow warrior Plenty-coups, "The enemy were like lice on a robe there, and hot for battle...we Indians charged the enemy, driving him back and breaking his line. But he divided and turned his ends around ours to get at Three-stars. When we saw this we turned back, with our wounded, because Three-stars needed us now." These Sioux curled around and past the Crows' and Shoshones' flanks just as the infantrymen reached the rear of the "friendlies." One group galloped to the east, down the big ravine, their target the cavalry's horses in the valley below. But the infantrymen and dismounted cavalrymen on the low bluffs sprang an impromptu ambush, hiding behind a small rise near the ravine's mouth. With admirable discipline, they waited until the charging braves came within 150 yards. Then they fired a volley, white puffs of black-powder smoke erupting to mark their positions. Stung by this fierce fire, the Sioux broke and made another split into two swarms as they retreated northward up each side of the ravine. There they streamed out on the ridge to battle the advancing bluecoats—some just in time to oppose Mills' bold first charge east of the ravine.

The warriors who had outflanked the Crows and Shoshones to the west attacked the three infantry companies and were repelled by fire. But in their fluid style, they merely galloped around the doughboys' exposed left. On this sprawling battlefield, they had no unified leadership and no apparent overall strategy. Perhaps none was needed. Throughout, the warriors exploited openings; threw force against weak spots; gave way when pressed; and attacked forces that seemed isolated from their comrades. They fought like water, flowing and flooding when permitted, ebbing back when resistance proved too steep. Early on, despite a certain reticence in military accounts, they seem to have driven some of the soldiers back almost into the creek itself.

Long decades afterward, the Cheyenne Wooden Leg remembered: "Until the sun went far toward the west there were charges back and forth. Our Indians fought and ran away, fought and ran away. The soldiers and their Indian scouts did the same. Sometimes we chased them, sometimes they chased us." Tiring, Wooden Leg dismounted and rested with other Cheyennes in a brush thicket—before Lame White Man, a Southern Cheyenne chief, rode into the open calling for brave actions. "It then became the turn of the soldiers and their Indians to get out of our way." Lame White Man had no war chief's status among these Northern Cheyenne. But a Plains chief did not lead by pulling rank. He led by example.

Sitting Bull, while apparently present to give encouragement, was too weak from his ordeal to partake of the fighting. Insofar as the Sioux and Cheyenne had an overall commander, it would have been Crazy Horse, moving over the field in a spotted calfskin cape flying from his shoulders, two or three grass straws stuck in his loosened hair, and dust rubbed over his spotted war-pony. Yet we cannot assume that even he gave detailed orders, or attempted to exert central command over the entire field. Nor can we be sure that he or any other Indian leader had an adequate idea of Crook's numbers; the Sioux and Cheyenne may well have been emboldened by the fact that only a portion of the white force was visible at any point of attack.

To thwart the Indians outflanking the infantry on the left, Colonel Evans ordered Captain Henry to detach two cavalry companies to the south side of the stream, holding a low ridge 500 yards westward. Henry quickly led companies D and F to the spot, holding it alone until two mounted companies under Colonel Royall himself drove the Sioux from the foot soldiers' left. Leaving his men behind on a knoll to hold this flank, Royall galloped back to order the rest of the 3rd Cavalry forward.

Having stopping the mounted braves pouring southward down the large ravine, Captains Burt and Burrowes attempted to spring another ambush, hiding their riflemen at the foot of the bluffs and leaving a gap between the two companies while the Shoshones and Crows feigned a retreat, hoping to draw attacking warriors into the trap. But the Sioux declined to fall for this familiar trick. By now the three companies of infantry on the skirmish line's left flank and the four dismounted companies of 2nd Cavalry on its right had begun their slow advance northward, their opponents laying on a hot fire as they gave ground. Many of the warriors were armed with breechloading rifles, including Winchester repeaters.

With Crook still not returned from his hilltop observation post, where he apparently hoped to manage the fight in Civil War fashion, Evans ordered Mills' battalion and Henry's remaining two companies to take the second line of bluffs. Under Royall's command, they did so, charging in a flanking movement from the southeast. The Sioux again gave way as the troopers topped the crest east of the gap—just as the infantrymen and dismounted 2nd Cavalrymen took the gap and that part of the ridge to its left. Fleeing westward along the ridge to a hill on the crest, later known as Crook's Hill or Crook's Point, they peppered the troops with bullets.

By now Crook had made his way back and ordered Captain Mills, with his own battalion and two companies from Henry's, to take this position. Mills deployed on open ground in column, facing west, before his leading three companies charged and took the hill. Pulling back to a cone-shaped mound 1,200 yards to the northwest, the warriors kept up an ineffective long-range fire. The infantry came up to occupy both Crook's Hill and the ridge to the east of it.

As Mills' men made their charge, Royall rode with three companies against the Sioux on a lower ridge, lying southwest across Kollmar Creek and parallel with the main crest. He drove them west along it, then stopped with four companies upon reaching some high ground near the head of the creek. Crook halted Mills before he could take the conical mound, instead ordering him to hold his position on Crook's Hill with a line of dismounted skirmishers. Piling up flat rocks along the southwest rim of the hill as impromptu breastworks, the men shot back at the warriors on the conical mound.

With Royall taking an enfilading fire from Sioux on the ridge to his left, a platoon of 18 men under Lieutenant E.H. Foster broke from Andrews' Company I and drove them off, charging far west along its crest and dismounting at a rocky knoll. He sent a volley at Sioux on a wooded ridge ahead of him, then mounted and charged up that ridge also, retreating from his isolated position when the Sioux attempted to cut him off. Andrews himself proceeded to the commanding high point at the head of Kollmar Creek, both he and Foster riding to rejoin Royall as the latter consolidated his men—and as the Indians again seized the rocky high point Andrews had just vacated, commanding not only the valley but the adjacent ridge. The warriors formed a line along the ridge to the west, concentrating their fire on Royall's command.

The Indians' unusual method of retreating to the west, across their enemies' front, had left most of Crook's men with nobody to fight. But Royall, on the left, could expect little support given the troops' present deployment; his useless "driving" of the Indians had merely left his own troops overextended. His position was separated by a canyon from Crook's main position almost a mile to the east. Indians swarmed upon the crest, firing down on his cavalrymen as other warriors circled around toward the left and rear of Royall's position, sheltered by hills and ledges.

By then (about 1030), the combat had evolved into three distinct battles, with Royall precariously holding on the west, Crook now on Crook's Hill with Mills' and Noyes' battalions and Van Vliet's detachment far away to the south and what might have been "the rear" had the Sioux recognized such distinctions. Due to the irregular ground, only Van Vliet's men could view the entire field. Crook ordered Burt and Burrowes' G and H companies to aid the embattled Royall.

*"Indian Skirmish Line," by Remington. Daring Indian warriors galloping along such a line proved almost impossible to hit.*

But, perhaps because they were too busy helping to hold the conical mound and fighting off Sioux themselves, the infantrymen did not obey until 1230.

Perceiving a dangerous gap between the two cavalry battalions on Crook's Hill, the commanding general ordered it closed. He also sent orders to Royall to link up with the left of his main force. But Royall, later asserting that he could not then retreat given enemy pressure, sent only Meinhold's company. This reached Crook's Hill under fire, but with only one man wounded. Perhaps Royall should have retreated with his entire command at once—especially since, with his fighting strength already reduced by the horseholders sheltering his mounts on the ridge's south slope, he was now forced to extend his dismounted line to cover Meinhold's absence.

With his position somewhat stabilized, and his wounded taken to a hastily established field hospital in a gully, Crook prepared to take the offensive. The Shoshones were placed on the left, on the south slope of Crook's Hill, and the Crows in reserve between the battalions along the crest to the east; the packers and a few miners, armed mainly with hard-hitting Sharps sporting rifles, clung to a rocky shelf 400 yards west of his central position. Perhaps because of the sheer ferocity of the attacking Sioux, Crook believed their camp to be no more than six or eight miles to the north, down the Rosebud's canyon to the east of the field. But he still failed to realize the danger at hand.

Crook pulled Mills' three companies from the line to make a demonstration downstream before moving into the canyon. Paying no heed to any Sioux actions, Mills was to take the village and hold it until Crook arrived in support. Five 2nd Cavalry companies later went in support of Mills, with 20 men from Company A accompanying the Indian allies on the flank to "keep up connections" as they proceeded down the long canyon. Crook also summoned Royall to join in the village attack.

Seeing Mills' apparent withdrawal encouraged the Sioux to mass and charge Crook's central position from west and

*Chief Washakie of the Shoshones, about 1880. Though already in his 70s, Washakie personally led his warriors into action at the Rosebud.*

north. One party galloped down at about 1030 through the gap between Royall's troops and Van Vliet's command on the south bluff. At the spring where Crook had played cards earlier that morning, they captured a herd of Army horses and, wrote Bourke, shot a half-grown Shoshone boy in the back, "taking his scalp from the nape of the neck to the forehead, leaving his entire skull ghastly and white. It was the boy's first battle, and when the skirmishing began in earnest he asked permission of his chief to go back to the spring and decorate himself with face-paint, which was already plastered over one cheek, and his medicine-song was half done, when he received the fatal shot." But the Sioux abandoned the horses when Van Vliet opened fire from the south during their return.

To meet the current onslaught, Lieutenant Bourke counter-attacked with the Shoshones and a cavalry platoon detailed to fight with them, while Randall's Crows rode to the left, the allied chiefs leading their warriors—Medicine Crow in a buffalo-horn hat, Washakie naked to the waist on a fiery steed, his proud eagle-feather warbonnet sweeping the ground behind his pony's tail. With shouts and war-cries, the braves and soldiers struck the Sioux.

The huge Sergeant Van Moll, of Lawson's A Troop, rushed into the fray—on foot—as the Indians galloped towards each other. The Regulars within range held their fire, untrained eyes unable to distinguish between hostiles and friendly Indians marked only by the red badges around their arms, while even the Shoshones feared to mistake Crow for Sioux. It was a savage contest in the trough of the valley, sometimes close enough for work with war clubs or coup sticks. Finerty, seeing that horses were shot dead "by the score," decided with an Irishman's appreciation for a good scrap that the astonishingly light human losses on both sides went far "to prove the wisdom of the Indian method of fighting."

The Sioux again fled westward, and with a sudden halt many of the Shoshones leaped from their horses to fire more accurately from the ground. When the Sioux rallied, the Indian allies and soldiers drove them further, to the head of Kollmar Creek, the Shoshones charging perhaps as far west as Andrews' Point. Since the main attack had been broken, and a superior vantage point gained for Crook's men, Bourke considered the Indian allies' charge to be "the turning-point of the Rosebud fight."

The Shoshones, realizing their exposed position, suddenly retreated with their wounded, and Bourke found himself virtually alone with his bugler, Elmer A. Snow. Both men mounted and galloped to safety behind the lines, Trumpeter Snow—later one of four men awarded the Medal of Honor for this action—crippled for life, both arms shot through and dangling useless. Realizing that the plucky Van Moll had been left to defend himself on foot, Bourke and Randall galloped back with a party of warriors to save him. But a small, deformed Crow warrior, known as Humpy, out-stripped all, rode into the midst of the enclosing Sioux, and grabbed Van Moll by the shoulder, motioning him to jump up behind. The surprised Sioux finally opened fire as Humpy and the big soldier dashed off, the troops' return fire forcing the braves back, the line cheering as rescuer and rescued passed through on their single pony.

Crook ordered three companies of infantry to form a skirmish line across the crest and down the valleys on either side of it, to chase the Sioux from their conical stronghold. It was 1100 when the line was formed, and the infantry advanced steadily, driving the Sioux before briefly occupying the crest. Van Vliet's two companies to the south, ordered to rejoin the main command, moved north to replace the doughboys in their earlier position as Crook consolidated his defenses. The miners and packers were recalled from their advanced position to reinforce Crook's Hill as Mills proceeded down the canyon.

Royall had received Crook's second message summoning him to join the intended village attack. Since the large ravine separated his first position from Crook's, he attempted to obey by retreating dismounted to the southwest, withdrawing his led horses first, to the next ridge on the south side of Kollmar Creek, and turning back a Sioux bid to seize the horses with carbine fire. When Crook again sent word to come on, Royall again withdrew his led horses first, the Indians on ledges to his left and rear—and on the ridge he had just left—firing into the dismounted cavalrymen. The Sioux made another try for the horses as Royall's men made their way to the southeast, and again the 150 troopers on the skirmish line beat them off, reaching a point south of Crook's Hill and a half-mile from union with the main force. As Royall began to change direction and finally cross the defile of Kollmar Creek from his third position, the Indians pressing him—and other warriors moving parallel with his line along the next ridge—attacked across the intervening hollow. When this failed, the Sioux followed with a flanking attack down the creek valley.

Royall had sent Lieutenant Vroom's company to take the advance and line a crest covering his route of retreat. But when Vroom mounted the bluff, he was surrounded and cut off by warriors who had massed on the ridge's southern side. He formed a circle on the crest for a last-ditch stand and lost five killed before the rest of Royall's detachment, led by Captain Henry's company, charged to the rescue and drove the Indians back. Royall, who had sent his adjutant to Crook with a plea for reinforcements, was helped in turn as Burt's and Burrowes' infantrymen double-timed it from their hill a half-mile away and deployed on a ridge to the northeast of his battalion. At Crook's command, the Shoshones and Crows also rushed in support.

During Royall's retreat, the Cheyenne warrior Limpy had his horse shot from under him; first taking cover behind some rocks, he hurried to retrieve his bridle before Young Two Moon made another of that day's many daring rescues. The two rode off with bullets kicking up the dust around them. Remarked Limpy in 1934: "When you are in a tight pinch like that it seems like you don't have no feelings. It seems like your feet don't even touch the ground."

Watching the two infantry companies make their move as the Sioux attacked Royall's men from the west and rear, Captain Henry (who like Royall's other officers had remained mounted throughout) was struck by enfilading fire, the bullet striking his left cheek and coming out his right, destroying the sight in one eye. Throwing blood from his mouth "by the handful," he reeled from the saddle. His troopers gave ground. But as Sioux rushed to count coup on the fallen soldier-chief and his wounded orderly, some literally riding over Henry, the Crows dashed to the rescue. "Our war-whoop, with the Shoshones,' waked the Echo-people!" remembered Plenty-coups. "We rode *through* them, over the body of one of Three-stars' chiefs who was shot through the face under the eyes, so that the flesh was pushed away from his broken bones. Our charge saved him from being finished and scalped."

The Homeric fighting over Henry's body lacked only a poet to sing of it. But finally the troops came up, as the captain was borne back to safety near the crest. Consoled by Finerty,

*Guy V. Henry. His health broken and left eye blinded after his Rosebud wound, Henry reluctantly went on an extended leave of absence, but returned to the Army and participated in the Ute War of 1879 as well as the Ghost Dance outbreak of 1890. During the Civil War he had won the Medal of Honor at Cold Harbor.*

Henry merely replied, "It is nothing. For this are we soldiers!"—and then, wrote the bemused reporter, "did me the honor of advising me to join the army!"

The Indian auxiliaries were pressed back in their turn by the Sioux, but nobly covered Royall's retreat as the soldiers reached their horses and mounted. As though to exploit this withdrawal, the warriors launched a large scale attack on the packers and soldiers on Crook's Hill. As Royall's men rode down the valley of Kollmar Creek, they were forced to cut their way through surrounding Indians before linking up with Crook, several men being killed after their horses were shot. Meanwhile a band of Sioux galloped past the scene of Royall's action and down the Rosebud to make a complete circuit around Crook's command, as though to mock the soldiers' futile reliance on linear tactics. Having finally realized his peril, Crook sent Lieutenant Nickerson to recall Mills from his search for the village. He would need every man he had just to hold on.

Mills' column had been moving cautiously down the long valley on the battlefield's extreme right, turning left at a sharp bend to continue down a menacingly narrowing canyon, the dust from Noyes' supporting column visible to his rear. The cavalry force was preparing for action when the buckskin-clad adjutant, black beard grayed by dust, galloped up with Crook's revised orders. To reach his new objective more quickly, Mills defiled as nearly as possible by heads of companies in parallel column. He surprised the warriors from the flank and rear, scattering ponies guarded mainly by young boys. The Sioux finally broke off the action and departed the field much as they had come, disappearing up various ravines, scattering—and "leaving us," wrote Finerty, "only the thirteen scalps, 150 dead horses and ponies, and a few old blankets and war bonnets as trophies of the fray." At first Mills pursued, uselessly, then rode to rejoin Crook.

Disappointed and still assuming a camp to be nearby, Mills asked: "General, why did you recall me? I had the village and could have held it." A dejected Crook explained: "Well, Colonel, I found it a more serious engagement than I thought," and added that he could not have kept his promise of support.

But even then, Crook was ready for a final, consolidated effort to destroy Crazy Horse's village. He began an advance, only to be told by the Crows and Frank Grouard that he would be ambushed if he went beyond the point where the Rosebud canyon narrowed. While later students have remarked on the degree to which white participants exaggerated the steepness and dangerous terrain of this passage, underbrush and fallen timbers then in evidence—as well as the day's nerve-wracking events—may have contributed to its menacing aura.

By about 1430, after six frightening, exhilarating hours, the battle was over. The Sioux and Cheyenne rode toward the

*Plenty-coups became re-nowned as his tribe's leading statesman following the end of inter-tribal warfare, but refused to speak to his biographer about life after the passing of the buf-falo. As chief of the Crows, he would urge his young men to enlist against the Germans in World War I—regretting that he was too old to fight himself.*

great village that Crook would never see, there to tend to the wounded, mourn for the dead, boast of their war-deeds, and display the scalps and trophies taken—with no feeling that their white foes had "driven" them from the field. Asked why Crazy Horse's forces had quit after seemingly doing so well, John Stands in Timber replied simply, "They were tired and hungry, so they went home."

It was not an answer to satisfy a West Pointer longing for battles of annihilation. But there was more here than the feeling that war should be pleasurable or exalt the individual; keeping up the pressure might have cost many more Sioux and Cheyenne dead. And in keeping the invaders from their camp, they had achieved their objective. They clearly felt that they had bested the bluecoats—as did some of Crook's own officers.

Fortunately for Crazy Horse, the Army's ability to make

Indians "bite the dust" never approached fictional standards, despite the approximately 25,000 cartridges expended by Crook's men. Crazy Horse allegedly conceded 36 warriors slain and 63 wounded—a believable figure given the amount of lead thrown and the 13 bodies which his men could not recover, but perhaps too high. While armies were supposed to keep records of such things, Crook's casualties remain a bit vague; while Crook officially reported 9 soldiers (all 3rd Cavalrymen fighting under Royall) and one Indian scout killed, with 21 wounded, Bourke unofficially put Army losses at 57, including 4 mortally wounded and many wounds "of no significance." Chief Old Crow was shot through the knee and permanently lamed. Plenty-coups later stated that the Crows had lost 1 man killed ("not really a Crow" since he was a Cree adopted by them) and 10 wounded, while the Shoshones apparently lost at least 1 warrior as well as their young boy.

Short of ammunition and unable to adequately care for his wounded, Crook prepared to fall back on his train. That night, before camping on the field, Crook's soldiers buried the bodies of their comrades, burning a fire atop the grave, and when the troops broke camp the next morning, the entire command marched over it, to wipe out all traces. Three or four Sioux were seen riding down to the battlefield, dismounting and sitting with bowed heads—weeping for their dead, the scouts explained. "They were not fired upon or molested in any way," wrote Bourke. But a Cheyenne found that morning, blinded and calling for water, was not spared: "The Crows cut him limb from limb and ripped off his scalp."

The Crows, disgusted with Crook's method of waging war, left for home, promising to return within 15 days. On the 19th Crook reached his Goose Creek wagon corral, and on 20 June, all but six of the Shoshones also departed, headed for Wind River. The next day the wagon train, with the wounded and two infantry companies, started back to Fort Fetterman.

Despite his regrets over the escape of the village—and later attempts to blame his failure on other officers, especially the supposedly laggard Royall—Crook claimed victory, with the meaningless assertion that his "less than a thousand" troops (minus civilians and Indian allies!) had driven their foes back "in great confusion." But Crook had not won: he had merely survived. True, he held the field—for what that was worth—only to abandon it the next day. But the Indians had inflicted a clear strategic defeat, obliging Crook to retire and abandon his mission. Slow to sense the urgency of his situation, he had left too much to others, and worried more about striking a non-existent village than about fighting the battle at hand—even when he was forcibly dismounted by his black charger being wounded under him. At best, he could claim for his soldiers equal honors in a stand-up fight, marked on both sides by the deeds of brave men. But was not the Army expected to prevail easily in such an open contest against mere savages?

General Sheridan was too charitable in terming it a victory. He was more accurate in dismissing it as "barren of results"—for the Army, at any rate.

# Gatlings and Long Toms:
# Tools of the Frontier Army

While two civilians at the Fetterman massacre used Henry 16-shot repeating rifles, and the doomed cavalrymen carried magazine carbines, the infantrymen who died with them still carried muzzleloading Springfield rifles, painfully reloaded with percussion caps and a paper cartridge containing powder and ball. But the revolution in metallic, self-contained cartridges soon caught up with the army at the 1867 Wagon Box and Fetterman fights. Here Red Cloud's warriors were repulsed by fierce fire from "Allin conversion" Springfields—surplus .58 muzzleloaders converted to fire a .50 metallic cartridge holding 70 grains of black powder.

The Civil War had already made breechloading carbines standard for cavalry, and by 1869 all U.S. mounted troops had metallic-cartridge weapons of various types, mostly war surplus. A uniform system was obviously desirable.

But the system was to be single shot; the factors behind this specification apparently included economy of manufacture, simple and reliable operation under field conditions, the fact that major European armies favored single-shot breechloaders, and "efficient use of ammunition"—since repeaters made wasting it too easy. (Only so much ammunition could be carried on campaign, and even *without* repeaters, seven 7th Cavalry companies managed to expend over 38,000 carbine cartridges at the Little Bighorn.)

The Ordnance Board headed by General Terry conducted exhaustive tests of 89 rifles and carbines, including the firing of deliberately maimed cartridges. While noting that every modern army would ultimately adopt magazine guns, the board recommended in 1873 the Allin-style Springfield "trapdoor" rifle and carbine, firing outwardly identical .45 cartridges of 70 and 55 grains strength. (When a prankster slipped a rifle round into a carbine, recalled one trooper, "you thought the sky fell in".)

The Springfield, particularly the rifle or "Long Tom," was an accurate, hard-hitting weapon, easily outranging repeaters firing less powerful cartridges; it could be sighted to 1,300 yards, though effective range was more like 250. It was also highly reliable, despite well-publicized complaints. Following the Custer disaster, Major Reno reported that out of 380 carbines used by his command's survivors, six displayed "a radical defect"; failure of the breech block to close caused the extractor to tear through cartridge heads during ejection, leaving a casing in the chamber. More often, shooters had to pry cases loose with knives after dirty and corroded copper-alloy shells (which developed verdigris deposits from contact with leather belt loops) became stuck in heated chambers. On Custer's battlefield, the victorious warriors found at least a few carbines with shells temporarily stuck fast.

But there is no evidence that ejection problems actually contributed to Custer's defeat. Nor would his men have necessarily fared better with repeaters. While a speedy second shot might prove vital at close-quarters, much Indian-fighting involved firing at longer ranges, sometimes supervised by officers with such commands as: "To the Front, Range 100 Yards, Volley Fire, Ready, Aim, Fire! Reload."

Even 7th Cavalry sergeant John Ryan preferred range over speed in securing a custom weapon for a steep $100—a .45 Sharps rifle with telescopic sight. Officers could purchase a special half-stocked model of the .45-70 rifle, although Captain Thomas French apparently killed or wounded five Indians at the Little Bighorn with either a standard issue gun or an older .50 model.

But the dread of being outgunned at critical moments was real. In 1873 the army's Tonkawa Indian scouts declined to turn in their Spencer repeaters (using removable seven-shot tubular magazines) for single-shot Sharps carbines, offering instead to pay for Winchesters if furnished cartridges. An officer of Ranald Mackenzie's 4th Cavalry, recalling one hot action against Comanches, exclaimed: "Thank God for those Spencers! My affection for them has never changed. It was not necessary that they should carry one thousand or twelve hundred yards, but kill at from five hundred down to twenty or thirty yards, in

what almost became a mix-up." After the Little Bighorn, with his Spencers replaced by Springfields, Colonel Mackenzie applied in vain for Winchesters to replace the Springfields, the Ordnance Department noting their inferior range and penetration. While denying that the Indians were better armed than U.S. troops, an ordnance officer conceded the "widespread predilection" in favor of magazine guns:

> ...Since the battle of the Little Big Horn, every frontiersman, with good reason or without, who has had the means, has supplied himself with a repeating arm. Indian conflicts are usually decided at close quarters, and in every encounter there comes a supreme moment when the side that slays the most, is victorious. At this crucial time, the magazine gun shows its superiority. Without taking the weapon from the shoulder, by a simple swaying of the body, round after round may be fired with baneful effect.

The trooper was often a poor shot, and on the second day of the Little Bighorn fight soldiers were forbidden to fire without an officer's permission lest they waste shells. The Army tended to neglect marksmanship, and commanders sometimes had to forego training for lack of cartridges. In 1872 the National Rifle Association finally spurred the Army to allocate 90 shells per year for practice. The canvas-looped Model 1876 Cartridge Belt came too late for that year's

Sioux campaign, but troopers were already carrying ammunition in the loops of non-regulation "prairie belts" of canvas or leather—the 5th Infantry's commander noting that his men had sacrificed their suspenders in making their own.

Phil Sheridan was to pronounce "all bayonets humbug," and while some infantry of Crook's and Terry's columns carried clumsy "trowel" bayonets, these were best used as detached entrenching tools. As for the cavalryman's saber, it was widely considered useless for Indian fighting; of the 7th Cavalry's officers, apparently only Lieutenant DeRudio actually carried one into the Little Bighorn fight. The main weapon for a charge, adopted in 1874, was Colt's 1873 Single Action Army revolver—the .45 "Peacemaker" of later legend, though the Schofield Smith and Wesson also saw service.

On the rare occasions when it was employed, artillery could easily demoralize Indians, the frontier mainstay being the highly portable, muzzleloading 12-pound mountain howitzer. More glamorous to Hollywood film makers, though seeing even less action, were the Gatling guns—crank-operated, multi-barreled weapons which could effectively grind out 50 shots per minute. General Miles would dismiss them as "useless for Indian fighting," arguing that they were cumbersome, jammed easily with overheating and black-powder residue, and did not outrange a rifle.

Custer had apparently hoped to employ Gatlings against Sitting Bull's village, only to be told by interpreter Fred Gerard that although Indians would not stand still while he did it, lobbing in some 12-pounder shells from a mile or two away could "make them scatter pretty lively." Custer would later be condemned for leaving his Gatlings behind, on the theory that their firepower would have proved a lifesaver. But considering the trouble the guns gave in traversing rough country, they might have saved his life in quite a different way—by so delaying his march that the Indians could have scattered before he reached them.

# Crows and Shoshones

Among the white man's most reliable allies were the tall, handsome Crows, or Absaroka, traditional friends since the days of the fur trade—though not above lifting an occasional white-owned horse. Having wrested their prime hunting grounds from the Shoshones in the late 18th century, the Crows found themselves caught between Sioux to the east and Blackfeet to the north. By the 1830s many whites were already predicting their annihilation. But they survived, partly through sheer fighting ability, partly through a shrewd alliance with "the yellow eyes"—the white tribe they recognized as the most powerful of all.

While Montana's white settlers had come to view the Crows as a valuable buffer against the Sioux, the government had been slow to make use of them. During Red Cloud's War, Colonel Henry B. Carrington, commanding Wyoming's Fort Phil Kearny, lacked specific authority to enlist Crows as scouts, and firearms with which to arm them; he had no Indian allies at the time of the Fort Kearny massacre. But the Crows still helped the Army by acting unofficially as couriers, passing on intelligence, and helping to beat off Sioux raids, a lieutenant at Fort C.F. Smith declaring that "no other Indians are braver or better fighters than the Crows." Still, issuing them weapons never became "official" policy, though all but two of the warriors

with Bradley had "good breech-loaders."

The war of 1876 offered the Crows a chance to recover lands seized by the Sioux—and virtually conceded to the invaders by the treaty of 1868. "Their hatred of the Sioux amounts to a monomania," asserted Finerty, and some were to treacherously slay five Sioux peace delegates in December of 1876. However, their warrior psychology—striking one student as "a queer blend of cruelty, vanity, greed, foolhardiness, literalism, and magnificent courage"—was characteristic of the Plains, and did not necessarily preclude truce, trade, mercy, or chivalry. When at the Rosebud young Jack Red Cloud was dismounted and frantically fled rather than coolly retrieve his bridle, three Crows disdained to kill the Sioux youngster; instead they took his father's Winchester and borrowed warbonnet, whipped him with quirts, and laughed at him.

But when Finerty and an officer protested the mutilation of a Sioux warrior after the battle, they too were met with laughter, before soldiers chased the Crows away. When one waved "a portion of the dead warrior's person," mocking in broken English his womenfolk's impending grief, "the whole group of savages burst into a mocking chorus of laughter that might have done honor to the devils and his angels. I lost all respect for the Crow

Indians after that episode." A *Chicago Tribune* reporter had similar thoughts after Terry's Crows, finding a dead Sioux baby hanging from a funeral basket in a tree, threw it down and trampled upon it; noting that they had earlier refused to take a message from General Crook, he sneered that "here, all their bravery seemed to return and prompt them to fall upon a dead child of their ancient enemy and master." Both reporters were unfair, of course. Ironically, the Crows could suffer in paleface eyes precisely because their role as *allies* gave such observers an intimate look at Plains warfare.

The Crows' insistence on making war in their usual style distressed their white comrades in other ways. Crook feared to discipline his allies for hunting or lighting bonfires lest they simply go home, while Gibbon gave his Crows a freedom contrary to his chief of scouts' possibly excessive instincts toward control, though Lieutenant Bradley managed to explain "the mystery of 'taps'" so that the bluecoats could get to sleep. While Finerty complained that "'They are numerous as grass' was the definite Crow manner of stating the strength of the enemy," Bradley thought his men capable of "excellent scouting work." But, he wrote, "The carelessness of these fellows at times is simply amazing. One would think that the Indian's life of constant exposure to danger would make caution and precaution so much his habit that he would never lay them aside, but it is quite otherwise." Bradley

even began to suspect that the Crows were not anxious to find the Sioux.

But the Crows also found fault, laughing at the infantrymen's attempts to ride and thinking it absurd that Bradley should feel it necessary to *see* a Sioux village after they had already estimated its population from the smoke. Incredulous that the whites should have trouble simply crossing a stream, they were inclined, as Bradley conceded, "to look upon it as a device to conceal our cowardice." After the Rosebud, even a white observer was struck by the contrast between the white wounded, lying exposed to the sun, and wounded auxiliaries shaded by improvised screens supported by sticks. Nor could the young warrior Plenty-coups understand why the maimed Captain Henry, rather than riding on a travois, was put on a litter between two mules, falling painfully when a rope broke: "No Indian would have done such a thing with a badly wounded man."

Any Crow reluctance to encounter a superior force of Sioux was perfectly in keeping with the normal Plains practice of attacking only when the odds, or a powerful "medicine," favored the attacker. The Army's previous performances had not encouraged confidence in bluecoat tenacity. White Mouth, reminding Gibbon that forces had previously set out and turned back after doing nothing, admitted: "We are afraid you will do it again." The Crows warred to their own medicine, whatever "road" it might take them down; those with Crook included not only an attractive female warrior, The Other Magpie, but also a *boté*, Finds Them and Kills Them, who normally lived and dressed as a female. Before the Rosebud fight, he donned a warrior's costume so that if slain he would not be laughed at by the Lakotas for hiding in a dress. During the battle Finds Them and Kills Them dashed up to a wounded Crow and held off the Sioux with rifle fire, shooting one Lakota just as The Other Magpie struck him with her coup stick and began to take his scalp.

The Shoshones, riding from their home in southwest Wyoming, had come to Crook with less coaxing—and with more Regular-style polish as they arrived in column of twos. Former enemies of the Crows, they were, wrote Captain Bourke, "not slow to perceive the favorable impression made, and when the order came for them to file off by the right moved with the precision of clockwork and the pride of veterans." In addition to some cavalry drill (perhaps attributable to Tom Cosgrove, an ex-Confederate who had married into the tribe), the Shoshones had also adopted the custom of keeping their .45-70 rifles in military-style gun racks.

Despite his advanced years, it was natural for the farsighted Chief Washakie to lead his warriors personally. Born sometime around 1800, he had become the leading man among the Eastern Shoshones by the 1840s, wielding an unusual and almost dictatorial authority. Though the benefits of embracing the whites were sometimes dubious, Washakie knew that they could not be stopped in their westward advance, and therefore sought a reservation in the Wind River Valley, located off the paths of both Oregon Trail and Union Pacific railway. The chief admitted that the Sioux might trouble his people, "but when the Sioux are taken care of, we can do well." Washakie recognized not only the white man's overwhelming strength, but the Indians' dependence on his technology. When some advised resistance to white land hunger, he scornfully displayed a revolver and noted that the Shoshones could make only bows and arrows.

By 1876 the Shoshones had not only their reservation, but a military post to protect it, Camp Brown—renamed Fort Washakie in 1878. Fortunately, however, they fought at the Rosebud like Shoshones, rather than as white cavalrymen. In 1900, Washakie died and was given a magnificent military funeral.

Whites of a later generation would vilify such men for the same conduct that had once earned them praise. But these warriors fought for themselves and their fellow tribesmen, rather than for some imaginary Pan-Indian nation. "When I think back my heart sings because we acted as we did," said Plenty-coups. "It was the only way open to us."

# Indians Armed

Even the Plains warrior's "traditional" weapons bore the mark of the white man's technology, for the horse culture had long been dependent upon European trade goods. Least affected, save when decorated with beads or other white-made items, was the stone war club, its head sometimes attached by a flexible hide shaft for a whipping effect; it was handy in mounted warfare as well as useful in dispatching wounded enemies. But other clubs featured one or more knife blades inserted in a wooden stock, and the famous fighting hatchet or "tomahawk" (originally a type of eastern war club) featured white-manufactured heads.

By 1876 the tomahawk had perhaps become more ornamental than useful, though of course even the knife, carried by all but young children as an indispensable tool, might be used occasionally (blade held underhand) for combat. The fabled "scalping knife," with blade sometimes Indian-made from file or saw, was simply any blade used to take hair.

The 1876 campaign was the last to prominently feature the war lance, tipped perhaps by a captured saber blade and sometimes wrapped in the fur of a swift animal such as the otter, to impart these qualities to weapon or user. Some tribes deemed a long lance unbecoming for a brave warrior. In the past lances had proved an effective counter to cavalrymen's sabers; but Plains warriors would occasionally carry sabers themselves, whether for fighting, counting coup, or, as with Sitting Bull's Brave Hearts society, as badges of rank and status.

Skilled since childhood, the Indian proved deadly with the short bow. Iron arrow points, whether secured in trade or fashioned from barrel hoops, were often barbed, detaching easily after penetrating; since a point could not be pulled out with the shaft, it might be removed by looping a wire under the point, or simply pushing it out the other side. A Dr. Bill, who devised several removal methods, reported in 1871 that victims with single wounds were exceptional; if one arrow struck home it was instantly followed by two or more others—one victim being hit by seven. Drawing from his quiver a handful of arrows, the warrior could discharge them faster and with greater accuracy than a soldier could fire bullets from his carbine. With no telltale smoke to reveal his position, the archer could even lob down "indirect fire" without exposing himself.

The bow had made the Plains horsemen so deadly to whites armed with muzzleloaders that the advantage enjoyed by gun-armed Indians over tribesmen lacking them must have been largely moral in nature; even the whites' adoption of Colt's revolver for horseback fighting proved a temporary advantage, since Indians soon obtained these also.

Firearms (in Lakota, *maza wakan* or holy iron) in Indian hands ranged from smoothbore muskets, to cap-and-ball revolvers, to the latest repeaters—variously acquired through trade, capture, gunrunning, or from the government as hunting guns or in fulfillment of annuities. Efforts to restrict the flow of weapons may have affected friendly Indians more than hostile, a Crow chief complaining in 1873 that the Sioux were "better armed than we are." General Crook believed that while 20 well-armed whites could whip a hundred Indians with muzzleloaders, "since the breech-loaders came into use it is entirely different; these they can load on horseback, and now they are a match for any man."

The most coveted weapon, ideal for mounted fighting, was the 1866 .44 lever-action Winchester rifle or carbine. Simply working the lever on this improved version of the 1860 Henry would eject a spent cartridge, chamber a round, close the breech, and cock the hammer for the next shot. With 12- and 15-shot magazines (and an extra round in the chamber), the Winchester offered awesome firepower—especially against a soldier with a single-shot weapon. The famous Model 1873 ".44-40" offered a more powerful centerfire cartridge, though still inferior at longer ranges to the soldiers' Springfields and owned by few warriors in 1876.

The Cheyenne warrior High Backed Wolf was carrying a Henry as early as 1865, and by the time of the Great Sioux War metallic cartridge guns were common among the warriors. But Army officers might exaggerate the number of Winchesters in Sioux hands, and Charles Windolph later estimated that about half the warriors at the Custer fight still relied on the bow, with "not more than 25 or 30 percent" carrying repeaters. With a minimum of 1,500 warriors, Custer might thus have faced 375 repeating rifles or carbines; but even in projecting a more conservative total of 192 repeaters on the same force, modern archaeologists noted that this represented "nearly one for every soldier on the field...it becomes readily apparent that Custer and his men were outgunned, if not in range or stopping power, then certainly in firepower." When over 300 warriors under Crazy Horse surrendered in 1877, only 117 firearms, mostly Winchesters and captured carbines, were given up; but Crazy Horse himself surrendered 3 Winchesters, and Little Hawk 2. From the dead Cheyenne chief Yellow Hair were taken a Winchester '73; a Smith and Wesson revolver; a Colt cap-and-ball "Navy" revolver; and a knife, lance, and shield.

The Indian's skill with firearms varied widely. Certainly he might make impressive snap shots from horseback, and some tell of men loading muzzleloaders at the gallop, with bullets held in the mouth. But one officer insisted that: "The marksmanship ability of Indians is woefully exaggerated. A white man who can shoot at all is more than a match for them as a class. They do not use elevated sights and hence at long range their aiming is guess work." A warrior might in fact remove a weapon's sights, as well as cut down the barrel and stock for convenience on horseback. While cartridges for practice or even combat might be in short supply, Indians pioneered the reloading of casings with percussion caps, powder, and lead bullets possibly molded by themselves; Crazy Horse supposedly ordered boys to collect spent casings from the Rosebud battlefield. But a man short on ammunition might still feel obliged to slip a .45 cartridge into a .50 gun—rupturing the case, at best.

As firearms came to dominate the Indian arsenal, its most spiritually significant element, the thick buffalo-hide shield, evolved accordingly. By the 1870s, the actual shield—though able to turn a glancing musket ball—had declined in importance, warriors sometimes attaching its "medicines" to their hair or body. His shoulder galled raw from an expedition where his shield swung against it, the Crow warrior Two Leggings subsequently carried "only the shield cover, or a miniature shield, because their medicine power was just as much protection"—against a breechloader's bullet, at least. About six inches in diameter, miniature shields were worn around the neck or in the scalp lock. Spiritual power in some form remained essential. Even when armed with the most "civilized" of killing devices, the Indian waged war to his own vision.

*Three Sioux pose for a studio portrait, one holding a Sharps carbine. While photographers sometimes kept weapons handy as props, the sabers—not usually thought of as characteristically "Indian" arms—may well have been owned by the warriors themselves.*

# CHAPTER IV

# Terry Seeks the Hostiles

## May-June 1876

Crook's experience had left him with a new respect for his opponents' abilities. The Indians' boldness, he reported to Sheridan on 19 June, "showed that they anticipated that they were strong enough to thoroughly defeat the command....I expect to find those Indians in rough places all the time, and so have ordered five (5) companies of infantry, and shall not probably make any extended movement until they arrive...." Exhibiting no particular sense of urgency, he idled with his strong force at Goose Creek, taking advantage of the bountiful hunting and fishing, but accomplishing nothing. Crook's refusal to take to the field removed the Wyoming column from the area of operations during a critical portion of the campaign. With no communication between Sheridan's columns, Gibbon and Terry would remain unaware of Crook's dubious battle—and anticipate no more trouble from their quarry than had Crook.

After setting out on 17 May, General Terry's formidable command of cavalry, infantry and Gatling guns made almost 14 miles over the rolling plains, stopping on the banks of the Heart River. Here, with Bismarck's gambling holes and sporting women sorely out of reach, the men were paid, apparently due to Terry's fear that debauchery, if not desertion, might follow soldierly affluence. And here General Custer's wife and sister camped before starting back with the paymaster on

# Weapons of the Plains

| Weapon Type c. 1876 | Cal. | WT | RPM | Range |
|---|---|---|---|---|
| Spencer M1865 Carbine ("Indian Model") | .56-50 | 7.5 | 21 | 300/500 |
| Sharps M1870 Carbine | .50-70 | 7 | 15 | 300/500 |
| Springfield 1873 Carbine | .45-70 | 7.5 | 15 | 300/600 |
| Henry 1860 Rifle/ Winchester 1866 Rifle | .44 Henry | 9.8 | 30 | 150/250 |
| Muzzleloading Percussion Rifle-Musket (Springfield 1861) | .58 | 8.88 | 3 | 300/800 |
| Smoothbore Flintlock (Type: Common British Indian trade musket) | .56 | 7 | 3 | 60/100 |
| Colt Single Action Army Revolver | .45 | 2.3 | 9 | 7/50 |

Key: **Cal.**, caliber in inches, with numbers after dashes indicating grains of black powder in cartridges—except for the .56-50, which indicates different diameters for the body and mouth of a "bottlenecked" casing. Like other Spencer cartridges such as the .56-52, the .56-50 actually featured a .52 bullet. With thinner casings, rimfire cartridges tended to be underpowered: the Spencer used 43 to 45 grains, the .44 Henry 28—though the standard centerfire Colt revolver cartridge contained 30. **WT**, weight of the unaltered weapon in pounds. RPM is the number of rounds per minute presumed sustainable by an experienced user; most numbers are open to minor argument and could vary widely according to test (or field) conditions and individual skill. Fouling after repeated firings was especially likely to slow the reloading process in muzzleloaders. Rate of sustained fire was not always relevant for a combatant; a warrior might be more concerned with husbanding his Winchester cartridges than with rapidly burning up a full magazine—assuming he had even that many shells and could ignore the cloud of white smoke obscuring his target after each shot. To reserve ammunition for critical moments of repeating fire, the Spencer had a magazine cut-off permitting the loading and firing of single shots. Similarly, while metallic-cartridge six-shooters, especially the "self-extracting" Schofield, could be reloaded much more quickly than "cap-and-ball" types, cavalry officers devoted little worry to this, viewing the pistol as a weapon for the charge or of last resort.

**Range**, in yards, gives conservatively estimated practical and maximum effective range—assuming unaltered weapons firing proper ammunition, but in the knowledge that marksmen of decidedly variable skill would often be firing at fast-moving individuals rather than at masses or lines of men. Some dead shots could always exceed the limits, as did buffalo hunter Billy Dixon in 1874, when he killed or wounded a stationary Indian horseman at a reported 1,538 yards—about eight-tenths of a mile—with his .50 Sharps buffalo rifle.

*In 1874 Terry had ordered the Black Hills expedition delayed until Springfield "trapdoor" carbines could replace the various patterns carried by the 7th Cavalry—Lieutenant Calhoun reporting that the new weapons seemed "to give great satisfaction." Together with the Colt Single Action Army revolver, it represented the first standardization of small arms since the Civil War, and with minor variations would remain the standard until 1892.*

the morning of the 18th. In the 1920s John Burkman, still treasuring his youthful days as Custer's striker or "dog robber," would tell of how his chief had watched Libbie Custer ride away, head bent, obviously in tears, until she was a distant speck on the plains. "Custer's face went white and he was awful sober. 'A good soldier,' he said, low and quiet, 'has to serve two mistresses. Whilst he's loyal to one the other must suffer.'"

While the Heart River was only about 30 yards wide and three feet deep, the troops had to "corduroy" its steep banks with logs to get Terry's wagon train across. This cost almost 3 hours, and so much exhausting effort that Terry stopped at 1315 to make his second camp on the Sweet Briar Creek, after less than 11 miles. Starting that day, the march was led by a battalion of three 7th Cavalry companies, another serving as rear guard while two battalions rode watchfully on the flanks of the train, and in open formation in rough country. The right wing, under Reno, consisted of Companies B, C, I, E, F and L, battalion commanders Captains Myles Keogh and George Yates; the left wing, under senior captain Frederick W. Benteen, of A, D, G, H and K, and M under Captains Thomas B. Weir and Thomas H. French.

While one company of the advance guard, led by Custer, went ahead to select the route and the site of that night's

*Mrs. Elizabeth Bacon Custer.* "With my husband's departure," *she recalled,* "my last happy days were ended, as a premonition of disaster that I had never known before weighed me down."

camp, the other two troops, accompanied by two light wagons loaded with tools and construction materials, reported to Terry's headquarters for pioneering duty, including bridge construction for creek crossings. Behind this pioneer detail rode Terry and staff, then an infantry company followed by the Gatling guns; the wagon train, four vehicles abreast; and another infantry company. Alongside the wagon train, civilian employees drove the ambulatory steaks of the beef herd and the remainder of the horses and mules. Fanning out in front of all were Varnum's Arikaras. To avoid dismounting more often than necessary for grazing, each troop of the rear guard would push in advance of the train until roughly half a mile ahead, then dismount before resuming its march half a mile behind. This left two troops of the guard actually riding alongside the train at any one time.

At times the march could be pleasant enough. The country was rich in antelope, and, wrote K Company commander

Lieutenant Edward S. Godfrey, Custer's troop of stag hounds "amused themselves and the command in their futile attempt to catch them." Company commanders encouraged the soldiers to hunt—not only to supplement the tedious rations, but to improve marksmanship. The far-ranging Indian scouts enjoyed the most success, selling some game to their white comrades.

Yet despite such diversions, the terrain must often have seemed a more forbidding enemy than even the mighty Sioux, who moved over it with such mocking ease. For the next four days, as Terry marched slightly to the north of the present Northern Pacific Railway line, his men found themselves pounded by rain and even hail, the rear guard frequently pulling out stuck wagons. And despite efforts to avoid the low areas along streams and instead march along the benches and plateaus bordering them, the trail became a mire, bogging down wagons to the wheelhubs as ravines poured torrents of water. The pioneer parties tried to overcome the obstacles in their path by building bridges, cutting away gullies, and forming sloughs by laying down brush and logs. During these tedious, time-wasting "crossings," wrote Lieutenant Godfrey, "the cavalry horses were unbitted and grazed, the men holding the reins. Those men not on duty at the crossing slept, or collected in groups to spin yarns and take a whiff at their 'dingy dudeens.' The officers usually collected near the crossing to watch progress, and passed the time in conversation and playing practical jokes."

The daily distances covered varied widely according to obstacles discovered and the ease with which Custer, riding ahead, could find a campsite offering adequate wood, water and grass while avoiding quicksand and slippery stream banks. With the march halted, men cared first for their mounts, only then setting up tents and setting out their horses' equipment three yards in front of them, save those saddles which troopers chose to use as pillows. With a main guard posted around the camp, the wagon train parked within, and with Varnum's scouts watching from nearby heights after sunset, the troops dug trenches for mess fires

# George Armstrong Custer

Last in a class of 34 (after the usual attrition and the resignation of Southern cadets), the Ohio-born, Michigan-raised Custer (1839-1876) was court-martialed even before graduation for a minor offense, but was shortly released to distinguish himself in the Civil War—starting as a second lieutenant and ending as a major general of volunteers. After Reconstruction duty in Texas and Louisiana, Major General Custer reverted to his Regular Army rank of captain before securing the lieutenant colonelcy (and generally the field command) of the new 7th U.S. Cavalry. During General Hancock's abortive 1867 Indian campaign in Kansas, Custer was again court-martialed and convicted: his offenses included absenting himself without leave to visit his wife and having some rather brazen deserters shot down on the spot.

Custer's one-year suspension of rank and pay was cut short when Sheridan recalled him for his first winter campaign. The 7th Cavalry's November 1868 attack on the Washita River was welcomed by Sheridan and Sherman; yet Custer was condemned not merely for attacking "peaceful" Cheyennes, but for slaying noncombatants (though he gave orders against this) and

with "abandoning" Major Joel Elliott, who with 15 troopers had ridden off without orders and been annihilated. Custer's subsequent, exhausting, but generally unrecognized operations on the Southern Plains managed to rescue two captive white women and coax many Indians into peacefully surrendering.

In his memoir *My Life on the Plains*, Custer displayed a common ambiguity when recognizing the Indian's displacement by "this to him insatiable monster," civilization. Terming him "a *savage* in every sense of the word," Custer still found "much to be admired" in his way of life, and fell quickly into contradiction: denouncing the stereotype of the "noble" red man, he lamented a few pages later that reservation life deprived the Indian of those qualities which "tend to render him noble."

But much about Custer was contradictory, and those who knew him, like those who would later write of him, tended to split into opposing camps of Custerphiles and Custerphobes. He impressed contemporaries as a military tyrant, or popular with his men and kind to them; methodical, yet boyishly reckless; honest to the point of naivete,

and then burned off the grass for a distance beyond, to guard against prairie fires. Grazing was done at a distance from camp, so that at night animals could be grazed within the enclosure. Stable call was sounded an hour or so before

or conniving and calculating; modest, or egomaniacal and ruthlessly self-centered.

After humdrum duty in Kentucky and the 7th Cavalry's move to Dakota Territory and the new Fort Lincoln, Custer had two fights with the Sioux during the 1873 Yellowstone expedition. In 1874 he commanded the famous Black Hills expedition, making what the Sioux would term "The Thieves' Road," and in 1875 helped conclude a reasonably effective peace between the Sioux and the Arikaras, Mandans, and Hidatsa.

Custer's violent death the next year eclipsed even his brilliant Civil War career, making him a heroic (and often absurdly idealized) figure to several generations. His devoted wife Elizabeth contributed to the legend with three books recounting her life with the general, and apparently managed to inhibit (as well as outlive) a number of critics.

After her death in 1933, debunkers quickly gained the upper hand. Frederic F. Van de Water's 1934 *Glory-Hunter* painted a hate-drenched portrait of Custer as a psychopath and military incompetent, and its interpretation quickly became the most influential. More recent scholarship, however marred by partisanship, has helped to restore some balance, exploring Custer's virtues as well as his less admirable characteristics.

But Custer's popular image has often been influenced less by scholarship than by his symbolic role—"in a peculiar sense," as Theodore Roosevelt wrote, "the typical representative of the American regular soldier who fought for the extension of our frontier." This very status—and a fame ironically derived from total defeat at Indian hands—later doomed Custer to play the symbolic scapegoat for America's past Indian policies. While a retired soldier could safely assert in the 1930s that Custer had been the Indians' friend and was now "loved and admired by them," he would become a genocidal caricature of an Indian hater.

Even U.S. Congressmen would denounce him to prove their own enlightenment, over a century after he had died fighting for his country. Perhaps the words of Shakespeare's *Henry VIII*, John Bourke's epitaph for General Crook, might better serve in our own time for General Custer:

> *Men's evil manners live in*
> *brass; their virtues*
> *We write in water.*

---

sunset, the men watering their horses, then washing down hardtack and bacon with black coffee, perhaps cooking on their own any game available.

For the officers, things were a bit easier, as strikers made their beds and arranged the furniture of camp: stools, tin washbasins and looking glasses. Officers generally dined together in messes of four, furnished with a small folding table, various cooking implements, and a mess chest with tableware. Retreat sounded shortly after sunset, "as much to insure the men having their equipments in place as to secure their presence," wrote Godfrey, for few wished to desert in such a wild country. The pipes came out, and the men "grouped around the fires and sang songs and spun yarns until 'taps.'"

Reveille usually sounded shortly after 0400, the regiment breaking fast with the inevitable hard bread, bacon and coffee, sometimes varied with beans or fresh meat cooked in Dutch ovens or camp kettles. With the forces of civilization given little time to ponder their present rude existence, the march began about an hour later.

On 19 May the Dakota column reached the rain-swollen Sweet Briar River and found that it could be neither forded nor bridged. Terry shifted his march toward the south, though the ground underfoot proved so soft that the men often had to hitch double teams to the wagons. With mixed rain and pounding hail as a final treat, the soldiers made another early, and quite miserable camp at the Buzzard's Roost butte, with the nearest wood five miles away, and even the "buffalo chips" too wet to perform their redeeming function of fuel. With only standing water in coulees and buffalo wallows available, many of the men could cook neither supper or breakfast. Only the arrival of mail from Fort Lincoln on 20 May relieved the general camp dreariness. After the column crossed the big Muddy Creek and camped on its Little Muddy branch, scouts rode out with return mail after dark, moving by night and concealing themselves by day.

In 4 days only 46 miles had been covered, and the slow pace continued. Starting at 0600 on 21 May (after building a bridge to cross the Little Muddy) and halting at 1700 that afternoon, the command made 13 1/2 miles—which Terry considered a noteworthy improvement. The first high buttes of the *Mauvaises Terres* could be seen to the west. On the morning of the

23rd, having camped on a branch of the Knife River, the Dakota column marched only eight miles and halted before 0900, ostensibly to exploit what Terry termed "a delightful camp" and rest the stock, but also, perhaps, because Custer—ranging far ahead chasing an elk—had discovered an Indian campfire, still burning. Scouting failed to uncover its makers. But at dusk, Terry's men could see a band of Indians some three miles away, moving slowly while silhouetted against a ridge line—presumably agency Indians in the process of gravitating toward the hostile camps.

On the 24th Terry, marching 19 miles, crossed the Northern Pacific's line of survey, halting at what was termed Stanley's Crossing of the Big Heart River—and throwing up breastworks for defense. On the 27th, 10 days after leaving Fort Lincoln, the soldiers reached the head of the easterly-flowing Heart River, surmounted the divide, and beheld in their full glory the Mauvaises Terres—the Bad Lands—skirting the canyon of the Little Missouri. A wild country it was, with fantastic natural formations that to some seemed like the ruins of a great city, patches of red sunlit clay glistening like dying fires. But its terribly desolate beauty could become merely dreary at closer range, especially to those marching over it.

Seeking to guide the command south to the head of the high-banked, tortuously-coursed Davis Creek and the only feasible route down the Little Missouri, both the esteemed Charley Reynolds and Custer apparently relied on memories of Stanley's surveying trail of 1873. But old tracks had been effaced by rains, and the column—"losing six miles," the annoyed Terry wrote—had to backtrack, though reporter Kellogg told of Custer's "fine memory" in setting things right by correctly identifying the landmark Sentinel Buttes.

While the troops made camp amid poor grass, sparse timber and alkaline water, Custer ordered the 7th Cavalry band to ascend a butte and play, perhaps simply to raise morale. Any stray bands of Indians within hearing must have marveled at the white man's music in these surroundings. But the Rees were to find no traces of their hated Sioux foes. On

*"Lonesome Charley" Reynolds—dubbed "Lucky Man" by the Arikara Indians for his success in hunting—was known for his solitary, soft-spoken ways.*

the 28th Terry built 8 bridges across Davis Creek and made 7 2/3 miles; on the 29th, as Crook's Wyoming column made its first day's march from Fort Fetterman, 5 more bridges, with 6 1/2 miles marched. At 0900, having officially progressed 165.87 miles in 13 days, Terry's men made congenial camp at the confluence of Davis Creek and the Little Missouri, dining on the abundant fish and again erecting earthen parapets. Since the spring weather had come so late, Terry had felt that he might still find the enemy on or near this favorite Sioux wintering spot, and here Custer forbade any discharge of firearms lest it alert warriors within earshot.

While Terry proposed to stay encamped at least two days to scour the area for the projected concentration of Indians, Custer proposed a scout to the south. Terry agreed and, as Custer wrote his wife, "left the matter to me." In fact, he left both route and distance to Custer's discretion, specifying only that his absence would "not extend beyond 7 a.m. of the 31st inst." Exercising his first independent command of the campaign, Custer took companies C, D, F and M, 5 pack mules and a picked 12 scouts under Varnum, riding over 20 miles up the winding river, which he crossed repeatedly—34 times in 50 miles, according to Custer, a mere 13 times each way according to Dr. James DeWolf. Horses struggled up steep stream banks and then slid down with legs braced.

Apparently neither Terry nor Custer cherished much hope of finding the Indians' main camp, especially since the latter had gone out with such a small force. Even as Custer reconnoitered, only to conclude that "all stories about large bodies of Indians being here are the merest bosh," Terry wrote to his sister expressing the fear "that they have scattered and that I shall not be able to find them at all. This would be a most mortifying & perhaps injurious result to me. *But what will be will be.*" The scout became almost a lark, Custer recording the good spirits greeting mishaps in the Little Missouri's quicksand and Dr. DeWolf writing: "Lots of fun seeing the horses mire and throw their riders. The General's nephew got thrown over his horse's head into a mudhole." Whatever his wilful tendencies, Custer returned by 1800 on the 30th—half a day early.

Told of the lack of hostile sign, Terry decided to move on, investigating conscientiously southward before linking up with his supply depot at Glendive Creek. He dispatched a message to Sheridan informing him that contrary "to all the predictions of the guides and scouts," no Indians had been found, nor any signs that they had been in the vicinity "within six months or a year." As he had made slower progress than anticipated, he would now push on westward—continually scouting to the left so that any Sioux returning to the agencies could not pass around his flank. But while Terry's misinterpreted intelligence concerning the Indians' location might have applied to various summer roamers even then gathering on the Little Missouri (some 50 miles south of Custer's farthest scouting), Sitting Bull's followers, and the main hostile encampment, were now on Rosebud Creek.

On 31 May Terry's column crossed the river at Sentinel Butte and made a rough ascent up its west side. Custer lingered to direct wagons over the ford—"playing Wagon Master," as Terry put it—and then disappeared with a small escort and his two brothers. But upon reaching the day's campsite, the Boy General found Terry perturbed by his unauthorized excursion. For with Custer gone and guide Reynolds busy hunting mountain sheep, the column had become lost, marching over not Stanley's old trail, as planned, but that of an Army survey of 1871. Why Custer did not remain with Terry is unknown, though he may have thought it impossible that the column *could* lose its way and simply gone exploring on his own. Finding that turning back would take too long, Terry had gone on; recording in his diary that Custer had departed "without any authority whatever," he reprimanded him for his ranging. Custer lamely, if perhaps somewhat cheekily, explained that he had assumed that his advance guard would "probably be sufficiently far in advance of the main column to constitute a separate command, and that I could be of more service to you and to the expedition acting with the advance....Since such is not the case, I will, with your permission, remain with, and exercise command of, the main portion of my regiment."

Considering his debt to Terry, and his precarious position with the highest executive authority, Custer seemed oblivious to the wisdom of reining himself in rather than striving for "separate" commands, or indulging his habit of stretching a subordinate's limits. It was a habit which tended to obscure his very real virtues—virtues which Terry hoped to exploit. While Custer simply took the command's errant marching as evidence that "my 'bump of locality' is of some use out here," Terry could hardly be blamed for not seeing it in quite that cheery way.

That night, into the morning of 1 June, came the summer snowstorm, to torment men shivering in their tiny "dog tents" or standing huddled around their fires. It lasted all day and into the next. Between one and two feet deep, the snow drifted halfway up some of the tents, deprived animals of grazing—and perturbed the Ree scouts, who thought the unexpected blizzard an evil omen. Terry decided to remain in camp lest the snow retard the wagons and "ball" up the feet of his animals, and Chief Medical Officer Dr. John W. Williams advised that he not march the next day either, though the men attempted some pioneer work.

Breaking camp on 3 June, the Dakota column made its best distance yet—25 miles—before halting at Beaver Creek. The snow had thinned as the command descended to lower elevations, and the weather proving so changeable that Terry would suffer sunstroke before the day's march ended. Terry had asked Custer to take the column as far west as he could that day, since about 1000 that morning two whites and an Indian, messengers from Stanley's Stockade, rode in with messages from Colonel Gibbon and Major Moore. From these Terry learned of Sioux in significant force south of the Yellowstone, and of their slaying of three hunters from the Montana column on 23 May. He also learned that two supply steamers had arrived at the stockade; while the *Josephine* had already unloaded and left, the *Far West* awaited Terry's arrival.

After arriving, Gibbon's messengers at the Glendive depot had gone further downriver and, after encountering the *Far West*, had ridden it back to the supply base through the first

*The steamer* **Far West.**

# Fire-Wagons at War

Seeing the first steamboat on the Missouri in 1819, an Indian remarked: "White man bad man, keep a great spirit chained and build a fire to make it work a boat." By 1876 the U.S. Army often found itself dependent upon such spirits. Following Colonel William Harney's 1855 show of force on the Plains, the next major campaigns supplied by steamboat were those of Sully and Sibley in Dakota against the Santee Sioux and their Teton cousins. Eight steamboats helped supply Sully's massive force of 4,000 men.

For a penny-pinching army, the most economical posts were those capable of being supplied by boats on the Missouri, at least when the upper river wasn't frozen. But troops in the field also relied on riverborne supplies, and as logistically tortuous as the campaign of 1876 proved *with* steamers, it would have been impossible without them. Even its impressive wagon train could supply only a part of the minimal eight tons per day needed by the Dakota column—including some 7,500 tons of grain for draft animals alone. The key to supplying the campaign's northern wing lay in stockpiling supplies by steamboat at Forts Lincoln, Rice, and Buford, then shuttling them to depots on the Yellowstone.

The advantages were obvious. A practical working load for traffic on the upper river was 200 tons of cargo—the rough equivalent of 133 six-mule wagons, minus the 60 pounds of fodder required daily for each team. The 40 or so cords of wood required daily for a steamer could be acquired en route, conserving cargo space. And steamers did not require lengthy rest periods, though there was always the risk of a breakdown or even a boiler explosion.

The sternwheelers used had narrow cross sections which made them more maneuverable in narrow channels and low water, both common to this theater. The most famous, the *Far West*, had been launched in 1870 and was fairly typical. A slim 33 1/2 feet in the beam and 190 feet long, it offered a low profile and drew 27 inches of water with a standard loading—permitting navigation, it was said, "on a heavy dew." A small, low cabin could house 30 passengers. Its captain, Grant Marsh, was already something of a legend on the Missouri.

When Crook's tentless troops met Terry's steamer-supplied soldiers, they were struck by the contrast between Terry's relatively plush situation and their own—all 300 miles from the nearest railroad. But such logistical support was a creature of circumstance, and the campaign would be cut short largely because the rapidly falling Yellowstone prevented the steamers from doing their part.

day's snowstorm. Moore had sent one of the men with two of his own couriers to deliver Gibbon's dispatch and his own cover letter, which assured Terry that the river was "in fine condition" should the boat attempt to proceed higher. But Moore had "no news of hostile Indians in addition to what General Gibbon gives in his dispatches."

And that was very little. As we have seen, Gibbon's dispatch told Terry nothing of Bradley's efforts at tracking the large hostile village, nor its last known location, nor even that Gibbon had actually tried to cross the swollen Yellowstone in order to attack it; Gibbon's one reference to a village, a skeptical postscript concerning the encampment up the Rosebud, actually cast doubt upon the very information it contained.

However, Gibbon's scout may have supplied further details orally, and it did seem that the Sioux were located farther west than Terry had surmised, toward the Powder, Tongue and Rosebud. Terry revised his plan to have Gibbon march down the Yellowstone. Instead, the Dakota column would make for the Powder River while keeping Gibbon opposite the Rosebud. He wrote orders for Major Moore to send a boatload of supplies to a new depot to be established at the mouth of the Powder—and for Gibbon to suspend his movement downriver. The two white scouts were promised a $200 bonus each to reach Gibbon at whatever point Terry's orders might halt him. With morning, Terry began the march to the Powder, 92 miles away, and for three days the Dakota column wound its way along Beaver Creek. But Terry still found no traces of Indians in what to the whites was a strange and barely explored country.

Finally, on the 4th, the troops broke out into a rolling, grass-rich plain like a verdant ocean—and the scouts found sign, roughly a week old, of a small Indian party, including three brush shelters or wickiups with leaves still green. On 6 June, the Dakota column crossed the middle fork of the Yellowstone tributary O'Fallon's Creek. Even Charley Reynolds became lost and led the unwary soldiers to the creek's south fork rather than the main stream. Backtracking,

Terry decided to strike out directly for the Powder rather than descend the Yellowstone—Custer suggesting that he could personally find a new trail by 1500 the next day. Despite the odds against it, Terry gave his consent. That day Colonel Michael V. Sheridan, brother to the divisional commander, wrote from Chicago relaying a report that 1,800 lodges of Indians were reported on the Rosebud, about to leave for the Powder River, below the site of Reynolds' fight, and that "they will fight and have about three thousand warriors. This is sent for your information."

While Custer set out on his mission with the 7th's Cavalry's Company D, Terry found his own route so rough that "We had at times literally to dig & 'pick' our way through...." As the troops crossed the rugged divide separating O'Fallon's Creek from the valley, Lieutenant Maguire observed a splendid vista of rolling country and yawning chasms, with varied-colored earth warped into "fantastic and weird shapes." Custer, with his marked talent for locating trails, found the only feasible route for miles around and missed making good his boast by a mere half-hour. After marching 32.3 odometer-measured miles (which seemed more like 50) in a hazardous descent to the valley of the Powder, Custer made camp. While others napped, their seemingly tireless leader wrote to Terry: "We arrived at 3:30. Considering the character of the country, the road is good, but will require some work." He also noted the discovery of a trail made by four Indians since the last rain. To rest his horses, Custer decided to bivouac, but advised Terry against joining him that day if he could find a suitable camp.

Terry, however, was too anxious to make up for lost time. He drove on, even swinging pick and shovel himself to help clear the way. Horses played out, and mules in harness dropped from fatigue. The exhausted column's last wagons finally straggled into camp at 2100, some 25 miles up from the Yellowstone confluence, in a grassy mile-wide valley watered by the Powder River, flowing yellowish with soil in suspension.

Custer's success in pathfinding impressed both Kellogg and Terry, who that night dispatched Ree couriers to the supply camp at the mouth of the Powder, to check on the whereabouts of the *Far West* and see if Terry's couriers had reached Gibbon. Earlier Terry had received Major Orlando Moore's 5 June dispatch from Stanley's Stockade, informing him that the *Far West* was en route to the Powder, "loaded as directed" with 75 tons of forage, 15 days' subsistence stores for 1,200 men, hospital stores and "private packages for the officers." Knowing of Terry's "appreciation of plenty of ammunition," Moore had also assumed the responsibility of placing aboard a store of cartridges including 10,000 half-inch Gatling rounds.

The hard-riding Rees were back the next morning, having started from the Powder River supply base just two hours earlier with a report which Captain Powell thought urgent. They had seen four Sioux en route, but these had fled. While Powell had seen no trace of Indians, two couriers who had attempted to reach Gibbon with Terry's earlier dispatches had hurriedly arrived at the base camp at 0600, saying that they had been discovered by a party of about 40 Indians (who, unbeknownst to them, were actually Bradley's Crow scouts) and so aborted their mission. Believing this information to be important, Powell had already dispatched it with a small boat to Terry's anticipated location near O'Fallon's Creek.

Distressed to learn that his couriers had failed to reach Gibbon, Terry decided to head for the Yellowstone that very afternoon, then use the *Far West* to make personal contact— rather than camp for a few days while weighing his options, as he had planned. Organizing a pack train for rapid movement, he committed to paper his three objects in marching: to discover whether any hostiles were below his present position; to find out whether the *Far West* had arrived with the necessary supplies; and to examine the valley en route "with reference to the practicability of sending our train down to the depot which is to be established at its mouth." Of course, this meant leaving Custer in temporary command of the column, whatever President Grant's preferences. Before leaving, Terry ordered the 7th Cavalry to prepare for an eight-day reconnaissance up the Powder, while his three infantry companies readied themselves to escort wagons down along the Yellowstone.

Arriving that evening with Companies A and I under Captains Moylan and Keogh, Terry found the *Far West* there as expected—and as needed, since his wagons bore provisions only sufficient to the Powder. Commanded by the doughty Grant Marsh, at that time the only river captain to have navigated the waters of the upper Yellowstone, it had arrived at Fort Lincoln on 27 May. There Marsh had the merciful inspiration to discourage Mrs. Custer and either Mrs. Calhoun or the wife of 7th Cavalry lieutenant Algernon Smith—or both—from boarding as passengers. After landing supplies at Stanley's Stockade (where Marsh found three 6th Infantry companies under Moore), the *Far West* had arrived at the mouth of the Powder on 7 June.

Terry was gratified to find that members of Gibbon's command had arrived a few hours before, including Major Brisbin and Captain Clifford—who with his infantry company was there by mistake, having assumed that he was to head on toward the Powder confluence even though Gibbon had wanted him to proceed only about 16 miles downriver, more or less paralleling the march of the other Montana troops.

It was presumably at this time that Terry, aboard the steamer, questioned the officers about the information regarding Indian movements which Gibbon had possessed but failed to report—as well as Gibbon's inactivity after his failed attempt at pursuit. Terry issued orders for Major Moore to transfer all supplies from Stanley's Stockade to the base camp at the Powder's mouth, and for Gibbon to have his command stand fast while he reported personally to Terry. Gibbon's snowbound command had been reinforced on 4 June by the Diamond R wagon train under Matt Carroll, along with previously detached units, guide Barney Bravo, two Crows, and Crow ponies from the agency to remount the scouts requesting them. Having heard nothing regarding his couriers, Gibbon had decided, despite the village observed up the Rosebud, to proceed down the Yellowstone toward Terry. His

*Captain Myles Walter Keogh, in the horsehair-plumed helmet and yellow-trimmed dress uniform introduced in 1872. Though sometimes envisioned as a devil-may-care swashbuckler, the gallant Keogh was prone to melancholia. In America a "certain lack of sensitiveness is necessary to be successful," he observed. "This lack of sensitiveness I unfortunately do not inherit."*

pace was leisurely. With Clifford's infantry company in Mackinaw boats, Gibbon set out on 5 June, marching only 57 miles in 4 days and stopping 17 miles below the mouth of the Tongue—to wonder what had become of Clifford's flotilla.

On the 8th Gibbon's Crows inadvertently scared off the scouts who could have earned $200 by delivering Terry's orders. But the next morning Gibbon received Terry's revised instructions from unpaid volunteer George Herendeen and a Crow scout. While the department commander steamed up-river, Gibbon rode down along the Yellowstone's north bank, escorted by a company of 2nd Cavalry and Bradley's scouts.

On board the *Far West,* Gibbon learned that Terry had neither discovered significant signs of a hostile concentration nor heard anything from Crook—who that very day was on the Tongue enjoying a brisk skirmish with the Indians who had fired into his bivouac. Terry, for his part, was able to quiz Gibbon on his actions and inactions. It was unfortunate that Gibbon, never having received Terry's cancellation of his earlier orders, had obediently but needlessly marched the

Montana column east of the hostiles' last known position up the Rosebud. He had to then retrace his steps to the Rosebud confluence; even if the enemy had crossed the Yellowstone to escape into the rough country of the upper Missouri's northern regions (and Terry's information was, after all, 15 days old), it was important to find out.

Terry therefore ordered Gibbon to hurry back to his old camp opposite the Rosebud, with the cavalry marching that afternoon and the infantry the next morning if not sooner. If it had not already departed, Gibbon was to prevent the Indian village from crossing the Yellowstone (though it is hard to see how he could have). Terry would return on the *Far West* in roughly a week, with Gibbon prepared to take the field when he did. In the interval, Terry would scout the Powder River to ensure against a hostile presence that far east and south. Gibbon, according to his own account, agreed to start his cavalry out that afternoon. But he decided to wait when a bad rainstorm blew up, finally dispatching his cavalry the next day despite muddy roads and intermittent rains.

Terry needed the best pathfinder available, and when the *Far West* stopped briefly at Gibbon's camp, Mitch Boyer—"a first rate half-breed guide," wrote Terry—boarded for the trip toward the Powder River confluence. Considering his Glendive supply dump too far to the east to be useful, Terry ordered that the rest of Moore's infantry march to the new Camp Supply at the confluence, while Captain Marsh transferred the remaining stores at Glendive.

Meeting with Custer and his other officers on the 10th, Terry explained the situation. Since no hostiles had shown themselves, either to the Montana column during its march along the Yellowstone, or to the infantrymen at Glendive Creek and the new supply depot, the Sioux were apparently to the west, up the Rosebud Valley—or, at any rate, had been there on 27 May. Unfortunately, they might have gone almost anywhere—further west toward the Big Horn, south up the Rosebud and toward the headwaters of the Tongue, north across the Yellowstone into the upper Missouri breaks, or eastward toward the upper Powder.

With his first priority the fixing of the Indians' location, Terry outlined his plan. While Major Reno took six companies of cavalry up the Powder to locate any hostile camps or isolated parties of warriors, the rest of the Dakota troops would march north to the new supply camp. The infantry would remain at the mouth of the Powder while the 7th Cavalry's remaining six companies rode up the Tongue and then to the upper Rosebud.

Custer apparently objected to the plan, and there were good reasons for doing so. The reconnaissance might either be misdirected, losing valuable time rather than probing toward the Indians' last known location, or warn the foe that the bluecoats were at their heels. Furthermore, should he actually clash with the Indians, Reno would have only half of the 7th available for any strike against a large encampment, while the other half remained idle in camp. Most of the officers also appear to have objected to the scout, which seemed to give theoretical Indians on the Powder precedence over any others.

Custer may also have protested, or at least been disappointed by, Terry's choice of Reno to command the scout. Perhaps Terry had made his choice to humble or rein in the obstreperous Custer, or simply to give Reno a chance at distinction—though had Terry expected any likelihood of fighting, Custer would have been the obvious choice. Terry's Special Field Order No. 11 characterized the mission only as a "reconnaissance," and rigidly prescribed its route. Reno was to reconnoiter the Powder River to the mouth of the Little Powder, then cross the headwaters of Mizpah Creek, descending it to its junction with the Yellowstone. There he could expect to meet the 7th's left wing as well as supplies of food and forage.

Terry planned, if "nothing new" developed before the cavalry was reunited, or if Reno ascertained "that the Indians are to the West of us," to "make a double movement," sending Custer with nine cavalry troops up the Tongue "and then across to and down the Rosebud while the rest of the Seventh will join Gibbon and move up the Rosebud." Major Moore's infantry would remain to guard Terry's supply camp and train. Such a plan would leave Gibbon's column the stronger of the two, though less mobile than Custer's all-mounted force.

Terry instructed Reno verbally to avoid the Rosebud, so as not to alarm the Indians presumed camped on that stream. But what was Reno to do if he instead chanced to find, and perhaps alarm, the main camp along the prescribed route? Terry did not inform him. Nor did he specify a date for Reno's arrival at the junction of the Tongue and Yellowstone, though his bow-shaped march of some 175 miles, at perhaps 30 miles a day, would have brought him to the meeting place on 16 June, when Custer was to arrive as well. But the fact that he was ordered to carry 12 days' rations may have left Reno with a different impression—and certainly gave him the ability to extend his march if he so chose.

That afternoon Reno, guided by Mitch Boyer, set out up the east bank of the Powder with companies C, E, F, I and L, a Gatling gun and crew under Lieutenant Kenzie, 11 pack mules per troop, and a detachment of Rees. Hoping to start his own march toward the Powder confluence, Terry dispatched two troops ahead to find a suitable wagon route, but after their failure turned on 11 June to his young subordinate: "He seems to think I have a gift that way," wrote Custer, adding that Terry hoped to get within 10 miles of the river's mouth that day and that the column's condition was the more "embarrassing" since the men had only one day's rations left. But despite his own unfamiliarity with the country, Custer again found (along with Company D, lost in the badlands since looking for a path the previous day) a trail permitting the command to camp that night on the banks of the Yellowstone. Now almost due west of Fort Lincoln, Terry had marched 318 miles, or an average of 15.9 per day.

On reaching the river, they found the *Far West*, along with Moore's infantry company, additional supplies, and a sutler selling straw hats and whisky to officer and soldier alike, though a canned-goods partition across a planking "bar" preserved military protocol by separating the two classes of drinkers. Even the Ree scouts were permitted one drink each. But while three-pint canteens could be filled only with a captain's orders, there were still drunks who, in lieu of a guardhouse, were herded out onto the prairie to sweat out hangovers.

On Monday 12 June, the steamer departed to pick up personnel and supplies remaining at the Glendive depot, where a skiff capsized while transferring a bag of mail from the Dakota column; 6th Infantry Sergeant Henry Fox, set to retire after 20 years' service, drowned. The soaked items recovered included Terry's dispatch to Sheridan, reporting "No Indians east of the Powder" and explaining his latest plan.

Preparations for the first phase of that plan, the Custer-Reno rendezvous, included training wagon mules to carry the packs for Custer's cavalrymen and discarding all nonessentials. Officers and men gave up their sabers to be crated and stored, for even the *beau sabreur* Custer apparently believed that they were of too little use against Indians to justify their rattlings on the march. The 7th's splendid mounted band would also stay behind, though the musicians' gray-white horses, like the steeds of some 10 or 12 noncommissioned staff personnel, would serve as mounts for some of the recruits who had marched all the way to the Powder River in their cavalry boots. But due to the lack of anticipated remounts, most of these would also stay in camp, along with Major Moore's three companies of 6th Infantry and the Dakota column's two 17th Infantry companies.

On the 13th the *Far West* steamed toward the Powder River supply camp, with the remaining stores and Captain Daniel Murdock's Co. D, 6th Infantry. Terry and his staff were installed aboard the steamer, with Captain Baker's C Company as a guard. After conferring with Terry aboard the steamer, Custer set forth at 0700 on Thursday 15 June, his band serenading the departing troops and concluding with "Garry Owen." With the 7th Cavalry's left wing companies, the rest of the Gatlings, and Arikara scouts—not to mention his two brothers and his nephew—Custer rode for the mouth of the Tongue while keeping four or five miles back from the river's edge.

Terry was to follow on the steamer that afternoon with rations for the command. But while Custer set a leisurely pace along the Yellowstone's south bank, assuming that Reno's men would not arrive at the Tongue confluence for several days, Terry found himself delayed by an engine breakdown. He did not arrive at Custer's chosen bivouac until the following afternoon.

By then, near the future site of Miles City, Montana, Custer's men had already come upon the remains of several Indian villages, complete with wickiups and lean-tos for pony shelters. A Sioux burial scaffold, its uprights colored black and red to show that an especially brave warrior lay there, was dismantled at Custer's orders and the body's wrappings pulled back for inspection by the black interpreter Dorman—who allegedly dumped the corpse in the river and, observed fishing at the same spot some time later, was suspected by the Rees of using it as bait. Godfrey recalled:

> The grounds where we camped had been occupied by the Indians the previous winter....The rude shelters for their ponies, built of driftwood, were still standing and furnished fuel for our camp-fires. A number of their dead placed upon scaffolds, or tied to the branches of trees, were disturbed and robbed of their trinkets. Several persons rode about exhibiting trinkets with as much gusto as if they were trophies of their valor, and showed no more concern for their desecration than if they had won them at a raffle. Ten days later I saw the bodies of these same persons dead, naked, and mutilated.

Among the collectors of Indian curiosities was Boston Custer, who wrote home to his mother how his brothers "Armstrong" and Tom, whether to find out more about the camp's inhabitants or simply aid in their relatives' souvenir-hunt, had helped him pull down "an Indian grave": "Autie Reed got the bow with six arrows and a nice pair of moccasins which he intends taking home." Noting that "with a little hard riding" Armstrong would probably overhaul the Indians, Boston predicted: "They will be much entertained."

There was evidence that the Indians had "entertained" at

least one luckless soldier at the site. In the ashes of an extinct fire lay a man's skeletal remains, along with remnants of a uniform—a cavalryman, Custer judged, since his overcoat buttons bore a "C," and his blue dress coat had a yellow cord running through it. "The skull was weather-beaten, and had evidently been there several months," wrote Custer, though it could presumably have been that of a 7th Cavalry trooper missing after Custer's fight in 1873 near that area. Custer felt sure that the man had been tortured, "probably burned," though the Arikara scout Red Star remembered clubs and sticks "all about him" as though he had been beaten to death: "Custer stood still for some time and looked down at the remains of the soldier."

At about 0830 on 17 June, the day of Crook's Rosebud fight some 150 miles to the southwest, Custer led his men to the mouth of the Tongue; the *Far West* later moored near the new bivouac. On the evening of the 19th the camp hummed with rumors after Terry received a dispatch from Reno, and learned to his displeasure that the major had been at the mouth of the Rosebud. He immediately sent his aide and brother-in-law, Captain Robert P. Hughes, to tell Reno to hold his position until Custer could join him. "Hughes returned. Reno gave him no reasons for his disobedience of orders," wrote Terry.

Reno had on the 11th crossed to the west bank of the Powder, above the confluence of Mizpah Creek and Ash Creek, another tributary of the Powder. Ree scouts galloped into that night's bivouac to report smoke to the northwest. The next day Reno found an abandoned pony and a recent campsite of some 26 lodges, whose owners had apparently traveled west. After making bivouac, Reno gained half a day by having his Ree and Sioux scouts ride ahead upriver to inspect the forks at the mouth of the Little Powder some 19 miles away. Crossing the Powder divide southwest to Mizpah Creek, Reno camped on the 13th on the upper Mizpah.

While Terry had ordered him to scout down that creek, Reno found that from the western divide he was able to see down into it for miles, spying no smoke or other signs of human life. Rather than proceed down the creek valley in obedience to Terry's orders, Reno decided to presume it empty of any camps and instead march boldly westward, possibly toward the point on the Tongue where Bradley had found a campsite on 16 May.

Boyer doubted that the soldiers would find any Indians en route. But an estimate of enemy numbers might still be gained by counting the old lodge sites. The next day, Reno rode to the divide separating the Mizpah from the broad, verdant valley of Pumpkin Creek. The scouts found some old trails, but it seemed that the hostiles were still farther west. On the 15th, the sixth day of his scout, the Gatling gun overturned as Reno descended toward the Tongue, and probing scouts found trails—but they were old. So far there was nothing to indicate any Sioux east of the Tongue.

On the morning of 16 June, Reno was eight miles down the Tongue when Boyer and the scouts returned from investigating the large campsite seen by Lieutenant Bradley on 16 May. Reno decided to delay his rendezvous with Custer, and to further disobey Terry by marching to discover where the village might be headed. Strict obedience was a fine ideal; but if Reno followed orders he would simply leave Terry with an absence of new intelligence. The command rode toward the Rosebud, the scouts riding ahead and apparently examining the site observed by Bradley on 27 May.

Boyer, counting 360 old lodge fires, estimated that 400 tipis, arranged in nine circles, had occupied the site, indicating at least 800 warriors and doubtless others able to fight when pressed. The circles, wrote Lieutenant Bradley, had been arranged "within supporting distance of one another, within which the Indians apparently secured their horses at night, showing they considered an attack likely and were prepared for it." The command followed a wide trail plowed up by lodgepoles until halted by darkness at 2330.

On the day of Crook's fight, which may have prevented the Indians engaged 55 miles away from hunting in the region or otherwise riding where they might have discovered him, Reno ascended the Rosebud, forbidding bugle calls and loud noises. In all, perhaps five old campsites were inspected by the scouts, including the great Sun Dance camp abandoned earlier that month. Apparently all had been used solely by Sitting Bull's winter roamers; while the spring migration of agency Sioux had peaked in mid-May, hunting and the cutting of new lodgepoles slowed their arrival, so that few had arrived in time for the Rosebud fight. But many more would come within the week.

Sent forward to reconnoiter the trail, scouts returned to report it continuing up the valley, and toward the south-west—suggesting the Little Bighorn valley as the Indians' destination. Reno could not be sure whether they would actually head there, or even how far ahead they were. But with rations low, and needing at least two days to return to the Tongue confluence, he decided against pushing further.

Reno hurried back down the Rosebud to the Yellowstone, following that river toward the Tongue rendezvous point to save time. On 19 June he pitched camp opposite and up the river from Gibbon, who sent two Crows to swim the river with a message and established communication with impro-vised signal flags. Gibbon wrote to Terry that afternoon that "the only remaining chance of finding Indians now is in the direction of the headwaters of Rosebud or Little Big Horn." Like his informant Reno, Colonel Gibbon now realized that Terry's notion of an enveloping "double movement", at least as originally envisioned, was no longer tenable.

On the 19th Reno wrote to Terry, assuring him that "I can tell you where the Indians are *not*, and much more informa-tion when I see you in the morning." But while admitting his disobedience, Reno had made the breathtaking blunder of neglecting to justify it. Terry wrote angrily (if we accept the printed text of a letter now missing) that Reno had acted "in positive defiance of my orders not to go to the Rosebud, in the belief that there were Indians on that stream and that he could make a successful attack on them which would cover up his disobedience....Of course this performance made a change in my plans necessary."

But whatever Reno's personal ambitions may have been, he

could have defended his deviation from orders on purely pragmatic grounds, had he not chosen a brooding silence instead. His scout had discovered significant information, and if his "performance" required a change in Terry's plans, perhaps it was because this information, however incomplete, revealed the futile hollowness of their premises. Terry now chose to act on the assumption that the Indians were moving toward the valley of the Little Bighorn.

On 20 June, Terry had Custer march to Reno's bivouac, the *Far West* reaching the reunited regiment an hour later. Joining Terry and Reno on the boat, Custer reportedly upbraided Reno for failing to actually find out the hostiles' strength and direction—and even for failing to pursue and attack them! Given later accusations that Custer was bent on hogging all glory for himself, it seems odd that he should have criticized Reno for not seeking a victory in his absence, especially since this would have involved even greater disobedience of orders. Custer's deepest concern seems to have been the risk of discovery taken without the gaining of more hard information. "I fear their failure to follow up the trails has imperilled our plans by giving the village an intimation of our presence," wrote Custer to his wife. "Think of the valuable time lost."

Custer himself would lose no time; Terry ordered him to march as far upriver as he could before dark. By 2030, with the Gatlings transferred to the *Far West* and the steamer paralleling the horsemen riding along the Yellowstone bluffs, the reunited regiment had reached a bivouac 14 miles westward from Reno's camp. The next morning the steamer arrived at Gibbon's camp.

Anticipating that Terry would dispatch his Montana column westward toward the mouth of the Big Horn, Gibbon had sent Captain Freeman with 7th Infantry companies E, H and K, plus six Crow scouts, to scout out the road ahead and perform any necessary pioneer work. Disembarking, Terry ordered the rest of Gibbon's command forward toward the Big Horn's mouth. Then Terry, Colonel Gibbon and Major Brisbin steamed toward Custer, who was marching briskly upriver.

Terry wrote to inform Sheridan of the current situation and to briefly outline his revised strategy. By now he had abandoned his earlier notion of dividing the 7th Cavalry between the Montana and Dakota columns:

> No Indians have been met with as yet; but traces of a large and recent camp have been discovered twenty or thirty miles up the Rosebud.
>
> Gibbon's column will move this morning on the north side of the Yellowstone for the mouth of the Big Horn where it will be ferried across by the supply steamer, and thence it will proceed to the mouth of the Little Horn, and so on. Custer will go up the Rosebud tomorrow with his whole regiment and thence to the headwaters and thence down the Little Horn. I only hope that one of the two columns will find the Indians. I go personally with Gibbon.

If Terry's expressed strategy seemed vague, it was because he could still not confidently predict where the Sioux might be found. The "so on" seemed to mean that if Gibbon found no hostiles on the Little Bighorn, he would be obliged to continue up its valley until either Custer or the Indians were encountered—Custer, in Terry's tentative projection, moving down that valley toward the Little Bighorn confluence. Terry made no mention of close cooperation between the two columns, merely expressing the "hope" that one would find Indians.

Such cooperation was not, at this stage, considered vital to safety. As Phil Sheridan had asserted, his subordinates shared his belief that each column could cope with any hostile force. And given the latest intelligence indicating perhaps 800 warriors, it seemed a reasonable belief, though Terry seemed unworried by the possibility that parties of summer roamers might add to their numbers. According to Godfrey (and despite a reputation for optimism), Custer was apparently alone in suggesting later that, if perhaps 500 men from the agencies arrived, he might face as many as 1,500 warriors; but from his study of Indian Department reports he felt sure that this was the maximum he could expect.

Nor did the enemy's capabilities intimidate the soldier chiefs. The military had long complained of the Indians' easy access to breechloading rifles, and before the march Charley

Reynolds had reported the Sioux to be preparing for possible war, accumulating Winchester repeaters and metallic cartridges. Many knew that the Plains Indian could be a superb individual fighter. Yet, like Crook, of whose chastening experiences they were ignorant, they shared the fundamental assumption that the Sioux would not give battle unless pressed, and that if caught they would be whipped. Only the scouts seemed to appreciate—and fear—the confident spirit of the Sioux, while the Army's fears were of a different sort. As Gibbon testified, Terry's overriding object was "to prevent the escape of the Indians, which was the idea pervading the minds of all of us."

Upon Custer's arrival, he was hailed aboard the moored *Far West* for the famous shipboard conference of 21 June, where Terry explained his plan. In the scenario which finally evolved, Gibbon's men would be ferried to the Yellowstone's south bank, then march southward after scouting the lower reaches of Tullock's Creek, which might be used as a route by Sioux travelling either north or south through the Big Horn region. The *Far West*, carrying Captain Baker's company as a guard, would head up the Big Horn as far as the Little Bighorn's mouth, or as far as possible given the river's condition.

Custer would take up the Rosebud all 12 companies of his 7th, unencumbered by wagons. But this highly mobile strike force was apparently not to proceed too quickly, and in order to keep the Indians from escaping to the south and east around his flank, he was to keep probing constantly to his left. If the Sioux became alarmed at Custer's approach and attempted flight, they might well head south toward the Big Horn Mountains, thus avoiding Gibbon's forces to their north, Custer marching from the east, and any unwanted clash with the Crows still clinging to their homeland in the west. Once reaching the mountains, it would be simple for the Sioux to break up into small bands, elude the clumsy bluecoats, and make necessary just such an extended campaign as Sheridan had feared. Thus Terry suggested that if, as he believed likely, the trail seemed to turn westward, across the

Chetish or Wolf Mountains into the valley of the Little Bighorn, Custer should take the unusual step of *not* following it. Moving instead farther south, he might go even as far as the headwaters of the Tongue River before turning to the west and south. Presumably this would give Gibbon's foot soldiers (who needed at least an extra day) time to get into position on the Little Bighorn. In performing these maneuvers, Custer would supposedly be able to block any Indian attempt to escape around his left.

After the Little Bighorn disaster, it was alleged that 26 June, when the men under Terry's personal command were expected to reach a "blocking" position at the Little Bighorn's mouth, was the date set for a predetermined, simultaneous attack by the Dakota and Montana columns on the great Indian village. But did anyone at the conference actually believe that cooperation between the two columns could take such a form? Not even the camp's present location was known for sure, let alone its location on 26 June. Given this uncertainty, the best chance of actually catching the Indians lay in Terry's earlier concept of simply turning Custer loose to follow their trail directly to the village, wherever it might be. In *theory*, a second column could block an Indian retreat if it occupied the perfect strategic position and moved from it only upon communication with the striking force. But any degree of coordination was unlikely while operating in a questionably mapped country with no roads, few known distances, and extremely challenging terrain—and in cold fact, under all but the most unlikely conditions, "blocking" Plains Indians with troops was simply impossible. One of the columns would have to strike first.

The contemporary evidence, uncolored by later attempts to absolve Terry of responsibility for disaster, makes it clear that he expected Custer to do it. Bradley wrote in his 21 June diary entry that it was "understood that if Custer arrives first he is at liberty to attack at once if he deems prudent. We have little hope of being in on the death, as Custer will undoubtedly exert himself to the utmost to get there first and win all the laurels for himself and his regiment." An 8 July New York

*One of the Gatlings that accompanied Terry's Dakota column.*

*Herald* article by a Montana column officer, possibly Major Brisbin, was even more explicit:

> It was announced by General Terry that General Custer's column would strike the blow and General Gibbon and his men received the decision without a murmur....The Montana column felt disappointed when they learned that they were not to be present at the capture of the great village but General Terry's reasons for affording the honor of the attack to General Custer were good ones. First Custer had all cavalry and could pursue if they attempted to escape, while Gibbon's column was half infantry, and in rapid marching in approaching the village, as well as pursuing the Indians after the fight, General Gibbon's cavalry

and infantry must become separated and the strength of the column be weakened. Second, General Custer's column was numerically stronger than Gibbon's and General Terry desired the stronger column to strike the Indians; so it was decided that Custer's men were, as usual, to have the post of honor and the officers and men of the Montana column cheered them and bade them God-speed.

Custer at first accepted the offer of Low's Gatling battery, but later declined them, pointing out that they would retard his march; no doubt he had recalled Reno's unhappy experiences on his scout, which had almost caused Reno to have his single gun cached and abandoned. At some point it was also suggested that Custer take along Brisbin's four 2nd Cavalry companies, but he refused these also—perhaps for less pragmatic reasons. Having allegedly assured Brisbin that his 7th could "handle anything it meets," Custer is said to have remarked that he intended the coming fight to be an exclusively 7th Cavalry battle, "and I want all the glory for the 7th Cavalry there is in it." Of course, actually giving Custer Brisbin's men would have stripped Gibbon of his mounted troops and, presuming one company left to guard Terry's base, would have left his column a mere five infantry companies—a force, as Terry admitted in his annual report, "too small to act as an independent body." Terry actually had over 12 infantry companies in his area of operations, including 5 guarding a Powder River depot also manned by close to 300 dismounted cavalrymen and civilian employees. Far too many men were to play no part whatsoever in his offensive operations.

Major Brisbin would later claim that he had suggested that Terry go in command of the mounted strike force *himself*. When Terry spoke instead of his desire to give Custer a chance to "do something" while still smarting under the President's rebuke, and noted his own lack of Indian-fighting experience, Brisbin took the unusual step of questioning the judgment of his dashing fellow officer. But while Brisbin obviously had no desire to serve under Custer, did Terry really wish to take on the role of cavalry leader, and return to his original strategy of pursuit with a single mounted column? Certainly Custer would have preferred not being hampered by either Terry *or* Brisbin. In any event, Terry chose not to adopt this uncomfortable solution.

Even Terry's redistribution of scouts reinforced the impression that he hoped for a successful first blow by the 7th Cavalry. Custer was loaned six of Gibbon's Crows, since his own Arikaras were unfamiliar with the country. Having selected "my six best men," Lieutenant Bradley commented: "Our guide, Mitch Bouyer, accompanied him also. This leaves me wholly without a guide, while Custer has one of the very best that the country affords. Surely he is being offered every facility to make a successful pursuit." With the scouts went George Herendeen, who not only knew the area, but might be called upon to act as a courier between the two columns.

Custer was well pleased with his new Crow scouts—"magnificent-looking men, so much handsomer and more Indian-like than any we have ever seen, and so jolly and sportive; nothing of the gloomy, silent red-man about them....In their speech they said they had heard that I never abandoned a trail; that when my food gave out I ate mule. That was the kind of a man they wanted to fight under; they were willing to eat mule too." In his eagerness to close with the foe, Custer had entertained just such a possibility. Addressing his officers after Terry's conference, he suggested that the mules carry extra forage, only to hear troop commanders Moylan and Godfrey protest that some would surely break down under the burden. Recalled Godfrey:

> He replied in an unusually emphatic manner, "Well, gentlemen, you may carry what supplies you please; you will be held responsible for your companies. The extra forage was only a suggestion, but this fact bear in mind, we will follow the trail for fifteen days unless we catch them before that time expires, no matter how far it may take us from our base of supplies; we may not see the steamer again;" and, turning as he was about to enter his tent, he added: "You had better carry along an extra supply of salt; we may have to live on horse meat before we get through." He was taken at his word, and an extra supply of salt was carried.

In addition to the 15 days' worth of hardtack, coffee and

sugar, the mules also carried 12 days' of bacon, as well as 50 rounds of carbine ammunition per soldier. Custer informed his officers that all wing and battalion formations were now abolished, with each company commander being responsible only to him.

The mood was somber after the meeting broke up. Some officers made their wills, others disposing verbally of their property, seeming to Godfrey "to have a presentiment of their fate." Among the strongest presentiments was that of Lonesome Charley Reynolds. Suffering from an infected hand and feeling sure that he was riding to his death, he tried to have General Terry release him honorably from his post. But Terry convinced him to carry on. Perhaps to defy or shake off the mysterious gloom, some of the younger cavalry officers indulged in a poker party aboard the steamer and stayed up past dawn.

That morning, 22 June, General Terry produced his final written instructions to Custer, which were to arouse such fierce controversy in the wake of disaster—perhaps since, after Terry's first and only use of the military imperative "you will," orders seemed to give way to suggestions. The document itself dismissed as "impossible" any attempt to give Custer "definite instructions" regarding his movement up the Rosebud—and Custer, far from feeling unduly restricted, was so pleased at Terry's expression of "confidence in your zeal, energy and ability" that he copied the passage into his last letter to his wife.

At noon on the 22nd, all 12 companies of the 7th U.S. Cavalry began their ride out—in the form of a regimental parade viewed by Custer, Terry and Gibbon, with massed trumpeters doing service for the 7th's famous band and the courtly Terry offering a pleasant word to each officer as he returned the salute. The previous day's gloominess seemed dissipated. Riding out were 566 enlisted men, 31 officers, 35 Arikara, Sioux and Crow scouts, and about a dozen packers, civilian guides and "citizens," among them the skylarking Autie Reed, the somber Charley Reynolds, the half-Sioux Boyer, and the black interpreter Isaiah Dorman. Including the band,

152 troopers had been detached from the regiment since 10 June. Still, it seemed a formidable fighting unit.

Despite their informal campaign garb and over a months' marching, the 7th Cavalry presented a ruggedly martial appearance beneath the swallow-tailed, gold-starred American flags used as company guidons. With black campaign hats, store-bought slouches, or even straw hats shading bearded faces, the troopers wore blue blouses or (issue-gray or otherwise) shirts and faded sky-blue pants, often with legs and seats reinforced by whitish canvas. Each trooper carried 100 rounds of carbine ammunition and 24 pistol cartridges on his person and in saddlebags. Most officers wore dark blue, wide-collared "firemen's" shirts, with perhaps a "7" and crossed sabers worked in silk on the collar; many wore fringed buckskin jackets.

At Gerard's suggestion, the Arikara scouts rode around singing their death songs, then fell in to lead the march. The "Forward" was sounded, and the regiment rode out in column of fours. Only the pack-mules proved an embarrassment, with some cargoes falling off even before the command left camp. Custer lingered behind the rear guard, shaking hands with Terry and Gibbon. Then, as he turned to ride off with his men, Gibbon made a half-joking suggestion, something like: "Now, Custer, don't be greedy! Wait for us!" Custer replied cryptically, "No, I won't."

And then he rode off to take his place at the head of his departing regiment, mounted on his whitefooted sorrel Vic— short for Victory. A sergeant carried his personal pennant of red over blue with white crossed sabers. The Boy General's hairline was receding, and his reddish hair cropped short. He wore a broad-brimmed light gray hat shading the fair skin of his face, a fringed buckskin jacket and pants, high-topped cavalry boots, and a hunting knife in a beaded, fringed scabbard. With two pistols on his belt, a Remington sporting rifle his saddle gun, he looked every inch the experienced frontier fighter.

Terry watched him go. Perhaps, as is claimed, the department commander commented as he rode back to camp:

"Custer is happy now, off with a roving command of fifteen days. I told him if he found the Indians not to do as Reno did, but if he thought he could whip them to do so." Perhaps he had his doubts about not reining in Custer more than he had. But whatever his forebodings may have been, Terry could not have known—perhaps not even have imagined—that the next time he saw George Armstrong Custer, it would be as a naked corpse upon a barren, bloody hill.

# Orders or Suggestions?

Custer's final written instructions, a source of seemingly endless inkletting, bear repeating in full:

Camp at Mouth of Rosebud River
Montana Territory
June 22nd, 1876
Lieutenant-Colonel Custer,
   7th Cavalry
Colonel:

The Brigadier-General Commanding directs that, as soon as your regiment can be made ready for the march, you will proceed up the Rosebud in pursuit of the Indians whose trail was discovered by Major Reno a few days since. It is, of course, impossible to give you any definite instructions in regard to this movement, and were it not impossible to do so the Department Commander places too much confidence in your zeal, energy, and ability to wish to impose upon you precise orders which might hamper your action when nearly in contact with the enemy.

He will, however, indicate to you his own views of what your action should be, and he desires that you should conform to them unless you shall see sufficient reason for departing from them. He thinks that you should proceed up the Rosebud until you ascertain definitely the direction in which the trail above spoken of leads. Should it be found (as it appears almost certain that it will be found) to turn towards the Little Bighorn, he thinks that you should still proceed southward, perhaps as far as the headwaters of the Tongue, and then turn toward the Little Horn, feeling constantly, however, to your left, so as to preclude the escape of the Indians to the south or southeast by passing around your left flank.

The column of Colonel Gibbon is now in motion for the mouth of the Big Horn. As soon as it reaches that point it will cross the Yellowstone and move up at least as far as the forks of the Big and Little Horns. Of course its future movements must be controlled by circumstances as they arise, but it is hoped that the Indians, if upon the Little Horn, may be so nearly inclosed by the two columns that their escape will be impossible.

The Department Commander desires that on your way up the Rosebud you should thoroughly examine the upper part of Tullock's Creek, and that you should endeavor to send a scout through to Colonel Gibbon's column with the information of the result of your examination. The lower part of this creek will be examined by a detachment from Colonel Gibbon's command.

The supply steamer will be pushed up the Big Horn as far as the forks if the river is found to be navigable for that distance, and the Department Commander, who will accompany the column of Colonel Gibbon, desires you to report to him there not later than the expiration of the time for which your troops are rationed, unless in the mean time you receive further orders.

> Very respectfully,
> Your obedient servant,
> E.W. Smith
> Captain, 18th Infantry
> Acting Assistant Adjutant General

It has been argued that, since Custer already knew how the campaign was to progress through attending Terry's conference on the 21st, these orders were drawn up to relieve the lawyer-soldier of any responsibility for failure—or, in Colonel William M. Pond's modern analysis: "No matter what Custer does, Terry is protected. If Custer does everything Terry thinks, and wins, Terry told him to, and the credit is his. If Custer does and is defeated, Terry told him to use his discretion and the blame is Custer's. On the other hand if Custer disregards what Terry thinks and wins, Terry gave him the discretion to do it, and credit is due Terry. If he loses, he disobeyed orders and again the blame is his alone."

Some regard the orders as so vague that Custer could *not* have disobeyed them, unless he disobeyed his own opinion as to his best course of action. Others believe that Custer's determination to strike the Indians on his own simply made him indifferent to his superior's preferences or the success of his plan, especially since he had supposedly told a friend (shortly after Terry had helped secure his reinstatement) of his determination to "cut loose" from Terry and operate independently.

Did Terry verbally modify these instructions? In 1896 Custer's friend Nelson Miles, then commanding general, cited an affidavit which had Terry, on the night of the 21st, tell his subordinate: "Use your own judgement, and do what you think best if you strike the trail; and whatever you do, Custer, hold on to your wounded." Miles thought this "a most reasonable" conversation. Others not only questioned the likelihood of such a talk (especially the gratuitous caution against abandoning the wounded!), but the affidavit's existence. Miles later identified his earwitness only as Custer's "servant"—and despite possessing a copy of the affidavit, Custer's widow mysteriously declined to defend its authenticity. Not until 1953 was it published by Colonel W.A. Graham and the affiant revealed as Mary Adams, Custer's black servant. But three surviving 7th Cavalry officers had told Graham in 1924 that Adams had *not* accompanied the Dakota column, and another eyewitness had "Maria," Mrs. Custer's housemaid, at Fort Lincoln. The affidavit, Graham concluded, was worthless.

However, in 1983 John S. Manion produced evidence which seemed not only to establish Mary Adams' presence with the column, but also explain "Maria" as Mary's sister, both women being employed as domestics by the Custers. But even this cannot establish the truth of the affidavit's *contents*, and the real nature of Terry's verbal orders—if any—remains another mystery.

# Custer in the Civil War

After his graduation from West Point, Second Lieutenant George Armstrong Custer was assigned to the 2nd U.S. Cavalry, and at Bull Run distinguished himself by coolly reforming a mob of fugitives trying to cross a congested bridge.

Serving on the staff of various generals, most notably the fiery Phil Kearny, Custer became one of America's first aerial warriors by reconnoitering from a balloon, while his more "conventional" exploits included capturing the first Confederate flag ever taken by the *Army of the Potomac*. Soon commanding general George McClellan asked him to join his staff as additional aide-de-camp and temporary captain. "Custer was simply a reckless, gallant boy, undeterred by fatigue, unconscious of fear," wrote McClellan. "His head was always clear in danger and he always brought me clear and intelligible reports...I became much attached to him." When McClellan was replaced, Custer joined the staff of 1st Cavalry Division commander Major General Alfred Pleasonton—sometimes acting as Pleasonton's representative in the field and giving orders in his name to superior officers. Chosen to command the Cavalry Corps in 1863, Pleasonton secured Custer a captaincy. But when Custer, yearning for a real field command, applied for the colonelcy of a Michigan cavalry regiment, he was turned down by Governor Blair as being too young, too Democratic and too loyal to the controversial McClellan.

Custer further distinguished himself during the cavalry fighting at Brandy Station, where he led three regiments through surrounding enemy horsemen, and at Aldie, where, cut off from his men, he literally slashed his way out with his saber. Intent on revitalizing a cavalry corps unable to cope with Confederate J.E.B. Stuart's gray cavaliers, Pleasonton recommended George Custer, Elon J. Farnsworth, and Wesley Merritt for the rank of brigadier general. Stunned but gratified to learn of his appointment on 28 June 1863, the 23-year-old Custer soon appeared at the head of the 3rd Cavalry Brigade—the Michigan Brigade—in a self-designed uniform of gold-braided black velveteen jacket, gold-striped black breeches, scarlet cravat, and a broad-collared blue sailor's shirt brushed by his reddish-blonde curls. Though 20-year-old Galusha Pennypacker was to be the youngest Union officer to wear a star, it was Custer who would become famous as "The Boy General."

Less than a week later, at the great cavalry battle east of Gettysburg, Custer's brigade played a key role in stopping a flank movement by superior numbers of "Jeb" Stuart's horsemen—spurred on by their chief's cry of "Come on, you Wolverines!" One observer of the 1st Michigan Cavalry's climatic charge recounted: "So sudden and violent was the collision that many of the horses were turned end over end and crushed their riders beneath them. The clashing sabers, the firing of pistols, the demands for surrender, and cries of the combatants, filled the air."

Custer's contemporaries noted his speed in assessing tactical situations, his quickness of decision, and his energy and good timing in making attacks. His followers sported red ties of their own as his style of leadership inspired officer and man alike.

After seeing Custer "plunge his saber into the belly of a rebel who was trying to kill him," a private commented, "You can guess how bravely soldiers fight for such a general." An officer recalled, "When Custer made a charge he was the first saber that struck, for he was always ahead." And while he might choose firepower over shock in dismounting his men to fight, Custer himself made it a point to stay mounted during such actions. Despite having 11 horses shot out from beneath him, Custer suffered only one minor leg wound.

Soon after Sheridan came east with Grant as chief of the *Army of the Potomac*'s cavalry and insisted on forging a more independent striking force, Custer became one of "Little Phil's" favorites. In the Shenandoah Valley campaign of 1864, Custer won new laurels at Winchester and was rewarded with the command of the *3rd Cavalry Division*. After helping to smash up Jubal Early's army at Cedar Creek, Custer went to Washington with 13 troopers—each bearing a captured

a Rebel banner. Presented with the flags, Secretary of War Stanton announced Custer's promotion to major general of volunteers.

During final operations in Virginia, Custer's division played a crucial role in slowing Lee's retreat, and at Sayler's Creek, on 7 April, Custer's cavalrymen captured 31 flags during a crushing defeat. The Confederate general Joseph Kershaw thought Custer so effective that he ordered his men to single him out as a target, only to be cordially entertained by the Yankee after his own capture. The next day, Kershaw saw his sinewy figure, with "quick-moving blue eyes" and an "air of hauteur," ride off at the head of his captured banners:

> As he neared his conquering legions, cheer after cheer greeted his approach, bugles sounded, sabres flashed as they saluted. The proud cavalcade filed through the open ranks, and moved to the front leading that magnificent column in splendid array.

Finally blocking Lee's line of march, the 25-year-old Custer received the first flag of truce at Appomattox—and a gift for Mrs. Custer bought by General Sheridan: the table on which Grant had drafted the surrender terms. Sheridan wrote to "Libbie" that "there is scarcely an individual in our service who has contributed more to bring about this desirable result than your gallant husband." Custer ended the war as the Union's most famous cavalryman, and perhaps its most colorful hero.

# CHAPTER V

# Into the Valley

## Sioux-Cheyenne Encampments 18-25 June

## 7th Cavalry 22-25 June

*F*ollowing their battle of 17 June, the warriors of the great Sioux and Cheyenne encampment apparently did not consider attacking Crook's bluecoats a second time, or even offering them serious harassment. Satisfied that the soldiers, whipped into at least temporary submission, no longer threatened the village, the Indians felt no need to crush their foes. An attempt against such a numerous and well-armed force might have cost many more lives—and to replace a warrior took a generation. While some young men who had taken no part in the fight rode out on the 18th to visit the battleground, the Sioux and Cheyenne prepared to move their village.

The women quickly dismantled the buffalo-hide tipis, the conical tents averaging 14 feet in diameter, and packed up for the march. Everything a family owned—from dried meat to ceremonial clothing to brass kettles—could be packed upon a travois of two lodgepoles, their unconnected ends trailing along the ground as a horse (or, for lighter loads, a dog) pulled it along. Soon the entire village was on the move, dogs gamboling among the travois, small boys driving ponies, all making a trail, said the Cheyenne Wooden Leg, that "could have been followed by a blind person. It was from a quarter to half a mile wide at all places where the form of the land allowed that width. Indians regularly made a broad trail when traveling in bands using travois. People behind often kept in the tracks of people in front, but when the party of travelers was a large one, there were many of such tracks side by side."

Some of the inquisitive young men inspecting the battle-ground found a fire's ashes above a place "where the ground was fresh," and dug up some dead soldiers tied in blankets. Opening up one, the Oglala Standing Bear found that "the man inside was young, and he had a ring on his finger that sparkled. I cut off the finger and I had the ring for a long time. One of our men scalped a soldier and started home with the scalp on a stick. When we got to the ridge we could see the soldiers of Three Stars retreating toward Goose Creek a long way off. A big dust was rising there."

Moving down Medicine Dance Creek to the waters of the Little Bighorn river, the villagers quickly resolved into their customary tribal circles and erected their lodges along its banks. Since the village chiefs had originally intended to keep moving south to follow the migratory pattern of the buffalo, the Northern Cheyennes, leading the march, were encamped up the valley to the south, with the Hunkpapas of the rear guard at the extreme northern end. But it was decided to stay along the Little Bighorn for a time. There was no hurry; the grass along the wide valley floor could support the massive pony herd, and no soldiers were approaching. That night the Indians celebrated their victory over the bluecoats and their Indian enemies.

Undiscovered by the Sioux were some Crow warriors and a Shoshone companion who, on their way home from Crook's encampment, had stumbled across one of the villages as it arrived near the head of the Little Bighorn. Desperate to avoid being sighted by any hunters, but unwilling to abandon a badly wounded comrade, the Crows strapped the man down tightly on his pony. Heedless of his agonized screams, they galloped for dear life, following the thread of streams when possible to minimize their "sign." By evening the visitors to the Rosebud battlefield had returned, to report that the soldiers were retreating southward and reinforcing the impression of security.

It must be kept in mind that the Plains Indians, always at war against one or more foes, did not think in terms of fighting clearly defined, decisive "wars" as the white man understood them— and, despite their indignation over the Black Hills and other encroachments, had no intention of prosecuting a long-term military campaign against the powerful forces marching to subjugate them. Neither Sitting Bull nor any other Sioux or Cheyenne leader had a systematic strategy for defeating Sheridan's soldiers, or even avoiding them; and while some warriors had harassed Gibbon's men, they seem to have known nothing of Terry's approaching Dakota column.

But the Indians had already shown the will to resist a bluecoat assault. Not content to rely too literally on Sitting Bull's vision of soldiers falling into their camp, they had taken the unexpected step of riding over 20 miles to keep Crook a safe distance away from it. And if the soldiers returned, the warriors could and would fight—not only those who had been in the village at the time of the Rosebud battle, but also newer arrivals.

For it was between 18 June and 24 June that reinforcements for any future battle began to ride in down Ash Creek on the trail from the Rosebud, and down the Little Bighorn River. Turtle Rib of the Miniconjou remembered that his band, under Lame Deer, entered the village on 24 June, from the direction of the Rosebud. Sitting Bull's following may have grown from 400 to nearly 1,000 lodges—thus, in the conservative estimate of the late John S. Gray, swelling in fighting strength to perhaps 2,000 if older boys took part. But no one kept systematic count at the time, and many estimates have been entertained. Wooden Leg, for example, told Dr. Thomas Marquis that there were roughly 300 lodges of Cheyennes, with an average lodge population of 7 persons, 2 to 3 of them warriors—and that the Cheyennes were outnumbered by each of the 5 Sioux tribal circles. Estimating the Cheyenne population at 1,600, Marquis put the entire village population at 12,000 Indians with between 3,000 to 5,000 fighting men, likely the largest concentration of Plains warriors ever to battle a common enemy.

The chiefs had anticipated moving farther up the Little Bighorn, roughly to where General Terry had expected them to be. But when ranging hunters returned with news of a large antelope herd grazing downstream to north and west, they changed their plans. On 24 June, the great assembly crossed over to the west side of the river and moved back *down* the valley of the Little Bighorn, the Cheyennes ahead, Hunkpapas far behind in the usual marching order. After eight or nine miles, the Cheyennes halted about two miles north from the future railway station at Garryowen, Montana, and the women began to erect the lodges.

The great camp extended for almost three miles along the west bank of the Little Bighorn, the Hunkpapa circle at its upper end, about two miles below the mouth of Ash or Reno Creek, and including a small number of non-Teton Sioux, Yanktonnais and some Minnesota Santees under Inkpaduta. Between the Hunkpapas and the Cheyennes were a combined circle of Blackfoot, Brule and Two Kettle Sioux, and those of the Miniconjous, Sans Arcs and Crazy Horse's Oglalas. Black Elk, later known as a *wichasha wakon* (holy man), was a Oglala boy of about 13 at the time: "It was a very big village and you could hardly count the tipis....On the westward side of us were lower hills, and there we grazed our ponies and guarded them. There were so many they could not be counted."

The night of 24 June social dances were held, drums pounding, singers chanting. People visited back and forth between camps. Soon they would move their camp again, to hunt. According to Cheyenne historian John Stands in Timber, a few Sioux and Cheyenne boys had taken a suicide vow: "This meant they were throwing their lives away—they would fight till they were killed in the next battle."

"There seems to have been a general impression that they

were to be attacked," wrote George Bird Grinnell in *The Fighting Cheyennes*, "but no specific information was at hand." Despite the seeming absence of soldiers in the area, the wary villagers had brought from their last village site five stray Arapaho warriors, out for Shoshone scalps when intercepted by Sioux braves and held for several days. "They took all our guns away," said the Arapaho Waterman, "and made us prisoners, saying that we were scouts of the white man, and that they were going to kill us." At the urging of Cheyenne chief Two Moon, the Sioux released the Arapahos, returned their weapons—and kept watch on them. All five would fight in the coming battle to prove themselves friends.

Overtaking the command as it marched out on 22 June, Custer galloped forward to place himself at the head of his regiment. He halted it, dispatching his scouts to ride ahead. Marching two miles, the 7th reached the shallow Rosebud Creek and forded the three-inch deep waters near its mouth before moving upstream, Custer keeping the command to the high ground or "second bottom" rather than the more obstacle-laden land nearer the stream. Ranging ahead, but careful not to stray dangerously far from the column, were two groups of Arikaras led by Soldier and Bobtailed Bull, each scouting one side of the stream. Still farther ahead rode Mitch Boyer and the Crows, so familiar with this territory.

The pace was leisurely, but even on this first day the improvised mule train straggled badly, especially during the numerous crossings at the bends of the Rosebud. Custer called an early halt after about 12 miles and implemented a new system. Henceforth he would hold each company responsible for its own packs, with French-born Lieutenant Edward G. Mathey of Company M reporting on the least efficient; that company would be obliged to eat dust by guarding the pack train.

The command made camp at the base of a steep bluff, with water alkaline but still potable. At sunset Custer had "officers' call" sounded, the officers assembling at their leader's bivouac and squatting around his bed. "It was not," recalled Godfrey, "a cheerful assemblage; everybody seemed to be in a serious mood, and the little conversation carried on, before all had arrived, was in undertones."

Custer laid out his orders for the march. To avoid detection, no trumpet calls would be made except during an emergency. Marches would begin at 0500 sharp, with Custer regulating only two things from his headquarters: when to move out of and when to go into camp. Other details, from silent reveille to halts for grazing, would be left to the discretion of the troop commanders, who were to keep their troops within supporting distance of each other. "He took particular pains," wrote Godfrey, "to impress upon the officers his reliance upon their judgment, discretion, and loyalty."

If Godfrey's 1892 account does not err, it was here that Custer suggested that the 7th might meet at least a thousand warriors, reinforced by perhaps an additional 500 young men from the agencies —though, if the Indian Bureau's reports were reliable, there would be no more. Custer also spoke of his rejection of the Gatling guns, and of Brisbin's cavalry. If any Indian force could defeat the 7th, he explained (or rationalized), it would be able to whip a much larger force, and a reinforcement of four companies would not save the regiment. More plausibly, he noted that with only one regiment engaged, there would be harmony, without the jealousy and friction caused by introducing another—though the 7th may have had enough internal jealousy and friction to make up for the 2nd's absence. Troop officers were cautioned, Godfrey recalled, "to husband their rations and the strength of their mules and horses, as we might be out for a great deal longer time than that for which we were rationed, as he intended to follow the trail until we could get the Indians, even if it took us to the Indian agencies on the Missouri River or in Nebraska."

An inharmonious note sounded when Custer stated his willingness to listen to suggestions, provided they came in the proper manner, but added that he would take action against insubordinate grumblers. According to Lieutenant Edgerly, the white-haired Captain Benteen asked if Custer

*Frederick W. Benteen. Describing a "very juvenile face and head, set on a most masculine body," a reporter suggested that "he might be mistaken for an overgrown drummer boy, but...Benteen is just as brave and manly a soldier as ever wore a uniform."*

had ever known of any criticism or grumbling from *him.* Custer replied, "No, I never have, nor on any other [campaign] on which I have been with you." Considering Benteen's blatant criticisms of Custer's actions during the Washita campaign, his commander's reply indicates an extra effort at diplomacy. Benteen's own reminiscence was more biting: "I said to General Custer, it seems to me you are lashing the shoulders of *all* to get at some; now, as we are all present, would it not do to specify the officers whom you accuse? He said, Col. Benteen, I am not here to be catechized by you, but for your information, will state that none of my remarks have been directed towards you...."

Lieutenant Edgerly found this expressed hope for his officers' assistance "very unusual in Custer. He usually made

## Frederick William Benteen

A Missouri resident in 1861, the Virginia-born Benteen (1834-1898) defied his Rebel father by securing a Union captaincy; having reaped a "harvest of barren regrets," Benteen reflected that while he had "fought for Old Glory and would do it again," he had "fought my own people." As lieutenant colonel of the 10th Missouri Cavalry, he accompanied General James Wilson's massive 1865 cavalry raid through the southeastern Confederacy. Serving briefly as colonel of the 137th Infantry Regiment, U.S. Colored Troops, he joined the 7th U.S. Cavalry in 1867 as a captain, and in 1868 earned a colonel's brevet by charging several hundred Cheyennes with 30 troopers, rescuing 2 captive children.

The cherubic, white-haired Benteen evidently despised Custer from their first meeting, and though he claimed never to have "fought him covertly," this was not always true. After the Washita battle, Benteen wrote a letter which, published anonymously in a newspaper, accused Custer of having doomed Major Elliott and his men by not searching for them; privately, however, he later admitted that had Custer found them, "they would simply have been found dead, as they were two weeks later." But Custer apparently still trusted Benteen's professionalism, the latter asserting that "he wanted me badly as a friend, though I could not be..."

His own dislike for Custer apparently ripened into a rich hatred in later years, as the Boy General became a popular hero and Benteen was blamed, with Major Reno, for the Little Bighorn defeat—though the intriguingly irascible Benteen would also became a caustic critic of almost *all* his brother officers. Distinguishing himself at Canyon Creek during the 1877 Nez Perce War, Benteen was assigned to the 9th (Colored) U.S. Cavalry upon his 1883 promotion to major, despite his scorn for black troops. Court-martialed in 1887 for drunkenness on duty, he found his sentence of dismissal reduced to a year's suspension due to "long and honorable service." Upon its completion he requested a medical discharge. In 1890, the last year such honors could be granted, Benteen finally became a brevet brigadier general for gallantry at Canyon Creek—and at the Little Bighorn.

his own plans, and looked for the help of his officers as a matter of course." Lieutenant Francis Gibson claimed that the request for suggestions "struck us as the strangest part of the meeting, for you know how dominant and self-reliant he always was, and we left him with a queer sort of depression." Godfrey confirmed this account: "This 'talk' of his, as we called it, was considered at the time as something extraordinary for General Custer, for it was not his habit to unbosom himself to his officers. In it he showed concessions and a reliance on others; there was an indefinable something that was *not* Custer. His manner and tone, usually brusque and aggressive, or somewhat curt, was on this occasion conciliating and subdued. There was something akin to an appeal, as if depressed, that made a deep impression on all present."

Perhaps the most deeply impressed was Lieutenant George Wallace. After comparing watches to get the official (Chicago) time, the officers went their ways. Walking in silence with Godfrey and Lieutenant Donald McIntosh, the half-Iroquois Indian commanding Company G, Wallace remarked: "Godfrey, I believe General Custer is going to be killed." "Why? Wallace, what makes you think so?" "Because," said Wallace, "I have never heard Custer talk in that way before." Edgerly thought Wallace overcome by a Scottish tendency toward superstition.

Perhaps Custer's unusual demeanor was caused by a dawning belief that the Sioux might be a tougher enemy than he had thought—or, what might have disturbed him even more, an uncertainty about just *what* to believe. Coming to the bivouac of the Indian scouts, Godfrey listened as Mitch Boyer, Bloody Knife, Crow scout leader Half-Yellow-Face and others talked:

> I observed them for a few minutes, when Bouyer turned toward me, apparently at the suggestion of "Half-Yellow-Face" and said: "Have you ever fought against these Sioux?" "Yes," I replied. Then he asked: "Well, how many do you expect to find?" I answered, "It is said we may find between one thousand and fifteen hundred." "Well, do you think we can whip that many?" "Oh, yes, I guess so." After he had interpreted our conversation, he said to me with a good deal of emphasis, "Well, I can tell you we are going to have a damned big fight."

The morning of the 23rd brought another ill omen—or perhaps several. For some distance the broken nature of the bluffs required the regiment to march along the Rosebud valley, crossing the stream five times in three miles and perhaps unable to fully appreciate the characteristic pink rosebuds in full flower along its banks. After two more miles riding along its right bank, the command came across the wide lodgepole trail Reno had discovered—though Lieutenant Gibson's description of it as being only two days old suggested recent accessions to the Indians' numbers. Three miles beyond, and some 18 miles from the mouth of the Rosebud, was found the large campsite reported by Major Reno. They passed two more campsites that day, Wallace noting that "they were all old, but everything indicated a large body of Indians. Every bend of the stream bore some traces of an old camp, and their ponies had nipped almost every spear of grass." Having followed Terry's suggested schedule for distances covered by making 33 miles in roughly 12 hours, the regiment camped about 1630 on the Rosebud's right bank at the mouth of Beaver Creek, the makeshift pack train straggling in after sunset. Since each campsite examined that day seemed to have been made successively by the same band of Indians (rather, as was later thought, by a single sprawling camp), the command had thus far discovered little more than had Reno's scout.

But the next morning, they found the great Sun Dance camp where Sitting Bull had seen his vision, the framework of a dance lodge still standing. In it scouts found hanging at least one relatively fresh white scalp, perhaps taken from Private Stoker of the 2nd Cavalry, one of Gibbon's slain hunters of 23 May; Custer inspected the scalp and apparently passed it on for the men to look at. More ominous, from the Arikaras' point of view, were symbols and pictographs indicating that the Sioux were confident of victory in some future engagement, including figures drawn in smoothed sand of soldiers and Sioux; according to Red Star, "Between them dead men were drawn lying with their heads toward the Dakotas. The Arikara scouts understood this to mean that the Dakota medicine was too strong for them and that they would be defeated by the Dakotas."

Here Custer called a conference and told his officers that the Crows, riding ahead, had discovered fresh signs, the tracks of three or four ponies and one Indian on foot. As the assembly prepared to break up, Custer's headquarters flag blew down, falling toward the rear. Godfrey stuck the staff back in the ground, only to see it fall again. Wallace saw it as a sure herald of defeat.

The troopers resumed their march on separate trails to reduce the telltale dust so easily raised from the dry soil— moving slowly so as not to overtake scouts meticulously scouring the path ahead. Custer, riding in the advance with two troops, found no Indians, but may have concluded that he was being watched. In fact, it seems likely that parties of Sioux and Cheyenne spotted the command on several occasions. But such parties, if indeed headed for the great village, may have reached it only after the information became redundant.

At about 1300 the command halted, having covered only 16 miles in 8 hours. Furnishing his six Crows with fresh cavalry mounts, Custer ordered them ahead to follow the trail as far as they could, sending a messenger back with any crucial revelations. They were to keep an eye out for diverging trails, especially toward the left and Tullock's Fork. Likewise, Custer dispatched Varnum with some Arikaras to investigate a trail behind them diverging to the left, brought to his attention by Herendeen; Custer stated, according to Herendeen, that "he did not want to lose any of the lodges, and if any of them left the main trail he wanted to know it." Likewise, Varnum later noted his duty to see that "no trail led *out* of the one we were following." This was consistent with Terry's anxiety to prevent any escape to the left.

But what the scouts found—small scattered campsites, fresh trails overlying the earlier—was evidence not of a large village breaking apart, but of new summer roamers converging to form a still mightier camp. Thus Varnum, having gone "an extra twenty miles for nothing," returned to report that the Indians thought to be splitting off had merely detoured to the left, to let their travois avoid some steep stream banks before returning to the main trail.

Custer was still resting his troops when Crow couriers rode back to report a recent Indian camp, finally resuming the march at 1700. Several more large campsites were passed, Lieutenant Wallace's official itinerary noting, "The trail was now fresh, and the whole valley scratched up by the trailing lodge poles." But Custer still had flankers watching for lodges leaving the trail. At 1945, having marched about 28 miles, the command camped on the right bank of the Rosebud, about 18 miles from the battlefield of 17 June.

Custer had that day committed his one clear breach of Terry's instructions by failing to scout the upper reaches of Tullock's Creek for Indians moving north or south through its valley and then sending George Herendeen (who was to have received a $200 bonus) down that way with the latest news for Terry. But Custer had apparently proposed sending him that morning, only to have him reply that farther up the Rosebud they could cut across a gap and strike the Tullock more economically. And by the time they reached that point, they became keenly aware that the Sioux were to be located in the valley of the Little Bighorn. Lieutenant Edgerly later observed that while great stress was later placed on Custer's alleged failure, "I believe that with the same orders and conditions, General Terry or any other good soldier would have done just what General Custer did."

Partly sheltered by a high cliff to its right, the command rested, but with mules unpacked save for necessary rations and supplies, and with the apparent understanding that if the trail turned west across the divide into the Little Bighorn valley, Custer might launch a night march. Two Cheyenne warriors, Big Crow and Black Whiteman, observed the unsuspecting bluecoats. But they were of Little Wolf's band, and that chief would not reach Sitting Bull's camp in time to give warning. At about 2100, three of the four Crows earlier dispatched—White Man Runs Him, Goes Ahead and Hairy Moccasin—returned to tell Custer that the village, without breaking up into its component bands, had turned up Davis Creek and crossed the divide between Little Bighorn and Rosebud. Unfortunately, the Crows had stopped short of following the trail to a point where they could confirm the camp's location in the Little Bighorn valley.

But they did tell Custer of a vantage point, a hill almost exactly on the center of the divide, used by the Crows during horse-stealing expeditions. From there they would be able to see the village in the morning and estimate its strength. Custer summoned his chief of scouts and told Varnum of his plans to move the command to the base of the divide later that night, arriving before morning at a point where the scouts would be able to locate him from the bluffs. Varnum reminisced:

> Custer said he wanted an intelligent white man to go with them and get what information he could from them & send him a message with that information. I said, "That means me." He said he did not like to order me on such a trip and that I had already had a hard day of it. I said he made me Chief of Scouts, and I objected to his sending anyone else unless he had lost faith in me. He said he thought that was about what I would say, and for me to go. He said I was to leave about 9 o'clock and get there before daylight. I would take the Crows & interpreters and I said I wanted one white man to talk to and asked for Charlie Reynolds, which he approved.

Varnum was to send a note from this "Crows' Nest" detailing what he had seen, returning at noon should he discover no hostiles.

At a council of officers, Custer detached Lieutenant Luther Hare for duty with the remaining scouts, leaving K Company officered only by Godfrey, its commander. With the signs not more than two days old, and the enemy allegedly no more than 30 miles away, he informed his officers of what he had learned—and, it is said, told them that they were probably about to go into the fight of their lives.

Custer now knew that the trail had not scattered, and was so fresh that it indicated a camp on the *lower* Little Bighorn, rather than on its upper reaches as Terry had expected, or on the Rosebud. At this point Custer had two radically different options. He could follow Terry's preferences and continue southward up the Rosebud before turning west to, and then down, the upper Bighorn, all the while continuing to guard against Indians escaping to the south or southeast around his left flank. Presuming that Gibbon and Terry were in their expected position (a situation which Terry had not in fact guaranteed), Custer could then move against the Indian village with Gibbon ostensibly acting as a blocking force. But such a movement, abandoning the pursuit of the trail for at least two days, would risk losing track of the Indians or being discovered by them. They could then move where they pleased, even backtracking on his own Rosebud route or launching an attack on Custer himself or an unsuspecting Terry. Or they could break up into fleeing bands—everyone's worst fear.

Custer ordered his officers to march again at 1100, following the Indian trail as closely as possible to the summit of the divide before daybreak. He would then hide the command throughout the next day, while his scouts explored the country in detail. A dawn attack would follow, Washita-style, on the 26th, the 7th Cavalry surrounding and surprising the encampment.

Custer's opportunity—to bring an entire cavalry regiment to bear against a large village—was a rare one, and one suspects that he would have been surprised at the suggestion that Terry might condemn such a deviation from instructions, given the "sufficient reason" cause. Furthermore, as Godfrey would later point out, "Custer knew the ridicule and contempt heaped on commanders who had given the enemy opportunity to escape when nearly in contact with them. Whatever may be the academic discussion as to his disobedience, I hold that he was justified by sound military judgment in making his lien of march on the trail."

Custer's unusual mannerisms and behavior during the past few days hinted at something other than mere blind overconfidence. Perhaps he worried about the personal consequences of failure to catch the elusive Sioux. Or perhaps the grave attitude of the scouts, with whom Custer enjoyed a closer relationship than did most Regular officers, had begun to impress itself upon him, whatever his facade of carefree aggressiveness. Perhaps he even regretted not bringing Brisbin's men, despite his remembered boasts that the 7th could defeat any Indians it might encounter.

The command rode out at 1100 or afterward, Custer in the

lead with Fred Gerard, Half-Yellow-Face and Bloody Knife. Even now, he emphasized having the scouts watch to make sure that no Sioux band, no matter how small, escaped to the left. Told of this, Bloody Knife, who regarded his friend Custer with little awe, remarked that he "needn't be so particular about the small camps; we'll get enough when we strike the big camp." The confused eight-mile night march was tiring for both men and horses as they struggled through ravines and climbed toward the divide; with no lights permitted and no moon, men pounded on tin cups to guide those behind them, or simply relied on the smell of rising dust to keep the trail. The pack-train, supervised by Captain Keogh's Company I, took nearly 90 minutes to get its animals across a creek, leading to an order for each company to lead its own animals—and Benteen's speculation that Job had never had much to do with shave-tail mules.

Halting at daylight, the troops concealed themselves in a wooded ravine between two high ridges, unpacking some of the mules and removing some saddles. While ordered to make coffee, many simply slept on the ground, reins over their arms. By 0230, Varnum's mixed party of Rees and Crows had reached the Crow's Nest, a rocky promontory of the Wolf Mountains offering a splendid view of most of the Little Bighorn valley. Their horses hidden in the convenient pocket at its base, the Crows scanned the landscape as the sun broke the horizon.

In the valley below, the boy Black Elk was awakened by his father at daybreak and told to help in taking the family's horses out to graze. "If anything happens," his father said, "you must bring the horses back as fast as you can, and keep your eyes on the camp." Black Elk obeyed, joining the other boys guarding the herd.

"As soon as it came daylight enough to see," recounted the Crow scout Hairy Moccasin, "we saw smoke and dust in the valley....The smoke indicated a village and the dust a pony herd...." The scouts also saw, with disapproval, the telltale smoke of the cavalry's campfires as the men cooked breakfast.

Since Varnum failed to see the ponies, the scouts told him

# Red Allies: U.S. Indian Scouts

From earliest colonial days, whites in America had sought Indian allies in war—even against rival Europeans—as red and white used each other for their own ends. But for most of the 19th century, the U.S. Army had recruited Indian irregulars and scouts in *ad hoc* fashion. In 1866 Congress authorized formal enlistment of "a force of Indians not exceeding one thousand" to act as scouts, and to be discharged "when the necessity for their services shall cease, or at the discretion of the Department Commander." They were paid as cavalrymen (with $12 monthly for using their own horses), furnished with uniforms (often retaining only the items they felt useful or becoming) and supplied with arms and ammunition; the government even issued a special "Indian Scout and Police" Colt .45 revolver, nickel-plated to inhibit rust, and revealing little faith in Indian habits of maintenance. Although the scouts formed a temporary portion of the army, perhaps enlisted for six-month periods, some were retained in service for decades and retired under the usual conditions.

In 1874 the Army had theoretically limited enlistees to 300, a number Congress fixed in 1876—unfixing it when it became obvious that the Sioux war was going badly. By January of 1877 Sheridan's division had nearly 700 scouts on its rolls, 494 of them in Crook's department. When Congress neglected to pay the U.S. Army for 10 months, Colonel Miles enlisted only 70 scouts (or "wolves" in the Plains sign language), terming the others "allies" and furnishing them rations and ammunition. Whatever their title, they were invaluable.

Some scouts served against their own tribe, and sometimes a tug of loyalties ensued; four Sioux rode as scouts with Custer's command, but one—having left after faithfully serving out his term—was reportedly found dead in the hostile camp, presumably slain while battling his former employers. Some, whether moved by a longing to resume the role of warriors or the hope of benefiting their people, were signed on almost immediately after their surrender; as a Cheyenne enlisted by General Miles ironically recalled, "My friend, I was a prisoner of war for four years, and all the time was fighting for the man who captured me."

Despite its risks, such a policy

to "Look for worms on the grass," as at that distance the immense herd would seem an undulating mass. While Varnum's untrained gaze still detected no ponies, he dispatched a note to Custer with two scouts at about 0445, reporting their find. Several Sioux were also seen less than two miles to the

had unique benefits—for as George Crook, its foremost advocate, later said of the Apaches, "To polish a diamond there is nothing like its own dust." Indians were better not merely at catching Indians, but at achieving "a broader and more enduring proposition—their disintegration." Cheyennes spying on Miles' Cheyenne scouts apparently feared just such a prospect, calling out to them to go home: "We can whip the white soldiers alone, but can't fight you too."

Custer could employ his Arikaras with no worry about divided loyalties; this once-feared Upper Missouri tribe had been forced by Lakota raids to combine with the Hidatsas and the remnants of the Mandans in a single village. Bloody Knife, Custer's favorite, was half-Sioux and a great personal enemy of Hunkpapa war leader Gall. Termed by one reporter "a tawny cynic," he had served Custer on two previous expeditions, never hesitating to tell off his white brother when the occasion demanded it. Unlike most officers, Custer could converse with his scouts in the Plains sign language and seemed, as Mark Kellogg observed, "Much at home amongst them;" the scout Red Star even noted that "Custer had a heart like

an Indian." Yet he did not share—at least openly—their fear that the Sioux would prove "too many," perhaps dismissing it as the usual Indian reluctance to engage superior numbers.

Though the Arikaras would be accused of "deserting" at the Little Bighorn, they did not flee before the action as prudence might have dictated, and suffered three killed as well as one, Goose, wounded in the hand. While some retreated to the troops' base camp, others stayed with Reno on the bluffs. In any case, it was the soldiers who were supposed to do the actual fighting—and their example was not inspiring.

While would-be civilizers feared that enlistment merely encouraged the Indian's warlike tendencies, some officers believed that it helped smooth assimilation into "American" society. And although Sheridan had argued that soldiers "should possess the attributes of civilized men," in 1891 one company of each cavalry and infantry regiment was ordered composed of "Indian soldiers." All such companies were mustered out by 1897. Perhaps, as was claimed, the experiment was a failure. But perhaps it merely meant that the Indian wars were finally over.

---

west of the scouts and an attempt was made to kill them before they could either discover Custer or pursue Varnum's two messengers. But the attempt failed—though the Sioux, apparently from a small party headed back toward their agency, did not ride to warn Sitting Bull's camp.

*These Arikara scouts posing with Custer in 1874 carry Colt .45 revolvers, perhaps the nickel-plated model issued to Indian scouts and police. Pointing at the map is Custer's Arikara "brother" Bloody Knife. Custer may have been heavily bearded during his last fight, as he appears here.*

Varnum's messenger Red Star reached Custer ahead of his badly mounted companion Bull, riding zigzag and with his pony's tail tied up to show that the enemy was discovered. Red Star's account suggests that Custer, who had earlier emphasized to the scouts the importance of seizing the enemy's horses, attempted to lighten the situation with his characteristic teasing humor:

> ...Custer sat down on his left knee near Red Star who was squatted down with a cup of coffee. Custer signed to Red Star asking him if he had seen the Dakotas, and he answered by a sign that he had. Then Red Star handed the note to Custer, taking it from his coat, and Custer read it at once and nodded his head. By Red Star's side was Bloody Knife and Tom Custer. Custer said to Bloody Knife, by signs, referring to Tom, "Your brother, there, is frightened, his heart flutters with fear, his eyes are rolling from fright at this news of the Sioux. When we have beaten the Sioux he will then be a man..."

Godfrey's remembrance of the conference bore a grimmer edge:

> The General, "Bloody Knife," and several Ree scouts and
> [Gerard] were squatted in a circle, having a "talk" after the
> Indian fashion. The General wore a serious expression and was
> apparently abstracted. The scouts were doing the talking, and
> seemed nervous and disturbed. Finally "Bloody Knife" made a
> remark that recalled the General from his reverie, and he asked
> in his usual quick, brusque manner, "What's that he says!" The
> interpreter replied: "He says we'll find enough Sioux to keep us
> fighting two or three days." The General smiled and remarked,
> "I guess we'll get through with them in one day."

Custer got up to take a look, and Red Star, his breakfast
unfinished, kicked over his coffee. Riding bareback, Custer
went to the several troops and gave orders to get ready to
move at 0800, but then ordered the command to hold fast. But
the regiment began moving out anyway at about 0845. After
marching at the walk for over an hour, the soldiers concealed
themselves in a deep wooded ravine. In the meantime, Custer
had ridden toward the Crow's Nest with a party including
Gerard, Red Star, Bloody Knife and two other Rees, to be met
by Varnum on the way.

Custer and the others climbed to a lower vantage point
than the Crows had at first used, and inspected the valley. But
by the time of his arrival, possibly after 2100, the camp smoke
had apparently dissipated, while the sun was higher and no
longer at the observers' backs, and the haze of summer heat
increasing. At first Custer, even while using field glasses,
insisted that he could see nothing. According to Varnum:

> Custer listened to Boyer while he gazed long & hard at the
> valley. He then said "Well I've got about as good eyes as any-
> body & I can't see any village Indians or anything else," or words
> to that effect. Boyer said, "Well General, if you don't find more
> Indians in that valley than you ever saw together you can hang
> me[.]" Custer sprang to his feet saying, "It would do a damned
> sight of good to hang you, wouldn't it" and he & I went down
> the hill together. I recall his remark particularly because the
> word damn, was the nearest to swearing I ever heard him come,
> and I never heard him use that but once before and that was in
> an Indian fight on the Yellowstone...

Custer finally accepted his scouts' powers of observation.
But he fiercely disputed—at first—their contention that Sioux
in the vicinity must have detected his command, and the

Crows' insistence that he could not wait until the 26th to attack. Custer rode back with the reconnaissance party to his troops, angered to discover that the Captain Tom Custer and the regimental adjutant, Canadian-born Lieutenant William Cooke, had for unexplained reasons advanced the command four miles before halting after 1000.

As if this were not enough, the returning Boyer saw two Sioux within 150 yards of a napping George Herendeen before they suddenly fled—presumably back toward their village. And just after the Boy General learned this disturbing news, Tom Custer reported that a squad of cavalrymen, riding back along the trail to retrieve hardtack fallen from an F Company mule, had sighted several Indians breaking open the boxes with tomahawks. The soldiers opened fire and saw the Indians retreat—not knowing that the braves were from Little Wolf's band and would not warn the village.

But Custer now felt sure that the Indians *had* seen his command, making it impossible to conceal the command for the next day and night and still prevent the camp's breakup and flight. At the Washita fight in 1868, he had not merely enjoyed superior odds against Black Kettle's villagers, but had been able to move his men into pre-assault positions with almost complete success before attacking from four directions. Custer's plan for a similar dawn attack now had to be scrapped for an assault in broad daylight by outnumbered troops still probing their way into the enemy's territory, perhaps even as the enemy scattered and fled.

Custer summoned his officers and announced that since further concealment was useless, he proposed to attack immediately. Company commanders were to assign one noncommissioned officer and six privates to their troop pack mules, inspect their troops and report as soon as they were ready to start. The companies would then march in the order in which they reported to Custer, the last one escorting the pack-train. Captain Benteen announced that his H Company was always ready, and so Custer gave him the advance; others reported themselves ready within two minutes, some, in their eagerness, not actually inspecting their troops first.

*Major Marcus A. Reno.*
*The Arikara scouts*
*called him "the man*
*with the dark face."*

Lieutenant Mathey's B Company ended up with the pack-train.

At about 1145 the column swung into motion, crossing the divide between the Rosebud and the Little Bighorn at noon, the summer sun beating down. Just a third of a mile beyond the crest, Custer called a brief halt before reaching the headwaters of Reno Creek.

Here he made his fateful division of the 7th Cavalry into three combat elements and a supply column. He himself would ride with Companies C, E, F, I and L, numbering 13 officers and about 200 enlisted men, plus four Crow scouts, Mitch Boyer, young Autie Reed, and Assistant Surgeon George E. Lord. Correspondent Kellogg, well aware that Custer would be at the center of any action, also went along: "I go with Custer," he had written, "and will be at the death." Custer seems to have had Captain Keogh command the first battalion or squadron of C, L and his own I, and Captain George Yates the second composed of E and F.

Major Reno received A, G and M troops, with 11 officers, about 130 cavalrymen, and the remaining Indian scouts, including the Crows Half-Yellow Face and White Swan; Custer had ordered all the Rees scouts to go with Reno—even, to the men's surprise, his favorite Bloody Knife. Reno also took with him Assistant Surgeon Henry R. Porter and Acting Assistant Surgeon James DeWolf, Charley Reynolds, Isaiah Dorman, George Herendeen and Fred Gerard. Captain Benteen's was the smallest command at about 110 men and 5 officers—his own Company H, plus D and K—and, curiously, unaccompanied by a surgeon. Lieutenant Mathey would lead the consolidated pack train escorted by Captain Thomas M. McDougall's Company B. But due to reinforcements from each company, he would actually command more men than Benteen—2 officers, almost 130 enlisted men, and 11 packers, as well as forage master Boston Custer and Custer's orderly John Burkman, denied the privilege of fighting with his chief.

With the coveted village still perhaps 15 miles away, and the element of surprise apparently vanished, Custer felt he had to attack as quickly as he could. But even here he apparently made at least a gesture toward satisfying Terry's plan. Advancing upstream as planned, he would probably drive any fleeing Sioux north, since the village, judging from the scouts' observations, apparently lay well below the mouth of Reno Creek. But any Indians rashly left behind him might, if properly alerted, escape upstream. From the head of Reno Creek, Custer found his view southeast into the Little Bighorn valley blocked by a line of ridges, perhaps concealing villages further upstream which could escape to the left of his advance.

This probably explains Custer's order to Benteen to ride to the left, investigating the line of ridges about a mile away for signs of Indians or camps in the upper valley before returning to join the trail of the main column. Before Benteen's column had disappeared from sight, Custer, realizing or suspecting that more than one line of ridges blocked the view, sent two supplementary orders. The first apparently told Benteen to proceed to the *second* line of bluffs should he find nothing; the

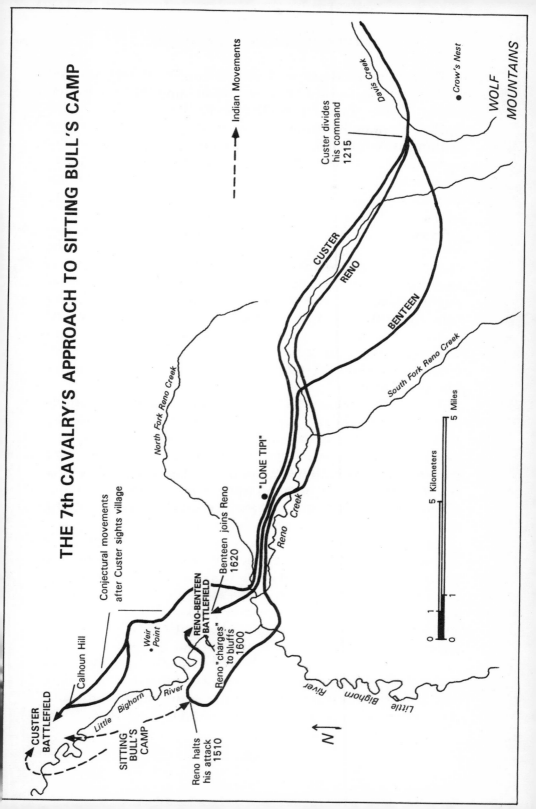

# THE 7th CAVALRY'S APPROACH TO SITTING BULL'S CAMP

WOLF MOUNTAINS

Crow's Nest

Davis Creek

Custer divides
his command
1215

CUSTER

RENO

BENTEEN

South Fork Reno Creek

North Fork Reno Creek

"LONE TIPI"

Reno Creek

Benteen joins Reno
1620

Conjectural movements
after Custer sights village

Calhoun Hill

CUSTER
BATTLEFIELD

Weir
Point

RENO-BENTEEN
BATTLEFIELD

Reno "charges"
to bluffs 1600

Little   Bighorn   River

SITTING
BULL'S CAMP

Reno halts
his attack 1510

Little Bighorn River

Indian Movements

5 Kilometers

5 Miles

N

next, to ride farther on and into the valley if he found no Indians on this second line. Despite his odd later claim that taking Custer literally would have meant pushing even farther onward if nothing were found—"My orders were 'Valley hunting *ad infinitum'*"—and that he did not know why he had been sent to the left, Captain Benteen knew quite well what to do, and did it. Custer was still probing, making a "reconnaissance in force" with his advancing regiment ready to react as the facts revealed themselves.

In column of fours, Reno's and Custer's commands rode forward, trotting much of the time. Reno crossed to the creek's left bank and the two columns rode almost parallel, at varying distances on opposite sides of the stream, Custer paying close attention to the scouts' activities. As the two columns approached the confluence of Reno Creek and the south fork of the Little Bighorn River, and the creek bottom widened, Custer motioned Reno over with a wave of his hat to the right bank. The two columns rode side by side only a few yards apart.

The point at which the Indians of the village first became aware of the soldiers' approach cannot be stated with certainty. But it was obvious that the bluecoats could do little to conceal their presence. Their horses' ironshod hooves raised dust so easily from the dry ground that at one point Cooke ordered part of the command trailside to reduce the massive clouds. But the dust was still seen by Indian women digging wild turnips east of the river.

At about 0215, on the north side of Reno Creek, at a still-disputed point west of the junction of the middle and south forks, the command came to yet another campsite and the so-called Lone Tipi—a single standing tent, in the company of a broken-down lodge. The tipi contained the body of Old She Bear, a Sans Arc slain at the Rosebud fight, to which the Sioux had ridden on 16 June from this campsite.

The Indian scouts in the advance had paused to count coup on the lodge with quirts, cut it open, consume meat and soup left for the dead warrior, or simply gather around the site. They began to strip for battle as Custer rode up, angered by this unexpected halt. Then rising dust was seen some four or five miles down the valley.

Lieutenant Hare and interpreter Gerard spurred their mounts to a nearby knoll, where Gerard saw in the distance a cloudy image of pony herds and milling Indians—some 40 or 50 of them, about three miles away, and apparently in full flight. He waved his hat, yelling back to Custer, his words carried strong by the north wind. "Here are your Indians, General," he cried, "running like devils!"

That Sunday afternoon, in the valley of the South Cheyenne at the base of the Black Hills, a patrol of 5th Cavalrymen under Major Thaddeus Stanton lay concealed along a well-beaten track used by agency Indians, to cut off possible flight to the hostile camps. General Terry marched onward with the Montana column toward the confluence of the Little Bighorn. On the *Far West*, pushing up the Big Horn River while Colonel Gibbon lay on board ill, men scanned the shore anxiously for signs of enemy warriors. In distant Philadelphia, those walking the Centennial Exhibition grounds could contemplate the forearm of the proposed statue "Liberty Enlightening the World," its torch thrust skyward.

And in the valley of the Little Bighorn, the 7th Cavalry's greatest battle was about to begin.

# Marcus A. Reno

Born in Illinois, Marcus Albert Reno (1834-1889) was graduated from West Point in 1857—having taken six years to complete the five-year program. As a brevet second lieutenant in the 1st Dragoons, he served on the Washington and Oregon frontier, seeing service against Northwestern tribes. After promotions to second lieutenant in 1858, first lieutenant in April 1861, and captain the following November, he found himself leading the renamed 1st Cavalry Regiment in the Maryland campaign of 1862. In 1863 he was injured at Kelly's Ford when his horse was shot from under him. Serving for a time on recruiting and staff duty and on the Cavalry Bureau, he rejoined the Army of the Potomac in May 1864 and for a time served as chief of staff of Sheridan's cavalry, as well as colonel of the 12th Pennsylvania Cavalry and commander of a mounted brigade. His brevets included colonel of Regulars and brigadier general of volunteers.

Promoted major in the 7th Cavalry in December of 1868, he commanded escorts for the Northern Boundary Survey in 1873 and 1874. Following the Little Bighorn slaughter, Reno's behavior as 7th Cavalry commander became bizarrely officious and obnoxious, and on 24 July Colonel Gibbon placed him under arrest after a dispute. General Terry apparently considered relieving Reno of command because, as Godfrey's journal put it, "Reno's self important rudeness makes him unbearable." Considering Reno's performance and the battle's outcome, it seemed an odd time for self-important airs.

After assuming command at Fort Abercrombie, Dakota Territory, Reno was court-martialed in 1877 for "conduct unbecoming an officer and a gentleman," including taking "improper and insulting liberties" with a fellow officer's wife. President Hayes commuted Reno's sentence of dismissal to two years' suspension.

Widespread public censure from Custer partisans led Reno to request a court of inquiry to clear his name regarding the Little Bighorn fight—just two days before the statutes of limitations on any possible charges expired. Five months later an unenthusiastic War Department finally ordered the court convened.

Convened at Chicago's Palmer House Hotel, the 1879 court was unable to subpoena the man who might have provided the most damaging testimony. Captain Thomas Weir had died less than six months after the battle, "terribly used up with liquor"—perhaps because of the horrors he had witnessed, or remorse over his own role. But the court did hear most of the surviving officers as well as a few enlisted men and civilians.

The three-man panel, chaired by Colonel Wesley Merritt, concluded after four weeks of testimony that: "While subordinates in some instances did more for the safety of the command by brilliant displays of courage than did Major Reno, there was nothing in his conduct which requires animadversion from this Court." It was not quite the Scottish verdict of "Not Proven," but was a decidedly halfhearted "clearing" of the Reno name. Merritt was quoted as privately remarking: "Well, the officers wouldn't tell us anything, and we could do nothing more than damn Reno with faint praise."

Even Colonel Graham, reluctant to believe that officers would deliberately perjure themselves, believed some had been "evasive" and all "more or less reluctant," answering only when specifically asked and volunteering no information. Yet the impression that the court was a whitewash was based not merely on the suspicions that the officers had "closed ranks," but also the evident reluctance of the panel (if not the court recorder) to probe for the truth with questions. Furthermore, even the evidence actually heard could have justified a harsher verdict, given Reno's rout-like "charge" to the bluffs and evident loss of command control during the Weir Point episode.

Certainly the Army, which had never sought to try Reno on any charges related to the battle, had nothing to gain by raking up the detritus of the Little Bighorn, especially since Reno—even if a court confirmed the worst suspicions of incompetence and cowardice—was due to rise to a colonelcy through seniority. There was also the honor of the 7th Cavalry to consider, as well as the reputations of its surviving officers. Captain Benteen, despite his lack of respect for Reno, later confessed that the court: "knew there was something kept back by me, but they didn't know how to dig it out by questioning, as I gave them no chance to do so; and Reno's attorney was posted 'thereon.'" Curiously, one piece of evidence submitted was a petition, dated 4 July 1876, and supposedly signed by enlisted survivors of the Little Bighorn, requesting the promotion of Reno and Benteen; in 1954 the FBI examined it and declared at least 79 of the 236 signatures "probable frauds."

One civilian witness, Fred Gerard, later claimed that the officers knew that anyone making himself obnoxious to the defense would incur the wrath of superiors "in certain department headquarters farther west than Washington and not as far west as St. Paul"—i.e., Chicago.

Later in 1879 Reno was again court-martialed for "conduct unbecoming," on charges including peeping through the window of his commanding officer's daughter and attempting to brain a lieutenant with a billiard cue. This time President Hayes failed to intercede, and Reno was dismissed from the service. Still striving for reinstatement, he died of complications due to tongue cancer, and was buried in an unmarked grave.

It was part of Reno's tragedy that he inspired neither the adulation nor the hatred surrounding the more renowned Custer; instead he seems to have been merely a sullen, unpopular figure to his fellow officers, and even his modern defenders have generally restricted their discussion to the Little Bighorn affair. But he won a posthumous victory of sorts in 1967, when the Army Board for Correction of Military Records met in response to an appeal from Reno's great-grand-nephew. For no apparent reason, the board simply jettisoned the considered opinions of Reno's colleagues and President Hayes, termed his dismissal "unjust," and ordered his records "corrected" to indicate an honorable discharge. One eminent scholar would term it "a very silly procedure." But it did entitle Reno to be buried in a military cemetery, and he was duly interred with the pomp and honors of war—at Custer Battlefield National Cemetery.

## Guidons of the 7th

*Instead of Spa we'll drink down ale,*
*And pay the reckn'ning on the nail*
*No man for debt shall go to jail*
*From Garry Owen in glory...*

The regiment would go on to patrol the Mexican border; battle Filipino *insurrectos*; fight Japanese, North Koreans, and Chinese. Even after the pentomic reorganization of the 1950s, men calling themselves "the Garry Owens" saw action in Vietnam and in Iraq. But the name of the 7th U.S. Cavalry, like the rising phoenix on its coat of arms, would always be linked with the crushing defeat at the Little Bighorn—and its glory days as "Custer's Seventh."

The long-haired lieutenant colonel had, of course, never been its senior officer. After its 1866 organization in Kansas as one of four new Regular cavalry regiments (two of them "colored"), it was initially commanded by Colonel Andrew Jackson Smith, who as chief of the District of the Upper Arkansas left matters largely to Custer. His successor was Colonel Samuel D. Sturgis; but thanks largely to the efforts of Phil Sheridan, Sturgis was on detached service for long periods, leaving Custer in effective command. And he would irrevocably place his stamp upon the 7th—including the Irish quickstep "Garry Owen," described as Custer's "favorite marching hymn."

From 1866 to 1876 elements of the regiment fought 33 separate engagements and skirmishes against

Indian enemies, most of them small if often fierce affairs. Following the Hancock expedition, the arduous Washita campaign and several years of frontier duty in Kansas, the 7th was scattered for 2 years among 3 Southern states, then reunited in 1873 for a move to Dakota Territory and the participation of 10 companies in Stanley's Yellowstone expedition. Custer's command then made its home at the newly expanded Fort Abraham Lincoln, D.T. But, the frontier being what it was, he could never have the regiment united under his direct supervision.

In 1876 the 7th was considered an excellent tool to employ in Indian warfare. With the average enlistee's age 27, there were still many Civil War veterans in the ranks, and the roughly 10 percent of recent recruits would later be exaggerated after the Little Bighorn fight. But the 7th, like all regiments, fell well short of its authorized strength of 80 men per company, and many men lacked both battle experience and sufficient combat training.

Nor were there enough officers. When the 7th marched out of Fort Lincoln, seven lieutenants and four captains were either on leave, physically incapacitated or on detached service. Two of the 7th's three majors were absent despite Custer's attempt to retrieve Lewis Merrill for the campaign and so avoid having Reno the most senior. Several of the remaining officers had severe physical handicaps; Lieutenant John J. Crittenden, actually a 20th Infantry Officer, was missing one eye from a gun explosion, while Lieutenant Al-

gernon E. Smith could not put on his uniform without assistance due to a wound-crippled left arm. The officers were a disparate crew, including West Pointers, appointees from civilian life and former enlisted men. Soft-spoken Donald McIntosh was half-Indian, with the look of a "fullblood." Many, including Canadian-born William Cooke, the self-confessed Italian political assassin Charles DeRudio (viewed by Custer as "the inferior of every first lieutenant in this Regt."), and Irishman Myles Keogh, were Civil War veterans.

Custer has been accused of dividing his officers, partly through his own favoritism, into pro- and anti-Custer factions. But aside from the fact that other regiments also suffered from factionalism, if to a lesser degree, there was a general tendency for officers at frontier posts to quarrel. In an army where captains and lieutenants might be unusually old and promotion grew slower with each cutback in army strength, pettiness, and jealousy were more likely to erupt than any Indian outbreak. Frontier conditions also encouraged officers to destroy themselves with drink, though it was apparently a combination of alcohol and the trauma of the Little Bighorn slaughter that helped kill Captains Weir and French before age 40.

While the 7th's performance on the battle's first day was seriously flawed, largely due to lack of command and control rather than any want of enlisted courage, a certain spirit seems to have been retained even by the battered remnant. A witness wrote of its appearance as Terry's and Crook's commands met, each company fanning out to launch "a sheaf of skirmishers" to the front: "Something in the snap and style of the whole movement stamps them at once; no need of waving guidon and stirring call to identify them. I recognize the Seventh Cavalry at a glance...."

The 7th went on to disarm agency Indians and participate in the tragic pursuit of the Nez Perce under Chief Joseph. But its most famous fight, after the Custer battle, was among those actions commemorated by the scarlet streamer "Pine Ridge." On 28 December 1890, aided by quick-firing Hotchkiss cannon and Oglala Sioux scouts, the 7th attempted to disarm a band of Miniconjous near Wounded Knee Creek, S.D.—only to be met by blazing fire from Winchesters wielded by braves convinced that their "ghost shirts" would repel bullets. After a horrific slaughter, a burial party reported 84 men and boys, 44 women, and 18 children dead on the field, while at least 7 of the wounded brought in by the military died. Despite orders to spare women and children, despite the whites' own losses of 25 killed and 35 wounded (those later dying of wounds apparently brought fatalities to at least 34), despite the reasoned work of scholars, the myth that Wounded Knee was a massacre of improbably unarmed Sioux (with the dead soldiers all shot by their own side!) has grown to unstoppable proportions—even to the claim that all was done to avenge Custer's defeat 14 years before.

# CHAPTER VI

# The Battle of the Little Bighorn

## 25-26 June 1876

*F*or Custer, the fleeing braves must have been the crowning proof that the Indians of the great camp, the prey which the soldiers had hunted for so long, were on the verge of escaping. He had to act—and act now.

Quickly he ordered the Arikaras to pursue the enemy and attempt the capture of their ponies. But the Rees balked—apparently because they thought Long Hair was sending them unsupported. With words and fluent gestures in the Plains sign language, Custer threatened to disarm any man wanting in bravery "and make a woman of him." But Gerard quickly explained that the soldiers would be with them, and they rode forward. Custer also issued orders for Reno.

As Lieutenant Wallace remembered them, the orders ran thus: "The Indians are two miles and a half ahead; move forward as fast as you can and charge them as soon as you find them, and we will support." Reno remembered an assurance that he would "be supported by the whole outfit." Custer also told Reno to take the scouts with him—perhaps meaning only the Rees, since four Crows stayed with Custer and the other two may have gone with Reno through a misunderstanding.

Later, it would seem clear to Reno that Custer had "in-

*Canadian-born William Winer Cooke's extravagant Dundreary whiskers helped conceal his youth; a Civil War veteran who commanded a sharpshooter detachment during the 7th Cavalry's Washita fight, he was 30 years old when he rode into the valley of the Little Bighorn.*

tended to support me by moving further down the stream and attacking the village in flank"—which would not have seemed a novel tactic to any Civil War cavalry veteran. However, he was also to claim that, on 25 June, he was sure that Custer's five companies would support him from the rear. If Custer ever did intend such an uncharacteristic maneuver, something was to change his mind.

But we cannot even be sure that at this point Custer still planned to attack the village proper, which might be already breaking up, or hoped to join Reno in pursuing and corralling fleeing warriors and their dependents. As recalled by Lieutenant Winfield Scott Edgerly, it was believed even before the division of the regiment that "some of the Indians were already leaving, some officers imagining they saw quite a party moving off to the right of the village."

As Reno moved out, Custer gave Lieutenant Varnum permission to join this leading attack element. Riding near Custer was Company G's Lieutenant Wallace, acting topographical officer. "I called back to him, 'Come on, Nick, with the fighting men. I don't stay back with the coffee coolers.' Custer laughed and waved his hat and told Wallace he could go & Wallace joined me." Both officers would survive the battle.

With the river still several miles away, Reno urged his men to keep their horses in hand, conserving critical strength for the anticipated charge. For a time, both Captain Keogh and Lieutenant Cooke rode with Reno's battalion, Cooke, doubtless evaluating the situation for Custer, going at least as far as the river before turning back, and ordering stragglers at the crossing to close up for the hot work ahead.

Reno's men began fording the swift water, cautiously crossing in column of twos a short distance upstream from where Reno Creek entered the Little Bighorn. Thirsty horses paused unbidden to drink, delaying the crossing, while some officers and men took advantage of the halt to fill canteens. Reno halted briefly to close up the confused formation in a narrow belt of timber, then resumed the advance out onto the valley floor.

Riding out ahead with Lieutenant Hare and the scouts to seek out the enemy pony herd, Ree interpreter Fred Gerard had seen, amid the increasing dust kicked up by ponies' hooves, mounted warriors—riding about and circling their ponies as though to signal that enemies were in sight, or to prepare for combat. Aware that Custer was "laboring under the impression that the Indians were running away and it was important for him to know that they were not, but were coming to meet us," He rode back towards Custer's command as Reno's battalion finished crossing. Seeing Lieutenant Cooke (but not Custer's column, concealed behind a knoll near the trail), Gerard told him that the Indians were showing fight and advancing to meet Reno. Saying he would report this, Cooke wheeled his horse about toward the column. He rode back toward the river, passing before he reached it Private Archibald McIlhargey, who bore a message advising that Reno now had the enemy to his front, in strength. Soon after Reno sent Trooper John Mitchell with a similar message, both couriers remaining with Custer's command.

Informed by Cooke of Gerard's revelations, General Custer advanced with his five companies. Making a sharp turn to the right, or north, he briefly watered his horses, probably at the north fork of Reno Creek—warning the men against letting them drink too much since they had much travelling to do that day. He had presumably decided to proceed down the river, then cross to its left bank and catch the Sioux between Reno's men and his own. If the Sioux, as Gerard had said, were advancing rather than running away, the village from which they poured, if not actually fleeing itself, would be all the more vulnerable, and it would be easier to outflank the warriors. Although the Crow scout Curley and Private Theodore Goldin later told stories of delivering written messages to Reno, presumably telling him of Custer's change in plans, Custer may in fact have decided that his companies would reach the Indians before any messenger could reach his subordinate. Or did he simply assume that Reno would realize that his promised support might take the form of a flank attack?

Custer could not know that the fleeing Indians pointed out by Gerard had been from yet another band of Cheyennes on their way to Sitting Bull's camp, or that they had veered off on seeing the soldiers, not to reach the village until that day's fighting was over. But at what point did the villagers actually realize that an attack by soldiers was imminent? Gathered afterwards over a span of many decades and under diverse circumstances, Indian accounts of the battle were to disagree on countless points. But almost all agreed that Reno's attack on the village came as a complete surprise.

If this seems a failure of proverbial Indian cunning, it was quite in keeping with the Plains tribes' usual lack of system in scouting and patrolling, even during periods of intensified warfare. Some warriors had observed dust clouds to the east that morning and suspected that the *Wasichu* soldiers might have kicked them up. Others would even recall spying soldiers east of the camp, riding along the eastern ridges toward its lower end. But the Indians may have been content to speculate on their identity—were they the whites whipped at the Rosebud?—because they knew of the soldiers' preference for dawn strikes over daylight attacks.

Even those few participants who later hinted at an Indian ambush never claimed to have personally participated in laying such a trap. Had they taken the danger seriously, the warriors would most likely have tried to keep the soldiers far from their camp, as they had at the Rosebud.

Certainly the persistent theory that the entire Little Bighorn battle was a gigantic ambuscade assumes remarkably consistent falsification in survivors' accounts. These portray an almost dreamy calm, typical of a Plains Indian village on a hot summer's day. While some hunters out early that morning had already returned with their quarry, others were still out, and some still lay abed in their tipis or brush wickiups. A few men and boys fished, others raced their ponies on the flat benches near the stream. Wooden Leg and his brother went swimming with other Indians of all ages and both sexes, afterwards going to sleep beneath some shade trees. The young Sioux Black Elk was tempted to do the same:

> Several of us boys watched our horses together until the sun was straight above and it was getting very hot. Then we thought we would go swimming, and my cousin said he would stay with our horses till we got back. When I was greasing myself, I did not feel well; I felt queer. It seemed that something terrible was going to happen. But I went with the boys anyway.

Major Reno's three companies trotted down the valley toward the village in parallel columns. Then Reno ordered Captain Myles Moylan's Company A and Captain Thomas French's M into line, with Lieutenant McIntosh's G in reserve. In the center of the line, about 20 yards ahead, rode Reno, while Indian scouts, led by Varnum and Hare, positioned themselves to the left of the line, perhaps 50 to 75 yards in front. To the battalions' right was the twisting river, masked by tall cottonwoods and thick underbrush along its banks; to the left, benchlands, beyond which lay a line of low hills.

The Cheyenne chief Two Moon, having washed down his horses and taken a swim himself, walked back to camp. "When I got near my lodge, I looked up the Little Horn towards Sitting Bull's camp. I saw a great dust rising. It looked like a whirlwind."

Pistols drawn, Reno's men galloped over the broad, level prairie, its grass clipped away by thousands of village ponies, the soil scarred by their hooves. In the valley widening before them, the soldiers could see massive dust clouds, and ponies driven downstream by herder boys. A small band of warriors, perhaps as few as 40 or 50, had apparently been caught unprepared in the valley. But instead of simply fleeing, they began setting fire to the grass behind them, kicking up dust by riding vigorously back and forth. Many moved to Reno's left, and warriors opened fire, a few shots striking the ground in front of Company A.

Ahead, above a timbered bend of the river protruding into the valley, dust floated skyward, and the tops of a few lodges could be seen. Thinking there were large numbers of warriors ahead, Reno responded by bringing G Company into line as the troopers galloped onward down the valley, the line losing order as the men cheered. Reno, practical but uninspiring, told them to stop the noise, as they would have work to do.

Black Elk was in the water when his cousin came down to water the horses:

> Just then we heard the crier shouting in the Hunkpapa camp, which was not very far from us: "The chargers are coming! They are charging! The chargers are coming!" Then the crier of the Oglalas shouted the same words; and we could hear the cry going from camp to camp northward clear to the Santees and the Yanktonais.

The sleeping Wooden Leg dreamed "that a crowd of people were making lots of noise. Something startled me. I found myself wide awake, sitting up and listening." He and his brother leaped to their feet, and heard shooting from somewhere at the upper part of the camp circles. "It looked as if all of the Indians there were running away toward the hills westward or down toward our end of the village. Women were screaming and....Through it all we could hear old men calling: 'Soldiers are here! Young men, go out and fight them!'"

Whatever their initial surprise, the warriors recovered quickly. Some went out to confront Reno, whether on a favorite war-pony—such being frequently tethered outside their owners' lodge—or even on foot. Others ran toward the pony herd, or stayed in camp to react to any future threat. Those not hurrying upstream to bid the soldiers defiance made such hasty war preparations as each man deemed necessary. Women and children ran downstream, scattering up hillsides to avoid the fight, though some women merely began to strike their lodges in case of retreat. Wooden Leg recalled the confusion:

> We ran to our camp and to our home lodge. Everybody there was excited. Women were hurriedly making up little packs for flight. Some were going off northward or across the river without any packs. Children were hunting for their mothers. Mothers were anxiously trying to find their children. I got my lariat and my six shooter. I hastened on down toward where had been our horse herd. I came upon three of our herder boys. One of them was catching grasshoppers. The other two were cooking fish...I told them what was going on and asked them where were the horses. They jumped on their picketed ponies and dashed for the camp, without answering me....

As warriors continued to arrive, kicking up dust and riding back and forth to rush their ponies and give them their second wind, the Arikaras rode in their irregular formation toward the village and the Indian pony herd—the objective indicated by Custer. Here they appear to have ridden down and killed a number of Sioux women caught outside the village. They managed to seize some ponies before the Sioux rallied and forced the scouts to pull back.

The warriors' initial aim seems to have been simply screening the village and covering its retreat as necessary, and at first only a relative handful rode to confront the oncoming cavalry. This proved enough, however. Major Reno would later claim that "the very earth seemed to grow Indians," and that with hundreds emerging from a coulee, and others circling around the left toward his rear, he could no longer risk a mounted charge. But others would assert that he decided this *before* many warriors were visible. Perhaps, at the point of decision, Reno feared not so much the braves visible through the eddying dust, but the possibility that they might lure him into a Fetterman-like trap, the very lack of resistance hinting at unseen hordes ready to swallow up his small command.

Other participants in the charge shared Reno's belief that the command would have been annihilated had it proceeded down the valley—though Edgerly believed that "If Reno had charged through the village, Custer would have joined him in a very short time, and Benteen later, and we might have had an expensive victory." The wife of Sioux warrior Spotted Horn Bull made this possibly hyperbolic comment: "The man who led those troops must have been drunk or crazy. He had the camp at his mercy, and could have killed us all or driven us away naked on the prairie."

But within sight of the Hunkpapa camp circle, perhaps 150 yards from the river, Reno ordered a halt. A number of horses bolted, at least one of them carrying a private into the boiling cloud of dust and mounted warriors—never to be seen again. The troops dismounted, every fourth man serving as a horse-holder, facing north with their line curving slightly to the left as they advanced a brief distance on foot. On the left and to the rear were the Ree scouts, their leader, Sergeant Bob-tailed Bull, the last man on the flank. After Sergeant John Ryan and 10 men from M Company checked some nearby timber and underbrush along the riverbank, the horseholders led the battalion's mounts into it for protection.

The 90 or so men remaining formed a skirmish line, at first only a few hundred yards long rather than the rough quarter-mile dictated by a standard five-yard interval. Reno's left reached toward some nearby bluffs, his right resting on a dry creek bed. Still keeping their distance—perhaps between 700 and 900 yards away initially—the Sioux exchanged fire with the soldiers, shooting mostly from horseback.

The dismounted troopers, tending to bunch up under fire, knelt or lay down, some using the mounds of a handy prairie-dog town as impromptu breastworks. Despite the extreme range, they worked their carbines rapidly, so depleting their ammunition that every second man was ordered back to the saddlebags for more, the other half of the line

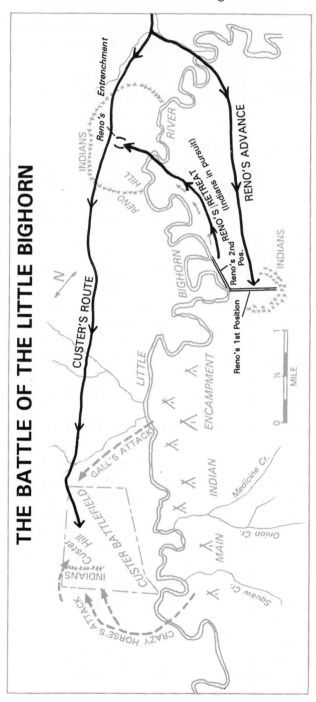

THE BATTLE OF THE LITTLE BIGHORN

repeating the process. Some weapons overheated, making ejection of empty cartridges difficult. Reno and other officers stood up straight or walked along the firing line, Captain French potting away at selected Indians with his Springfield rifle. The normally abstentious Charley Reynolds, sure that he was doomed, asked for a slug of whisky from Fred Gerard's flask.

While in the valley, Lieutenant Varnum caught a glimpse of men on gray horses—the Seventh's Company E—riding along the bluffs on the other side of the river, moving at a trot. Others saw a man atop the eastern bluffs waving his hat, and identified him as their chief, some of the men calling out, "There goes Custer." Curiously, in 1879 several officers were to officially deny (but later confirm) that they had seen anything of Custer's command at this point, while Reno apparently saw nothing.

More warriors joined the fray as they rode the long distance from the furthest camps, or completed their warlike preparations; Wooden Leg, in his best clothing, painted his face with a blue-black circle, with red and yellow paints applied inside it, his father urging him to hurry as he held his mount. Hastily combing his hair but neglecting to oil or braid it, Wooden Leg galloped on into an atmosphere "so full of dust I could not see where to go. But it was not needful that I see that far. I kept my horse headed in the direction of movement by the crowd of Indians on horseback." As swift-riding warriors began to infiltrate along the riverbank and into the timber, Reno pulled Company G from the line, leading it in probing the dry channel and a clearing in the woods through which tipis were visible. The remaining men extended their intervals to plug the gap. But the Indians could still ride effortlessly along the line, curling around the left flank to come up behind the soldiers. After perhaps 15 minutes, Reno's men filed into the crescent-shaped growth of cottonwoods anchoring his right, about 25 yards at its widest.

In the woods, Reno's dismounted men faced west and southwest, sheltered by a dry cut-bank and the timber itself. It seemed the best defensive position available. But the dense

*During Reno's retreat, Wooden Leg seizes the weapon hanging from a soldier's carbine sling before pulling it over his head: "...he fell to the ground...I do not know what became of him. The jam of oncoming Indians swept me on." As with most pictographic autobiographies, emphasis is on the individual warrior's exploit.*

timber and underbrush also made it easier for Reno to lose overall control of his command, and for the Sioux to filter into the woods despite his best efforts. Within half an hour, as the warriors began to make their way towards him from the eastern stream bank, Reno decided to retreat to the bluffs on the far side of the river. From there, presumably, he would attempt to link up with Custer.

Without having his trumpeter transmit a command, Reno issued verbal orders, apparently telling troop commanders to withdraw their men to the clearing and mount in columns of fours, facing upstream. But no party was told off to cover the impending retreat, and even Reno's orderly only realized a withdrawal was under way when he saw G Company men running toward their horses—some of them unable to mount in time.

In the clearing, Bloody Knife sat his pony near Major Reno. Suddenly warriors no more than 50 feet away loosed a ragged volley. "Oh my God, I have got it!" cried a soldier, toppling from his horse. A bullet smashed into Bloody Knife's head—splashing brains and gore into Reno's face. A shocked Reno ordered his troops to dismount—then to mount!—before riding headlong out of the timber. The battalion thundered after him in a rough triangle, Company A on the right and slightly ahead, G on the left, and M behind; but it soon became strung out. In its wake were left several dead, a few wounded, and some 12 to 15 troopers, several scouts and civilians missing—along with Company G's commander.

Should Reno have tried to hold the timber? Some with him agreed with Reno's claim that the position was untenable, others feeling sure that the command could have held out providing their ammunition was husbanded carefully. "If they had charged on him," testified Lieutenant Hare, "the command would not have stood it but for a few minutes, but Indians don't do that." The warriors themselves were surprised by Reno's hasty departure. "We could never understand why the soldiers left the timber," a Cheyenne told George Bird Grinnell, "for if they had stayed there the Indians could not have killed them."

Kill them they did. As Reno led his men at a rapid gait along the dry riverbed before starting for the bluffs at least half a mile away, the Indians directly to his front scattered before him. "But soon," said Wooden Leg, "we discovered they were not following us. They were running away from us....We stopped, looked a moment, and then we whipped our ponies into swift pursuit." The warriors closed in on their flanks with exultant war-cries. Lieutenant Varnum saw, for several hundred yards behind the main formation, the soldiers "scattered in twos & single file & the Indians surrounding on the flank with their Winchesters laying across their saddles and pumping them into us." A Cheyenne compared it to "chasing buffalo—a great chase." Galloping warriors disdainfully clubbed soldiers from their mounts, or struck them with quirts. "It seemed not brave to shoot him," said Wooden Leg of a man he had bludgeoned with a whip handle and dragged from his horse. "Besides, I did not want to waste my bullets." Some soldiers emptied their pistols into their painted foes; others simply galloped on. It seemed a rout, with every man for himself.

But some tried to bring order from chaos, or save stranded comrades. Halfway to the river, Captain Moylan tried to check his company's gait and close up ranks to protect the men in the rear. Dr. Porter cried: "For God's sake, men, don't run. There is a good many officers and men killed and wounded and we have got to go back and get them." Varnum, riding to the head of the column—and realizing the deadly folly of fleeing before mounted Plains warriors—also urged the men not to run. Replied Reno: "I am in command here, sir."

Others sacrificed themselves, or made a stand. Lonesome Charley Reynolds, left behind in the timber but galloping to overtake the soldiers, had his horse shot down under him and took cover behind it. Despite his injured hand, many expended cartridges would be found near his body; unable to fend off the doom he had foreseen, Reynolds fought to the last. Isaiah Dorman also had his horse shot down a short distance from the timber. The Sioux chief Runs-the-Enemy saw "a black man in a soldier's uniform and we had him. He turned on his horse and shot an Indian right through the heart. Then the Indians fired at this one man and riddled his horse with bullets. His horse fell over on his back and the black man could not get up. I saw him as I rode by." But perhaps he did get up; German-born Roman Rutten saw him making his stand on one knee, coolly firing his sporting rifle: "Isaiah and I were intimate acquaintances, and as I passed him he looked up at me and cried out, 'Goodbye, Rutten.'" The big interpreter's tortured body, an object of interest to those who had never seen a black Wasichu, would be found mutilated, his own camp kettle and cup filled with his blood, an iron cavalry picket pin driven through his genitals. Perhaps some old Santee friends had particularly resented his riding with the bluecoats.

Lieutenant McIntosh had lost his horse in the timber; but Private George McCormick surrendered his own, perhaps because he had a better chance dismounted, but allegedly stating that McIntosh was more important—and that he would release the horse if the officer refused it. McCormick hid in the timber, and survived. After McIntosh had tried to rally his men, Private Rutten saw him leave the timber: "He was singled out by himself, and he was trying to urge his horse along but was not succeeding well. His lariat was dragging, which seemed to bother the horse. McIntosh was surrounded by 20 or 30 Indians, who were circling around him, apparently determined to get him."

Reno's men had ridden straight for the ford they had first used to cross the Little Bighorn. But Indian pressure from their right forced them along a narrow trail to the nearest bluff. Their horses leaped down five feet or more into the water, splashed across the river in disorderly flight, and miraculously scrambled up the near-vertical eastern bank— some of their riders clinging to their necks, others on foot grasping their tails as they were pulled up. Indians shot down at the congested mass of humanity and horseflesh from the bluffs, or rode across the stream to club fleeing bluecoats and yank them from the saddle. The Arikara scout Red Bear saw Bob-tailed Bull's terrified horse cross the river after the soldiers, reins and lariat flying free, tail and mane floating in the wind, and saddle "all bloody in front." One plucky G Company corporal shot an Indian—then actually took the time to take his scalp, waving it in triumph as he rode up the bank. "If we've got to die, let's die like men!" cried Lieutenant Hare to the men near him before giving a rebel yell. "I'm a fighting son of a bitch from Texas!"

But Reno made no attempt to cover the panicky crossing or help men struggling in the water. As Lieutenant Benny Hodgson, Reno's adjutant, tried to cross, a bullet broke his leg and passed through to kill his horse. A trooper, probably Trumpeter Henry Fisher, stuck out a stirrup. Young Hodgson grabbed it and was towed across the river—only to be shot dead as he started up the eastern bank.

Several men who started up one of the ravines leading to the top of the bluffs, but failed to see warriors waiting there for them, were shot and killed—including Dr. DeWolf, warned just too late. The warriors scalped him in full view of the soldiers. Atop the bluffs, the men hastily prepared to receive an attack. Judging by Wallace's official itinerary, the troops had reached the top at about 1530, some fifteen minutes after leaving the timber in what Reno called a "charge." Had the Indians pressed their attack and been willing to suffer heavier casualties, they could easily have annihilated Reno's command, which now numbered perhaps a mere 60 effectives.

Of those left behind in the timber, Lieutenant Charles DeRudio proved the ranking man, his party including a Private O'Neill, Fred Gerard and the part-Pikuni Blackfoot scout William Jackson. From their place of concealment, they saw Reno's men flee, then witnessed another column of cavalrymen—Benteen's—ride down close to the river before turning right and disappearing behind a bluff. Many warriors could be seen riding away from Reno's men, responding to heavy fire which the men could hear downstream.

George Herendeen, his horse shot down outside the timber, returned to find another party of 13 soldiers, some with horses. He had them turn the mounts loose after securing the ammunition in their saddlebags. While in the timber, Herendeen could see Indians "shooting at Isaiah and squaws pounding him with stone hammers. His legs below the knees were shot full of bullets only an inch or two apart." Later that afternoon, with the Indians mostly dispersed, Herendeen led his companions across the river to Reno's battalion.

And what of Custer? Having watered his horses, he led his five troops, mostly at the trot or gallop in columns of twos, up across the ridge, parallel to the line of bluffs screening the Little Bighorn's right bank—though his precise route is controversial due to disparate accounts by the few surviving men who rode with him. After perhaps a mile Custer reached the top of the bluffs bordering the river's east bank, just north of that was later known as Reno Hill. For the first time, he could get an idea of the village's vast size—and also see Reno's men advancing down the valley. Sergeant Daniel Kanipe, of Tom

Custer's Company C, noted: "At sight of the camp, the boys began to cheer. Some horses became so excited that some riders were unable to hold them in ranks, and the last words I heard Custer say were, 'Hold your horses in, boys; there are plenty of them down there for all of us.'"

Perhaps recognizing the pack train's vulnerability and anxious to have its spare ammunition, the general had his brother Tom give Sergeant Kanipe a verbal message to convey: "Go back to McDougall and bring him and the pack train straight across the country. Tell McDougall to hurry the pack train to Custer and if any of the packs get loose cut them and let them go; do not stop to tighten them." Ammunition packs were not to be cut loose. "And if you see Benteen, tell him to come on quick—a big Indian camp."

As Kanipe rode off, Custer led the two battalions farther northward, just behind the bluffs, riding so rapidly that four men of Tom Custer's company found their horses dropping out. Two later survived to join Reno's command. At some point Varnum, with Reno in the valley below, glimpsed Company E's gray horses as they passed along the skyline. Custer turned to the right, down Cedar Coulee, a long ravine tending toward the north, the five companies squeezed into a single column as the ravine narrowed. After about a half-mile the ravine emptied into a broader coulee, later known as Medicine Tail, which seemed likely to end in a ford.

But before entering Cedar Coulee, Custer had again halted his command and ridden to the crest of a promontory, afterwards known as Weir Point, where he saw Reno skirmishing below—though it may have been Mitch Boyer, atop the peak inspecting the valley, whom some saw from below as he waved his hat. Custer now knew that Reno had not charged effortlessly through the Indians, and that Benteen could be of use only if recalled from his scouting mission. His messenger would be his orderly trumpeter, John Martin, a young Italian whose original name had been Giovanni Martini; perhaps inspired by Martin's poor command of English, Custer's adjutant hastily scrawled out a message in pencil. He tore the leaf from his notebook and handed it to Martin:

> Benteen
> Come on. Big village. Be quick.
> Bring packs.
> W.W. Cooke.
> PS Bring pacs [*sic*].

Custer's last messenger would later say that as he began his ride back he saw the two battalions begin to gallop down the coulee, and noticed the gray-horse troop in the center. Later he would hear firing and, turning around, see Indian warriors waving buffalo robes and shooting.

He had gone only a short distance when he met Boston Custer—riding back from the pack train. "Where's the General?" asked the young man. "Right behind that next ridge

*Custer's last message to Benteen, with Benteen's own "translation" in pen in the upper right-hand corner. "I have the original," he wrote to Mrs. Benteen, "but it is badly torn and should be preserved." Once thought to have been destroyed in a fire, the order was finally placed on exhibit at West Point.*

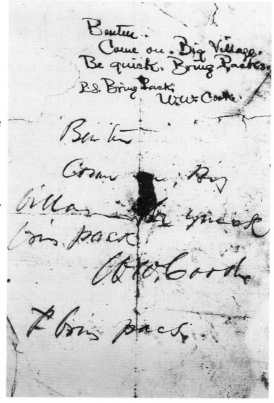

you'll find him," said Martin. Boston galloped to join his brothers while Martin continued on his mission. At one point he was spotted by warriors, but galloped to safety oblivious to the fact that a bullet had struck his horse.

After Martin had left, the only surviving witnesses to Custer's actions would be Indians. But four of these were his own Crow scouts. With the enemy located, Custer had released them, young Curley staying with Mitch Boyer while the other three—Goes Ahead, Hairy Moccasin and White Man Runs Him—prudently took their leave. They apparently rode to a bluff overlooking the river, stopping long enough to see some of Reno's valley fight and fire some long-range shots themselves. Rounding up some Sioux ponies, then picking up a Ree scout on Custer's back trail, they saw dust clouds and heard noises indicating Reno's retreat before riding another mile upstream toward Benteen's oncoming battalion.

Curley, often miscalled the "only survivor" of the Custer battle, was later frequently interviewed as to what he saw, provoking the usual diverse interpretations. In the late John S. Gray's recent reconstruction of the command's movements, Custer halted at the juncture of Cedar Coulee and the upper Medicine Tail. Here he was joined by Boston, who presumably told him that Benteen, encountered just above the Lone Tipi site, was marching his way. Curley and Boyer, watching from the heights for signs of Reno, saw his retreat from the timber, then joined Custer in Medicine Tail Coulee, about one and one-fourth miles above its mouth. Presumably motivated by Boyer's account of Reno's rout, Custer again halted, dividing his command into two battalions and sending two companies under Captain Yates down the coulee to the Miniconjou Ford, also known as Ford B. Leading the other three companies up out of the coulee, Custer halted yet again on a ridge forming its north rim, now called Luce Ridge. Gray theorized that from his vantage point with Custer, Curley watched the two separated companies as they exchanged fire with dismounted Indians concealed in brush on the far bank, then attempted a feint downstream and up toward Calhoun Ridge. Indian horsemen from the village began fording below and above the small band of troopers, forcing them to slow their advance by throwing out dismounted skirmishers—in Gray's view, an attempt to draw the Indians from the beleaguered Reno and buy time for the arrival of Benteen; from Luce Ridge, Custer commanded the back trail by which Benteen could easily reach him.

To conclude what we might term Gray's "Curley synthesis," Custer used heavy volley firing to repel Indian horsemen riding up Medicine Tail Coulee, then moved at a trot to rejoin his two detached companies, along the present Nye-Cartwright, or Blummer, ridge while firing again at Indians to his left. Mitch Boyer finally urged Curley to flee and take the news to Gibbon's supply base, but insisted on remaining with Custer himself. Curley escaped to the east, finding a dead Sioux and taking from him a blanket and a Winchester rifle. Pausing to look back from a hill over a mile from the field, Curley witnessed enough of the fight's last stages to convince him that Custer was doomed.

After leaving Custer's trail, Benteen's three-company battalion had ridden into and down a small valley. Crossing a small branch of the Little Bighorn in column of twos, the command rode toward the first line of bluffs, the rough and torturous country tiring the horses and sometimes requiring a march in single file. Lieutenant Gibson of Company H led a small detail in scouting the advance and actually climbing the bluffs. Sent to the top four times within six miles, Gibson saw only more bluffs, and Benteen, according to his own account, proceeded onward to the next line. Seeing neither valley nor hostile Indians, Benteen concluded that there was nothing to be found in this direction.

This impression was reinforced when Gibson, surveying the landscape with field glasses from a high ridge, could finally see up the Little Bighorn valley, but found his view downstream toward the great village blocked by various promontories and the river's irregular course. Since his subordinate could see neither lodges nor enemy warriors, Benteen decided to return to the trail.

Turning to the right, he soon found himself on the main

# No Survivors?

While the Custer battle fascinates largely due to the power of "the myth of annihilation," a recurrent element in that myth is the lone survivor, escaping to tell the tale. Initially, this role fell to a genuine member of Custer's command—the young Crow scout Curley, who had witnessed the opening stages of the battle. His early departure quickly became an escape through hordes of Sioux while improbably swathed in a Lakota blanket. Custer's first biographer, Frederick Whittaker, revealed that Curley had offered to show Custer an escape route; but that hero had "waved him away," riding back "to the little group of men, to die with them." Since Curley neither read nor spoke English, he made a convenient hook on which to hang bosh, causing other Indians who heard of them to call him a liar—even as he became a minor celebrity as the "only survivor" of the Custer massacre. Curley was interviewed many times regarding his role in the battle, by careful scholars and hack journalists alike, until shortly before his death in 1923. But his own view was perhaps best summed up by the words recalled by the Crow-speaking Tom LeForge: "I did nothing wonderful; I was not in the fight."

Others were glad to fill the part of survivor modestly refused by Curley. "It is astonishing the number of fakes who pose as 'heroes' as to Custer's last battle and campaign," complained General Godfrey in 1918. "The plains and Rockies are full of them..." One battle student collected over 70 accounts by "survivors." But of all those hoping to explain how they had escaped dying with everyone else (one obligingly pointing out on an Anheuser-Busch "Custer's Last Fight" lithograph the dead horse he had hidden beneath), only a few have been taken seriously by scholars. One, Frank Finkel, suddenly revealed his secret around 1921, telling a credibly unheroic story of his horse bolting through the surrounding Indians and carrying Finkel to safety. While skeptic William Boyes later suggested that Finkel, under his claimed alias of

trail along Reno Creek, with the pack train approaching from about a half-mile to the east. Boston Custer, having left the train, came up behind the column and recognized Lieutenant Edgerly: "He gave me a cheery salutation as he passed and then, with a smile on his face, rode to his death...." About a mile farther on, Benteen paused to water his mounts at a morass or "seepage of water." Along the march Captain Benteen and Lieutenant Godfrey had several brief glimpses of the gray horse troop.

Frank Hall, had deserted from the 7th Cavalry over a year before the battle, Finkel's claims were championed by respected theorist Charles Kuhlman—who, however, found them plausible partly because they confirmed his own beliefs about the battle's course.

Others may have escaped from the battlefield—only to die lonely deaths elsewhere. LeForge told of finding skeletal remains on several occasions while an Army scout, while Indian veterans recalled a soldier galloping from the field with warriors in hot pursuit, only to shoot himself when he seemed on the verge of escape. On 3 August, a trooper's dead horse and carbine were found near the landing site used by Terry's troops just west of the Rosebud's mouth, and five days later, at least several miles up the Rosebud, a slain cavalrymen's body. Markings on a white hat and cartridge belt identified him as Company C private Nathan Short. But did he escape from the fight wounded only to die later? Or did Custer send him as a messenger to Terry shortly before the fight, with Short destroying his failing horse and becoming lost before falling prey to Indians?

The only undisputed survivor of the Last Stand is, of course, Myles Keogh's claybank horse Comanche, found badly wounded on the field. Instead of being destroyed, as were other injured cavalry mounts left behind by the victorious Indians, Comanche was placed aboard the *Far West*. Nursed back to health, he became to the 7th Cavalry a mute symbol of the massacre, led on ceremonial occasions with reversed boots in his stirrups, until his death in 1891; stuffed and mounted, he continues to draw tourists to the Dyche Museum at the University of Kansas. But even Comanche's silent claim as "sole survivor" has been challenged by the theory that a wounded Company E gray, Nap, also survived the fight, without achieving renown. (Horses captured by the Indians somehow don't count.)

As to whether any soldier escaped death, we are left with what Dr. Brian Dippie calls the "irresistible paradox about Custer's Last Stand: because there were no survivors, one can never be certain that there were no survivors."

Benteen provoked unease among some of his officers by spending perhaps 20 minutes or more watering his horses, for it was here that some first thought they detected distant gunshots—probably those of Reno's command. Captain Weir urged Benteen to start out immediately in the direction of the sound, but to no avail. So Weir mounted Company D and rode off without permission, to be followed shortly by the other troops. Soon after Benteen's battalion finally left the morass, the first mules of the pack train reached it, several

*Comanche, held by his devoted keeper, blacksmith Gustave Korn. Like the horse, Korn had survived the Little Bighorn fight; when he was killed at the battle of Wounded Knee in 1890, Comanche reportedly became disconsolate, dying within the year. The horse on the left may be Nap, another possible survivor.*

thirst-crazed animals charging into the spring and becoming mired as they sought the alkaline water.

Marching three miles at a slow trot, the command passed the Lone Tipi—which had been set ablaze, probably by Arikaras. But first Benteen encountered Sergeant Kanipe with his verbal orders for McDougall, and sent him back along the trail to the pack-train toiling about a mile behind. Kanipe called out, "We've got them, boys," as he rode past his comrades, naturally leading some men to infer that Custer had already struck a successful blow.

Finding a split in the cavalry trail at the point where Reno and Custer's battalions had separated, Benteen remarked: "Here we have the two horns of a dilemma." Believing that the sounds of gunfire were coming from the left, Weir—in accord with the military maxim "Ride to the sound of the guns"—urged Benteen to take that trail, and actually struck out that way himself without orders. Benteen instead decided to go to the right.

Perhaps a mile south of Reno's final defensive position and just short of Custer's final watering place, moving at what Benteen called "a stiff trott," the column encountered Trumpeter Martin. (According to Edgerly, this happened *before* the trail forked, in which case, as Benteen critic Gary B. Gouin comments, Benteen might have "de-horned" his dilemma by interrogating Martin.) Benteen showed Cooke's message to Weir. But with the comment, "If I am going to be of service to him I think I had better not wait for the packs," he ignored the apparent instruction to fall back for the lagging pack train (and Custer's possible intent to simply bring the *ammunition* packs with him) and continued onward at a quickened pace. "It savored too much of 'coffee-cooling,'" he explained later, "to return when I was sure that a fight had taken place."

In fact, Martin's possibly misunderstood statements, by giving the impression that the Indians were "skedaddling" and that Custer or Reno had already seized the camp, may have led the captain to believe that he had missed out on the scrap. Since Martin had seen no such fight, his claims of victory (if not distorted by his garbled English) must have been inspired by what he, and perhaps every other man there, was sure *would* happen when the 7th U.S. Cavalry met the undisciplined savages. Edgerly summed up the prevailing illusion in writing that Martin's information, "although very satisfactory to the old Indian fighters, caused the hearts of some of the younger men who had not won their spurs to sink as they had looked forward with great hopes of glory to what we all thought would probably be the last Indian fight of any consequence in this country, and it now appeared probable that it would all be over before we could get near enough to see it and certainly before we could take an active part in it."

In encountering a party of Ree scouts driving off some stolen horses, Benteen was told of "Otoe Sioux" (many Sioux) and of what the scouts termed a big "pooh-poohing" in the valley. Leaving the pack train lagging out of sight, Benteen's men could hear firing, and quickened their pace still more.

Finally they began galloping, drawing their revolvers in hot anticipation of meeting the foe. But as they swung from column into line and came within sight of the river near Reno's first crossing, they saw instead heavy smoke from burning prairie grass, masses of Sioux warriors, and blue-coated figures struggling to reach those already atop the bluffs above the stream. The Indians also saw Benteen—who put their numbers at some 900 in the river bottom and perhaps half as many downstream—and broke off their pursuit of Reno's routed battalion, leaving only a comparative handful of marksmen to harass the troops. Benteen rode for the bluffs.

Reno, his straw hat gone and a red handkerchief tied around his head, rode out to meet him, crying, "For God's sake, Benteen, halt your command and help me. I've lost half my men." Reno "was in an excited position," testified Lieutenant Edgerly. "As we came up, he turned and discharged his pistol towards the Indians." As these were some "Nine hundred yards beyond any effective range," Edgerly considered it "done in a sort of defiance of the Indians." Lieutenant Varnum, moved by grief and impotent rage over the death of his friend Benny Hodgson, seized a carbine and also fired at the distant warriors. Lieutenant Hare, seeing his company commander, gripped Godfrey's hand and assured him: "We've had a big fight in the valley, got whipped like hell and I am—damned—glad to see you." Commented Benteen of Reno's battalion: "A more delighted lot of men you never saw."

Benteen asked Reno where Custer might be, but Reno said merely that he had gone downstream with his five companies, and nothing had been heard from him since. With some of Reno's demoralized men still scrambling to reach the bluffs—though the plucky G Company corporal, badly wounded, still waved his fresh scalp as he walked up—Benteen decided to halt and aid Reno. Perhaps he felt he had "come on" sufficiently to fulfil his orders; or that Reno as ranking officer, could compel his presence there; or simply that Reno's desperate plight justified not joining Custer. The retreat had been a disaster, with Reno losing not one-half, but roughly one-third of his men. At least 3 officers and 29 soldiers were dead, with 18 men missing and perhaps 10 or 11 wounded.

Benteen found the men scattered, with no defensive line drawn up. But when a few Indians, hampered by the range and perhaps their indifferent marksmanship, began firing at the combined battalions from positions on the far bluffs, Captain Weir dismounted his troop as skirmishers and drove them off with fire. Godfrey also formed his men in a skirmish line facing the river. Most of the Indians had already disappeared downstream.

Benteen's men were ordered to divide their ammunition with Reno's, and Reno dispatched Lieutenant Hare, pressed into service as temporary adjutant, to the pack train for more. With the lives of perhaps 350 men at stake, Reno seemed preoccupied with the disposition of Lieutenant Hodgson's body, first personally taking a detail down the bluffs (at least confirming that Hodgson was indeed dead) before the warriors turned back the party with fire. He then detailed Lieutenant Varnum to bury him. Varnum, perhaps himself overwrought by Hodgson's death, begged off by saying that he would have to wait for the spades carried by the pack train.

Meeting the train perhaps a mile after it had passed the Lone Tipi, Hare cut out two pack mules bearing a total of 4,000 cartridges and hurried back to the bluffs, a trooper leading each mule while another whipped it from behind; but despite fears of depleted ammunition, the men seem to have helped themselves from only one of the 1000-round boxes.

Even after the ammunition arrived, Reno refused to make any move toward linking up with Custer until *all* of the packs arrived, though he might have tried moving in their direction. A sergeant later justified the decision on the grounds that Reno needed extra blankets to haul those wounded men unable to ride.

Captain McDougall's pack-train arrived soon after, having cut loose some packs to speed its progress. Passing the Lone Tipi, the train had met the Rees with their captured ponies and a part-Indian scout, perhaps William Jackson's brother Robert, who assured them that there were too many Sioux and that he was heading for the Powder River cantonment. McDougall noted that when he reported the train's arrival, Reno, still preoccupied by the death of Hodgson, paid no attention.

By this time, the men had begun to hear shots from downstream—even Godfrey, who was rather deaf. Reno would at first report bluntly: "We could hear firing in that direction and knew that it could only be Custer." But later, perhaps realizing the implications of such an admission, he denied hearing all but a few scattered shots. Others heard volleys. Varnum exclaimed: "Jesus Christ, what does that mean?" It seemed to him that Custer was having a "pretty warm time" of it.

But there was apparently little thought that he was in danger. As Godfrey remembered it, "We were satisfied that Custer was fighting the Indians somewhere, and the conviction was expressed that 'our command ought to be doing something or Custer would be after Reno with a sharp stick.' We heard two distinct volleys which excited some surprise, and, if I mistake not, brought out the remark that 'Custer was giving it to them for all he is worth.' I have but little doubt now that these volleys were fired by Custer's orders as *signals of distress* and to indicate where he was." Whether or not this was so, Reno's inactivity in the absence of real Indian pressure, his failure to ride toward the sound, left 7 of the 7th's 12 companies—3 of which had seen no action—virtually out of the fight.

At the firing, recounted Edgerly, "Col. Weir, my captain, came to me and asked me what I thought we ought to do. I told him I thought we ought by all means to go down to Custer's assistance. He thought so, too, and I heard the first sergeant express himself to that effect. He then asked me if I would be willing to go down with only D troop, if he could get permission to go. I told him I would...."

When Weir rode off with an orderly toward the firing, Edgerly assumed that he had gotten permission, and fol-

*Captain Thomas Weir exposed himself needlessly in walking up and down the firing line on Reno Hill, but survived to become "terribly used up with liquor" following the campaign. Fearing to commit his account of the "Weir Point" episode to paper, he planned to tell Mrs. Custer what he had seen—but died less than six months after the fight, aged 38.*

lowed him with the troop. But Weir "afterwards told me he had not, and had not even asked for it...." Trumpeter Martin's account portrayed Weir as not merely acting alone, but flagrantly disobedient, having angry words with Reno and pointing down the river before leaping onto his horse and riding northward alone. At about the same time, Hare was returning after hurrying the spare ammunition forward.

Atop the promontory that would later bear his name, Weir looked to his left to see the Little Bighorn valley and innumerable tipis. To his front, he could see across the intervening Medicine Tail Coulee to the distant heights. Partly obscured by dust, on a ridge later known as Custer Hill, could be seen horsemen, Stars and Stripes guidons waving above them. "That is Custer over there," he told a sergeant, and ordered his company to mount. "Here, Captain," responded the sergeant, "you had better take a look through the glasses; I think those are Indians." Weir looked—and had his men dismount. Apparently Hare rode up with instructions from Reno to open up communications with Custer, whereupon Weir sent him back to report Indians to his front.

French's Company M set out in the lead to join Weir, followed by Godfrey's K and Benteen's H—Benteen ignoring Reno's orders and trumpet calls to the contrary. Later Wallace left for the point with the seven unwounded men of Company G, deploying them as skirmishers between D and M. Companies K and H deployed to the east and northeast, to present enfilading fire against any warriors riding through the gorge to the north of the point. But it was a poor defensive position, Benteen remarking: "This is a hell of a place to fight Indians. I am going back to Reno to propose that we go back to where we lay before starting out here." Reno himself was on his way to Weir Point with A, B and the pack train, the advance including men who had lost their mounts and wounded cavalrymen carried by six men to a blanket—though Hare pointed out that they might have been kept back with the reinforced pack train.

What could they see of Custer's battlefield? Benteen was to claim, perhaps simply because of poor eyesight, perhaps for other reasons, that the site was invisible from Weir Point—though it can be seen quite clearly with the naked eye. Godfrey observed, amid the dust, individual riders and bands of stationary horsemen, and "From their grouping and the manner in which they sat their horses we knew they were Indians...." Pointing his glasses at what seemed a reddish-brown patch of ground, he saw that its "appearance was changeable," and that this undulating mass—like the "worms" the Crows had tried pointing out to Varnum—was a vast pony herd.

Some of the officers apparently saw more than they would later admit. There is little doubt that Edgerly destroyed the portion of a letter to his wife dealing with the Weir Point episode, though later he would write of seeing Indians shooting as though at objects on the ground, with one part of the hill black with warriors and women. Not until 1910, as a retired brigadier, would he state that, "We could see the

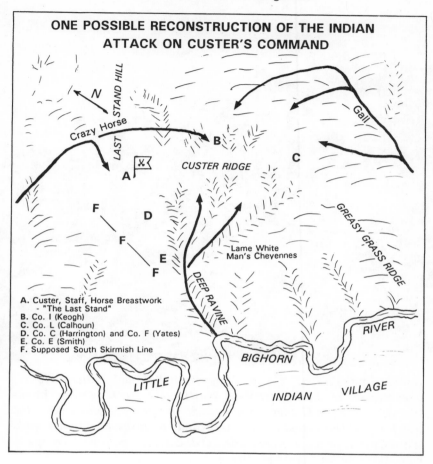

ONE POSSIBLE RECONSTRUCTION OF THE INDIAN ATTACK ON CUSTER'S COMMAND

A. Custer, Staff, Horse Breastwork
 - "The Last Stand"
B. Co. I (Keogh)
C. Co. L (Calhoun)
D. Co. C (Harrington) and Co. F (Yates)
E. Co. E (Smith)
F. Supposed South Skirmish Line

bodies of Custer's men and horses with swarms of Indians." Sergeant John Ryan recalled bluntly in 1923 that he could see "parties whom we supposed to be Indians, riding back and forth, firing scattered shots. We thought they were disposing of Custer's wounded men, and this afterwards proved to be true."

By then, perhaps, the fight of Custer's five companies had all but ended in a cloudy tumult best described in the words of Indian participants. The last steps were the slaughter of the wounded and the stripping and mutilation of the dead. Most, perhaps, perished quickly amid the dust and lingering pow-

*John Mulvany's 1881 "Custer's Last Rally," though ludicrously over-praised by a patriotic Walt Whitman ("...nothing in the books like it, nothing in Homer, nothing in Shakespeare....") was actually less fanciful than most early "last stand" pictures. Mulvany's awkward Custer, unlike his comrades, still carries a sword—perhaps a concession to the heroic tradition.*

der smoke, with a quick shot from a captured service revolver, or the crushing blow of a warclub. Some were less fortunate. A young Cheyenne woman later called Kate Bighead, searching for her nephew Noisy Walking, recalled seeing a dazed soldier sitting on the ground before three Sioux grabbed him and stretched him onto his back. "They went at this slowly, and I wondered what they were going to do. Pretty soon I found out. Two of them held his arms while the third man cut off his head with a sheath-knife...I saw several different ones of the soldiers not quite dead. The Indians cut off arms or legs or feet of these, the same as was done for those entirely dead."

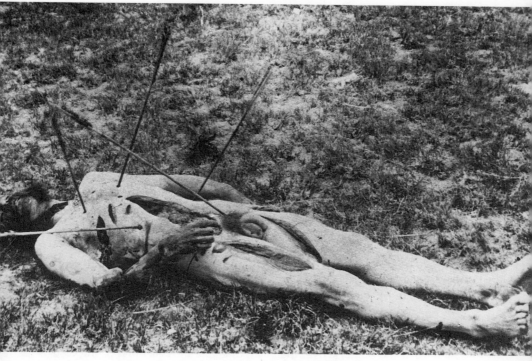

*A grisly example of war on the Plains. English-born Sergeant Frederick Wyllyams, slain in 1867 during a 7th Cavalry fight with Cheyenne, Sioux, and Arapho warriors. A portion of his scalp lies above his left arm. Many of Custer's men at Little Bighorn shared a similar fate.*

Young Black Elk, who had already slain one of Reno's wounded soldiers and gone to show his mother the scalp, eagerly arrived on the scene: "Before we got there, the Wasichus were all down, and most of them were dead, but some of them were still alive and kicking. Many other little boys had come up by this time, and we rode around shooting arrows into the Wasichus. There was one who was squirming around with arrows sticking in him, and I started to take his coat, but a man pushed me away and took the coat for himself." However, the boy took a bright, beautiful yellow object hanging on the soldier's belt. After its ticking ceased, "I

# What Happened?

The result was all too clear. But the course of Custer's last fight was quite another matter. The most obvious clue, to those whites who first viewed the stricken field, consisted of the dead bodies of men and horses. But these alone could suggest only so much about Custer's defense, and eyewitnesses could clash on details; though both numbers suggested that the Indians fought mostly on foot, Captain McDougall counted five or six dead Indian ponies on the field, while Captain Benteen recalled only two. Benteen cited the positions of the dead to suggest that the fight had been "a rout, a panic, till the last man was killed; that there was no line formed...you can take a handful of corn and scatter it over the floor and make just such lines....Only where Custer was found were there any evidences of a stand." Others disagreed.

Popular writers could and did concoct heroic death-struggles, the epic moment demanding that the doomed troopers slay more than their own number of foes; Frederick Whittaker, writing in 1876, depicted Custer fighting "like a tiger with his sabre," in the very act of running a redskin through as Rain-in-the-Face shot him. But even Whittaker cited "several Indians" for his tale. Those seriously attempting to reconstruct the fight would likewise depend on the only living witnesses.

While Sioux and Cheyenne veter-

ans were interviewed from 1876 until well into our own century, their accounts seemed so contradictory that W.A. Graham, having collected "50 or 60," found it impossible to "reconcile them sufficiently to form a coherent narrative," unless he "summarily discredited some as false and accepted others as true," which Graham was unwilling to do.

Others were less hesitant, though Indian participants could not even agree on how many of their comrades had fallen; thus (to cite only two) while the Sioux Kill Eagle stated that 39 had been slain by Custer's men and 14 by Reno's, with 14 wounded dying later, Low Dog gave the *total* killed as 38, with many fatally wounded. Since no Indian had the task of reporting casualties, estimates exceeding a hundred cannot be discounted.

This wide disparity in accounts—influenced by such factors as cultural differences, poor translation, fear of reprisals or the desire to please, and the typical warrior's emphasis on the individual rather than the tactical in warfare—meant that almost anything could be defended as "the Indian side of the story." The diligent Dr. Thomas Marquis even accepted the Cheyenne tale that almost all of Custer's men had committed mass suicide—though Marquis' chief informant, Wooden Leg, retracted his suicide story when questioned by others: "He laughed and said there were just too many Indians." Perhaps, as one student suggested, Cheyenne veterans in U.S. service as scouts or police felt the need for an alibi for Custer's death which later assumed a life of its own. But other Indian narratives exhibited a fine indifference to white sensibilities; one, from Pretty-Shield, widow of the Crow scout Goes Ahead, destroys the cherished vision of a fighting Custer being among the last to die by having him shot crossing the river and presumably carried to Custer Hill.

One possible reconstruction, offered by the renowned Robert M. Utley, has Custer splitting his command shortly after dispatching Martin to Benteen, sending two companies under Captain Yates down Medicine Tail Coulee, while Captain Keogh's battalion occupied the high ground separating Medicine Tail from Deep Coulee to the north. Custer may have intended holding the nearest ford, relieving pressure on Reno while using Keogh to cover Benteen's approach.

Reaching the river, Yates was repelled by a small band of warriors firing from the opposite bank. With Indian reinforcements arriving, Gall led his Hunkpapas across the river as Yates retreated, dismounting his men to fight; the troopers ascended Deep Coulee's north slope toward a low, flat hill, forming the south end of a high ridge—afterwards Battle Ridge—overlooking the Little Bighorn valley. After a lengthy exchange of fire, Keogh moved his men north to link up with Yates;

but the Indians stampeded their horses (and extra ammunition) when they too dismounted. Keogh finally joined Yates on the ridge's southern end, Calhoun Hill.

With Indians crossing lower down the valley to fire from a deep ravine into the men on Calhoun Hill, Custer—to counter the threat "or perhaps even to find another ford by which to charge the village"—sent Company C down the ridge to the head of the ravine. But they were quickly overrun by Lame White Man's attack, the survivors fleeing toward Calhoun Hill. Aside from this, the Indians generally refrained from charging mounted, instead using the grass, sagebrush, and dips in terrain for cover as they fired rifles, or sent arrows arcing down onto groups of soldiers lacking any cover. Yates' two companies moved northward along the ridge.

Finally Crazy Horse, having crossed the river below the village and sweeping up in a wide arc to lead his warriors up Battle Ridge, crushed Keogh's Company I against Gall's men. After the other groups of soldiers were destroyed, the climax ensued on the western slope of Custer Hill. After a group of soldiers (whether in panic or desperate counterattack) broke toward the head of a deep ravine, and the river beyond, only to be wiped out, some 40 survivors shot their horses for breastworks and died fighting.

Thus the "last stand"—except for those ready with their own theories.

wore it around my neck a long time before I found out what it was and how to make it tick again." The youngster ascended the hill, where he shot an arrow into a wounded soldier's forehead.

Iron Hawk, aged 14, was another Sioux boy who witnessed the aftermath:

> The women swarmed up the hill and began stripping the soldiers. They were yelling and laughing and singing now. I saw something funny. Two fat old women were stripping a soldier, who was wounded and playing dead. When they had him naked, they began to cut something off that he had, and he jumped up and began fighting with the two fat women. He was swinging one of them around, while the other one was trying to stab him with her knife. After awhile, another woman rushed up and shoved her knife into him and he died really dead. It was funny to see the naked Wasichu fighting with the fat women.

Wooden Leg, walking among the dead, "observed one face that interested me. The man, perhaps thirty or more years old, had long whiskers growing from both cheeks and extending below his chin: 'Here is a new kind of scalp,' I said to a companion. I skinned one side of the face and half of the chin, so as to keep the long beard yet on the part removed." Afterward Wooden Leg went to see a wounded friend, the same young man sought by Kate Bighead. Asked how he was, Noisy Walking replied "Good," though he had been hit by three bullets and also had stab wounds in his side.

Black Elk saw that his cousin Black Wasichu, hanging on his pony's side while fighting, had been shot through the right shoulder at such an angle that the bullet lodged in his left hip. "He was my cousin, and his father and my father were so angry over this, that they went and butchered a Wasichu and cut him open. The Wasichu was fat, and his meat looked good to eat, but we did not eat any."

The Arapaho Left Hand, who had fought to prove that he was not a spy, found that he had accidentally slain a Hunkpapa warrior. But it was not the only tragic error during the final fury of rubbing out Long Hair's soldiers. Fatally shot during a rush near the hill where the soldiers made their final stand, Lame White Man, the Southern Cheyenne leader who had lived so long among his northern cousins, was mistaken for a bluecoat scout and scalped by a Sioux. "The Cheyennes never made any inquiries among the Sioux concerning the case," said Wooden Leg. "We just kept quiet about it."

Perhaps even Sitting Bull, who had "made medicine" during the fight, was surprised by the scale of his prophesied victory. The soldiers of this band had been rubbed out, and yielded up a vast store of treasure, from clothing and silver coins to decorate hair or bridles, to boottops cut away to make handy leather pouches, to greenbacks used as saddleblankets for mud horses made by children. Best of all were the weapons: over 200 carbines and revolvers, and plenty of ammunition to fit. Very soon, warriors would ride south to use their new weapons against the remaining soldiers. Other Indians brought travois to take away the bodies of the dead and wounded amid lamentations that tempered the joy of victory.

At just what time Custer's fight ended cannot be determined, though to British student Francis B. Taunton the evidence suggests "that 'D' Company certainly witnessed the last hour or so of Custer's battle and the companies who later joined them may have seen the last thirty minutes of the fighting." Certainly the officers on the point suspected that Custer, like Reno, had been whipped, and perhaps badly whipped. But did even those watching the dim figures from Weir Point suspect the full truth? As Taunton writes: "None ever admitted so and certainly the extinction of five companies of cavalry was unparalleled in Indian warfare in the 19th century." Yet Reno's command now possessed all the reserve ammunition and mule-borne supplies, and "deep down it must have been asked: how could Custer sustain [even] a three-hour engagement with only 100 rounds of carbine ammunition per man?"

In later years, of course, the officers "consoled themselves and each other" with the propositions that Custer and his men were dead before they could have reached them, and that there were too many Indians between the two commands to have effected a rescue. But given Taunton's suggested recon-

# "Revolting to Civilized Perceptions..."

"Indian warfare," wrote General Crook in his parting message to the Bighorn and Yellowstone Expedition, "is, of all warfare, the most dangerous, the most trying, and the most thankless. Not recognized by the high authority of the United States Senate as war, it still possesses for you the disadvantages of civilized warfare, with all the horrible accompaniments that barbarians can invent and savages execute."

Unlike many eastern tribes or the Apaches of the Southwest, the Plains Indians did not customarily reserve prisoners for torture, instead simply killing or, on occasion, releasing or adopting male foes. But they routinely gang-raped female captives, slew women (as Sitting Bull recorded in pictographs of his war deeds), and mutilated the dead; the throat-cutting gesture used to denote "Sioux" in the Plains sign language also signified decapitation, an old Lakota custom. (Captain W.P. Clark, investigating such practices, found no evidence for the supposed belief that mutilation was intended to similarly maim the victim's spirit.) In the November 1876 attack on Dull Knife's Cheyenne village, troops discovered a Shoshone woman's arm and a bag containing the right hands of 12 Shoshone babies, while Lieutenant Bourke secured a necklace displaying 10 fingers and a human scrotum.

There is even an allegation that Custer was maimed with an arrow thrust up his penis.

From the soldiers' vantage point such practices merely confirmed the convenient image of the "wild" Indian as a savage—and if they aroused less bitterness than one might expect, it was precisely *because* he was considered unenlightened and hence less morally culpable. Lieutenant Bradley contrasted Little Face's kindheartedness in weeping over Gibbon's slain hunters and donating blankets for their burial with his tale of a legendary warrior stealthily beheading an Assiniboine girl. The "fate of this poor, innocent maiden, under circumstances so revolting to civilized perceptions, actually appeared to Little Face a good joke and caused him in the telling of it to chuckle with delight."

Alert to Plains customs, the Regulars tried to carry off their dead when practicable, or at least disguise their graves. Reno's alleged proposal for the unthinkable—abandoning his wounded to the Sioux—would inevitably arouse contempt in any who heard of it, W.A. Graham commenting, "Such a plan could emanate only from one so crazed by fear as to have lost all sense of self respect and soldierly honor."

While white frontiersmen or volunteers often embraced an exterminationist or "nits make lice" philosophy, Regulars generally made some attempt to preserve civilized standards. While women and young boys sometimes took up arms during village attacks, Colonel Carr confessed to his wife that he had "always been horrified at the idea of killing Indian women and children." While he had verbally forbidden it, "I did not deem it necessary to give written orders, because my command did not require any restraint in that direction. Poor things, I do not blame them for fighting for their husbands and fathers, right or wrong—many white women would do the same." On occasion Regulars attempted to restrain the excesses of Indian allies, perhaps while expressing disappointment at their failure to inculcate "civilized" habits of warmaking. Yet the very use of such allies made such excesses likely, just as any village attack risked noncombatant lives. Others might die as an indirect result; after the Dull Knife fight, 11 Cheyenne babies froze to death as the shelterless Indians fled.

Some soldiers did kill wantonly, whether for purposes of retaliation, adaptation to standards of "savage warfare," or simply because they viewed the Indian as a racially inferior being. Some took scalps, and Buffalo Bill used Yellow Hair's as a promotional gimmick for a play. At times witnesses were forced to ponder ruefully the pretensions of "civilized" man. After Ute John scalped the slain women at Slim Buttes, a regretful Finerty felt himself "compelled to state a few—a very few—brutalized soldiers followed his savage example. Each took only a portion of the [remaining] scalp, but the exhibition of human depravity was nauseating." Another reporter confessed that his "faith in the superiority of white humanity received a terrible shock." Trooper William White noted how a "foraging band of civilized people," seeking robes and blankets from tumbled scaffolds for Reno's wounded, also grabbed souvenirs; Dr. Paulding only ceased tugging at a dead man's beaded moccasins when the skin began to slough off the legs. But Finerty, seeing infantrymen pull down a Sioux burial scaffold for firewood, waxed philosophical: "Thus the relationship of all men to each other in point of savagery was established."

Lieutenant Bourke, presented with an Apache's ears and scalp, had the ears framed and used the scalp for a lamp mat, only later realizing "how brutal and inhuman I had been." Destined to become a noted anthropologist, Bourke regarded such practices as mutilation as natural in a hunting society, and was too honest to whitewash the civilized: "We enlightened people who prate so much about our goodness and elevation would do just the same," he admonished. Indeed, the whites "had little more morality than the savage, mean as he is; but we have a great deal more bread and butter."

*"Yes, I killed a great many," said Pizi, or Gall, giving a graphic account of the Custer fight to 7th Cavalry officers marking its 10th anniversary. The powerful Hunkpapa war leader had long made war upon the whites, once being bayoneted and left for dead by soldiers. Two of his wives were killed during Reno's initial attack.*

struction, with Weir reaching the point at roughly 1700 and elements of Custer's command still alive at 1800, an early demonstration toward the Indians might have disrupted their attack and saved a remnant of Custer's men—though any chance to save most of them, if such a chance existed, had doubtless passed before Weir even started out. Small wonder, then, that some officers later suffered from "a tendency to accelerate the movement northwards and terminate the existence of firing (what firing?) at the earliest opportunity."

Wrote Godfrey of the dusty panorama viewed from Weir Point, "While watching this group the conclusion was arrived at that Custer had been repulsed, and the firing was the parting shots of the rear guard. The firing ceased, the groups dispersed, clouds of dust rose from all parts of the field, and the horsemen converged toward our position."

By this time Weir had left his company—perhaps to confer with Reno, who never quite managed to reach the point. As cavalrymen and Indians traded fire, Reno ordered a withdrawal toward his original position, Benteen explaining in a tribute to his foes that "there were a great deal too many

Indians, who were 'powerful' good shots, on the other side. We were at their hearths and homes—they had gotten the 'bulge' on Reno, their medicine was working well, and they were fighting for all the good God gives anyone to fight for." But Reno rejected Benteen's idea of holding the Indians off while seeking a better position. Led by the pack mules, the soldiers pulled back, Benteen leaving a guidon at Weir Point for the benefit of Custer's command—or its survivors.

The retreat proved a messy affair, Godfrey later noting that companies M and D retreated too rapidly, and that had he not dismounted his own troop to make a temporary stand, the Indians might have pressed home their advantage. But Godfrey found himself "losing control" of his men as he attempted to have them retreat by odd and even numbers moving alternately to the rear: "At first there was a semblance of conformity to the drill, but it was not long till all were practically in one line." Men who had at first halted, knelt and fired deliberately would do so hastily, some then not bothering to stop or fire at all. Finally "Reno sent me orders to hurry back; I gave the command, Double time, March! and to my amazement some of the men started off like sprinters."

The retreat featured only one fatality. When Company D's Farrier Vincent Charley fell wounded through the hips, Edgerly told him to get into a ravine out of danger and promised that he would come back for him with a skirmish line. But when told of this, Captain Weir inexplicably—and inexcusably—told him that orders were to fall back and refused to send a line forward, leaving the farrier to the Indians. He was later found dead, a stick rammed down his throat.

So little confidence did Reno inspire that during the retreat Captain McDougall quietly suggested to Benteen that he should assume command. Benteen merely grinned. But for most of the fight he remained the dominant figure, with Reno largely inactive.

The warriors pursued closely, the troops barely having time to form a skirmish line on "Reno Hill" before meeting the warriors with gunfire. All soldiers were ordered to the line, leaving only the packers to care for the animals. Also on the line were the Crows Half-Yellow Face and White Swan, as well as those Arikaras who had not left for the Powder River base. "The men threw themselves on the ground," recalled Major Reno, "having no protection except the 'grease weed' which was no protection whatever." Reno had the packs unloaded and breastworks built for the wounded. Benteen ordered Wallace's company into position: "He said," recounted Benteen, "he had no company, only three men. I told him to go there with his three men and I would see he was supported..." The warriors abandoned their charge under the soldiers' hot fire.

The vaguely horseshoe-like position consisted of two roughly parallel ridges, the westernmost overlooking the river, separated by a small depression around which the troops formed their perimeter. Placing the wounded in the depression, Dr. Porter set up his field hospital, partly screened by horses and mules also placed there for protection. At the perimeter's southern end, Benteen's company formed a triangular addition, with a further hairpin-like extension line stretching beyond it to cover the southern approaches.

It was perhaps already past 1900. But the Sioux riflemen—so numerous that many had no room to shoot and had to stay out of range as spectators—had close to three hours of daylight left, and the soldiers had little cover save for objects such as saddles and the pack train's cargo. "For the most part it wasn't any real protection at all," admitted Private Windolph, "but it made you feel a lot safer...." Edgerly told of a soldier eagerly throwing himself down behind the first box of hard bread set down on Benteen's line: "He had hardly gotten his head against the box when a bullet came tearing through it, killing the man instantly. Strange as it may sound here, nearly every man who saw this laughed."

The position had obvious disadvantages. The nearest water was a good hundred feet below it, the river banks accessible through a narrow ravine. And while located on high ground, it was not the *highest* ground; some five hundred yards to the northwest of the perimeter's edge, Indian riflemen on "Sharp-shooters' Ridge" had an excellent view of the entire perimeter. Company M's redoubtable 1st Sergeant John M. Ryan felt obliged to give one Indian stationed there "credit for being a good shot."

> While we were lying in the line he fired a shot and killed the fourth man on my right. Soon afterward he fired again and shot the third man. His third shot wounded the man on my right...I thought my own turn was coming next. I jumped up, with Captain French, and some half a dozen members of my company, and, instead of firing straight to the front, as we had been doing...we wheeled to our right and put in a deadly volley, and I think we put an end to that Indian, as there were no more men killed at that particular spot.

Fortunately, most of the Indian marksmen were less proficient. The white-haired Benteen gallantly inspired his men by strolling about with perfect indifference to hostile bullets, but would ultimately suffer no more than a nicked thumb. Other officers also exposed themselves. Godfrey, "horrified" to find himself wondering whether the small sagebrush he lay behind would "turn" a bullet, got up and walked along the line, cautioning his men not to waste ammunition and ordering the best marksmen to fire while others supplied them with loaded carbines. Reno too would walk the line on occasion, but otherwise did little to inspire, much of the time apparently remaining in a shallow pit.

Corporal George Lell was gutshot. Knowing he would die, he said he wanted "to see the boys again before I go," and asked to be propped up. "So they held him up to a sitting position," recounted Windolph, "where he could see his comrades in action. A smile came to his face as he saw the beautiful fight the Seventh was making. Then they laid him down and he died soon after..." Before darkness fell, the command suffered 11 more men killed and wounded. After a number of mules and horses had been shot down, Lieutenant Mathey formed a picket line for the survivors by tying ropes to the dead animals' legs.

At about 2100, the gunfire ceased, save the odd shot from this or that hopeful brave. Most withdrew to camp, where

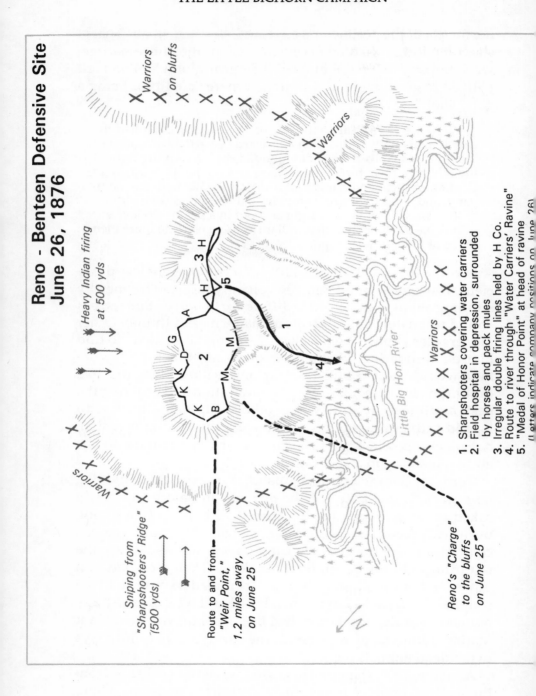

Reno - Benteen Defensive Site
June 26, 1876

Warriors on bluffs

Warriors

Warriors

Heavy Indian firing at 500 yds

Little Big Horn River

Warriors

1. Sharpshooters covering water carriers
2. Field hospital in depression, surrounded by horses and pack mules
3. Irregular double firing lines held by H Co.
4. Route to river through "Water Carriers' Ravine"
5. "Medal of Honor Point" at head of ravine
(Letters indicate company positions on June 26)

Sniping from "Sharpshooters' Ridge" (500 yds)

Warriors

Route to and from "Weir Point," 1.2 miles away, on June 25

Reno's "Charge" to the bluffs on June 25

N

*Henry Renaldo Porter, 1886. The only surgeon who survived to treat the wounded of Reno's command, the 26-year-old Porter worked without rest—then accompanied the wounded on the* Far West.

they could celebrate and contemplate the next day's action. The soldiers saw their large fires blazing in the valley below, and could even hear the beat of drums and what Godfrey called "demoniacal screams." But any celebration was mingled with the sounds of grief. The dead included Noisy Walking, whose wounds proved fatal that night.

During the cool and cloudy night, marked by a few brief rain showers, the soldiers used knives, tin cups, the few axes and spades available, and bare hands to scratch out rifle pits or build up crude earthworks. But Benteen failed to have his own company entrench, apparently due to both the men's exhausted condition and his own belief that the Indians would depart that night.

Men imagined strange things in the darkness—saw columns of troops, or heard hoofbeats. Perhaps the distant trumpet calls were real, albeit those made on a captured instrument by some Sioux or Cheyenne musician. But the men, however haunted their imaginations, seem to have had

## "The Old, Old Legend of Our Race..."

"I don't think I'll write any more than has been written on the Custer massacre," predicted John Finerty in 1890, adding that "the Custer business has been written, so to speak, to satiety." But fascination with the tragedy, and its central figure, was to produce over the next century an amazing literature, out of all proportion to either's significance. With the countless books, pamphlets, and magazine articles on Custer and his last battle would come much more "Custeriana" helping to keep his name a household word—poems, plays, paintings, lithographs, and films. But why such an enduring interest in the loss of a few hundred men slain by Indians?

The circumstances of Custer's defeat presented to the American public the raw materials of epic. It was a particular *type* of defeat—a last-ditch fight in which a small band of defenders, led by a famous hero of many battles, had gone down against superior numbers of exotic and savage foes. What the Alamo was to Texans, the Little Bighorn might become for the Republic at large—America's answer to Ther-

mopylae. The terrible facts, relayed by telegraph and newspaper with a swiftness unimaginable in earlier times, laid the foundation even as they were transmuted—interpreted, altered or twisted to fit a pre-existing epic pattern, embracing such seemingly diverse figures as Roland, Leonides, and Davy Crockett. Where fact did not provide an element necessary to the pattern, fiction, and Victorian excess did, answering some deep inner need in those telling the tale. As Bruce Rosenberg discovered in his *Custer and the Epic of Defeat*:

> When these narrative elements are combined into a coherent story—the sword, the hilltop, the last to die, the heavy toll of the enemy, the call for help, treachery, the hero's pride, and the one survivor...a legend of heroic aspect has been created.

Thus even Custer's alleged "betrayal"—by Reno, Benteen, corrupt Indian agents, or President Grant himself—might serve as simply another mythic ingredient. In 1876 Walt Whitman, with a poet's recognition of deeper truths, could write

no idea of the magnitude of Custer's defeat. Some apparently felt that, having been repulsed, he had ridden off to join General Terry while abandoning them—though Custer would have been an eccentric commander indeed to abandon seven companies while riding off with five. Others believed that he too was besieged. Major Reno attempted to get a

that the fall of Custer's men, "with their slaughter'd/horses for breast-works," merely

> Continues yet the old, old
>     legend of our race,
> The loftiest of life upheld by
>     death,
> The ancient banner perfectly
>     maintain'd
> O lesson opportune, O how I
>     welcome thee!

But the heroic legend co-existed with, fed upon, and was sometimes challenged by what historian Robert M. Utley would term "The Great Debate"—the controversy over the fight and the events and personalities surrounding it. Custer was condemned as well as praised by contemporaries, and later generations of Custerphobes and Custerphiles would argue facts and theories with equal heat. "The Custer Myth" can in fact be many things, and the story of the Last Stand has served as an example of heroism for American schoolchildren; a moral tale of hubris punished; and a textbook example of military incompetence. The Custer name can even stand as shorthand for utter disaster or insurmountable odds.

For the nation at large, the heroic myth might seem most useful; even Benteen wrote that if Custer's grave monument at West Point made "better soldiers and men" of the cadets, "why the necessity of knocking the paste eye out of their idol?" Perhaps such idealization is no longer possible, Rosenberg observing in 1974, "We have not seen the time when the French condemned Roland for oppressing underdeveloped nations, nor have the Greeks defamed Leonides for his ruthless treatment of the 'barbarian.' What is happening now to the reputation of Custer is unique in heroic legend."

Yet even if Custer's personal legend has been shattered, there persists a need to find a symbolic "meaning" in the cultural iconography of his Last Stand. Some have even hoped to use the battle to dramatize the plight of the American Indian. But the awkward fact that the Indians annihilated the soldiers keeps getting in the way; as Rosenberg remarks, to view such an event as symbolizing the most destructive aspects of white racism "takes a greater suspension of disbelief than most Americans are able to muster."

message to Custer, but the Indian scouts he sent probably never even made such a risky effort before returning.

Reno himself, seen on several occasions holding a flask by various eyewitnesses, is alleged to have been drunk that night, striking a packer and then raising a carbine while threatening to shoot him. An even more shocking story was later told privately by Captain Benteen; Reno had proposed that all those able to ride should mount up, all non-portable property be destroyed, and a forced march be made to the Powder River base camp. Those wounded men unable to ride would simply be left behind. Benteen grimly refused.

Daylight came early, between 0200 and 0300. Warriors surrounded the perimeter on foot, pushing as far as they could without exposing themselves. At times, when the soldiers failed to return fire, warriors attempted a rush, to be driven back by barking carbines. Occasionally even mounted-men dashed up close to the perimeter, then rode off. The Crow White Swan, though badly wounded, responded to one charge by pulling himself along with his rifle to get a shot at the Sioux; dragging him back to safety, his white comrades would find him again crawling toward the skirmish line.

Movement was dangerous, but even men lying flat could be hit. While Benteen's unentrenched company suffered the most men wounded, their position was inherently the most exposed, and some losses were apparently caused by warriors firing *over* other positions and into Company H; other companies tended to take too much cover, or lie down on the reverse slope of their positions, thus limiting their own fields of fire (sometimes to fewer than 25 yards to the front) and failing to keep the Indian riflemen at a distance. But Benteen himself remained unscathed; when a bullet knocked off one bootheel, he remarked, "Close call; try again." A private remembered hearing him announce, "Men, this is a ground hog case; it's live or die with us. We must fight it out with them." At one point warriors got close enough to the southeastern tip of H's line to throw rocks at the soldiers. Realizing the danger, Benteen led a charge to drive them back.

Thirst was magnified by the harsh Montana sun and clouds of black-powder smoke mingling with the dust. Some men, trying to eat biscuits, blew the chewed remains out like dry flour. Pebbles were placed in mouths, and a few raw potatoes and cans of fruit were used to ease suffering. The wounded cried piteously for water.

Near Benteen's line on the western side of the perimeter,

lay the head of a small coulee, later termed Water Carriers' Ravine. It led down to the river—and was occupied by warriors. Reinforcing his company with troopers from M, Benteen led another charge of H and M and drove out four Indians from the ravine, killing several. Private Thomas Meador was shot to death as the soldiers withdrew; the Sans Arc warrior Long Robe ran boldly up to touch him with a coupstick, only to be killed himself before he could get away.

Collecting water for the wounded was considered so dangerous that the officers refused to order anyone out. But there were plenty of volunteers—some of whom hoped for a drink themselves. Crossing an open space under long-range fire, the men were sheltered by the ravine itself until they reached the last 30 feet of ground leading to the river and could be shot at from bushes on the opposite bank.

After the first party returned unscathed, Benteen detailed four good marksmen to cover their approach, standing up at the edge of the river bluff and drawing some of the Indians' fire. "Some soldiers came to get water from the river," remembered Wooden Leg, "just as our old men had said they likely would do. The white men crept down a deep gulch and then ran across an open space to the water...." Wooden Leg claimed to have killed one of these, possibly a man who tried it before the first "official" party was dispatched. Mike Madden of Company K suffered a shattered leg; given a drink of whisky after Dr. Porter had performed an amputation, Madden supposedly asked him to "cut off my other leg." Waiting Cheyennes saw one underwear-clad soldier run down to duck his head in the river and drink while filling the vessel in each hand: "Half the time they could not see him because of the water splashed up by the bullets." But he survived. Twenty-five cavalrymen would ultimately receive Medals of Honor for helping to secure water and other acts of valor.

The heaviest Indian firing subsided by noon—possibly as a ruse, or in temporary withdrawal at the news of the advancing Terry-Gibbon column. This gave Benteen a chance to secure spades and finally entrench Company H. But to the

*William Slaper, former private of Company M, at Water Carrier's Ravine, 1926. Though he helped secure water for the wounded, Slaper was not one of those awarded a Medal of Honor.*

north, opposite Company B, Indians fired from a ridge into Benteen's position, and Benteen (or perhaps Reno) led another charge to drive them off. The Indians instead forced the soldiers back with heavy fire.

A few sharpshooters continued to harass the troops that afternoon as the great Indian camp broke up, First Sergeant Ryan driving some away from a bluff with long-range shots from his heavy Sharps rifle. Finally, the relieved soldiers saw the great column depart, Benteen estimating the hostile strength to have been that of a Civil War cavalry division: "It started about sunset and was in sight till darkness came. It was in a straight line about three miles long, and I think half a mile wide, as densely packed as animals could be." To Edgerly, the ponies of the herd made the valley resemble "a great brown carpet being dragged over the ground."

Reno's men gave their departing foes three cheers—but stayed in position, as an occasional sniper shot cracked through the dry air. That night, Reno moved the camp to get away from the bodies of men and beasts and to better command the approaches to the Little Bighorn. The men fortified it as best they could, and buried their dead. They would sleep on their arms that night. But the battle was over.

# A Few Custer Myths

"The Custer known to the average American is a Myth," wrote W.A. Graham in 1953, "and so is Reno; and so also Benteen." But, just as his "Last Stand" has come to seem synonymous with the Little Bighorn fight, so has Custer himself proved the greatest generator of myths—even for many who may never have heard of Reno and Benteen. A few of the most popular, or simply the most bizarre, are addressed below.

## Custer Hoped to Become President by Defeating the Indians

This hoary tale, which shows no sign of dying, was inspired solely by the testimony of the Arikara scout Red Star. His 1912 narrative had Custer claiming that even a small victory over the Sioux would make him "Great Father" and thus permit him to help his Indian comrades. (Significantly, Fred Gerard, who would have interpreted any such statement, never mentioned any Presidential fantasies voiced by Custer.) As elaborated in David Humphreys Miller's exceptionally mendacious *Custer's Fall*, the myth has Custer hoping to galvanize the St. Louis Democratic convention with news of his great victory; the fable was embellished by the overimaginative Mari Sandoz's last and worst book, *The Battle of the Little Bighorn*. But a victory over Indians in 1876 would probably have impressed only frontier voters, and there is no evidence that Custer had

any notion of running. Furthermore, news of a victory would not have reached St. Louis in time to effect the convention. Naturally enough, the myth has been accorded respectful treatment in such films as *The Great Sioux Massacre* (1965) and *Little Big Man* (1970).

## Custer Fathered an Indian Baby

Both white and Indian sources suggest that after the Washita fight Custer enjoyed a sexual relationship with the young Cheyenne captive Monahsetah, daughter of slain chief Little Rock—and alleged mother of Custer's son. But Monahsetah (about whose charms Custer waxes eloquent in his memoirs) seems to have given birth less than three months after meeting Long Hair, and even the gossip-mongering Colonel Benteen termed her son "simon-pure" Cheyenne. A *second* child was allegedly born to Monahsetah late in 1869, but documentation is lacking.

## Custer Was Betrayed by His Scouts

Though betrayal seems a vital, or at least popular, element in many heroic legends, it is usually Reno and Benteen who are accused of letting Custer down—some even suggesting, implausibly, that his subordinates *deliberately* plotted his demise. But as early as 1 August 1876, the *New York Herald* had a treacherous "half-breed" scout leading Custer into an ambush, the cunning Sioux even tying up the grass so as to entangle the legs of soldiers' horses. Perhaps that staple of Western fiction, the wicked "half-breed," helped inspire a 1952 theorist who suggested (for no apparent reason) that Mitch Boyer had treacherously murdered Custer. Montana rancher Henry Weibert has recently attempted to revive this story—while failing to explain why not merely Boyer, but also the Crow scouts, would wish to help their Sioux opponents. While the canard has, fortunately, not attained popularity, it demonstrates how "conspiracy theories" can happily persist in the complete absence of supporting evidence.

## Custer Committed Suicide

Long predating publication of Dr. Thomas Marquis' "mass-suicide" theory, this notion was popularized by Colonel Irving I. Dodge's book *Our Wild Indians* in 1882; Dodge asserted that the hero's body was not mutilated because Indians (according to Dodge, anyway) never touched the body of a suicide. Yet witnesses testified that Custer's wounds (neither likely to have been self-inflicted by a right-handed man) bore no powder burns. Nothing daunted, David H. Miller suggested that they could have been wiped away by other officers—a physical impossibility. Commented Godfrey: "There was no sign for the justification of the theory, insinuation or assertion that he committed suicide."

Certainly envisioning such a deed clashes with the usual vision of Custer fighting to the last. Yet it has been suggested that, however uncharacteristic it might seem, the image also preserves the hero inviolate. Like Roland, Custer dies—but no foeman can kill him.

As scholarship and society evolve, earlier myths are supplanted by others, or simply fade away. Part of it has to do with shifting public tastes, as well as popular attitudes toward martial valor and the Indian wars; we may find ourselves more receptive to the notion of a glory-grasping presidential hopeful than to Sitting Bull's alleged description of "the Long Hair" standing like a "sheaf of corn with all the ears fallen around him." But as long as Custer continues to grip the imagination, so shall myths swirl about him like the smoke of battle.

# A "Fiend Incarnate" (Allegedly)

The elaborate mutilation of Tom Custer's body suggested to the 7th's survivors that he had been singled out for attention, and inspired speculation concerning his slayer's identity. The Hunkpapa warrior Rain-in-the-Face had allegedly said that he would kill Tom Custer and cut his heart out for arresting him. It was naturally assumed that he had done so. No less a bard than Longfellow duly immortalized the tale, though poetically substituting Tom's better-known brother as the victim of *The Revenge of Rain-in-the-Face*:

> But the foeman fled in the
>     night
> And Rain-in-the-Face, in his
>     flight
> Uplifted high in air
> As a ghastly trophy, bore
> The brave heart, that beat no
>     more,
> Of the white chief with
>     yellow hair.

Even Mrs. Custer accepted the tale of how "that incarnate fiend" had removed the heart of "our brother Tom," though she made no mention of the allegation that he had eaten it as well.

The subject of this legend had been born around 1836, near the forks of the Cheyenne River in Dakota. Rain-in-the-Face's name was apparently inspired by a childhood nosebleed, the blood streaking, rain-like, the paint on his face; on a later occasion, real rain similarly streaked his paint and reinforced the name. (Like many warriors,

Rain-in-the-Face had more than one name, also being known as He Who Takes the Enemy.) Though known as a valiant warrior who had borne unflinchingly the pain of a particularly gruelling Sun Dance, he was not destined to become an outstanding war leader.

During the Yellowstone expedition, as two 7th Cavalry companies battled an estimated 300 Sioux and Cheyenne, a sutler and veterinary surgeon wandering some distance away were slain by a small party—including Rain-in-the-Face. In December of 1874, General Custer, learning that an Indian boasting of the killings was at the Standing Rock agency, requested General Terry's permission to arrest him. Since no court had military or civil jurisdiction over acts committed by Indians in the Yellowstone country, the arrest has been seen as an Army attempt to embarrass the Indian Bureau for failure to control its charges. Inside the trader's store Tom Custer personally seized the warrior from behind to prevent him from using his Winchester.

The captive not only admitted the killings to General Custer, but would do so later to other whites. While to some the slaying of two unarmed men seemed peculiarly horrible, artist and photographer DeCost Smith, noting the Hunkpapa's "evident pride" in crushing one man's head with a stone, surmised that to Rain-in-the-Face their helpless state merely signified his own good "medicine." While he could not logically be expected to recognize such "noncombatants," especially with a fight raging nearby, the "murderer" stayed lodged in the post guardhouse.

But what could Custer do with him? The problem was solved, with or without Custer's foreknowledge, in April of 1875. The Lakota—apparently in collusion with his guard, but perhaps benefitting from an outside effort to free a fellow prisoner—ducked through a hole in the wall.

When he finally surrendered in 1880 with a band of Hunkpapas, he was a cripple, and would remain on crutches for the rest of his life; while carving out a pistol ball he had evidently shot into his own leg while hunting buffalo, he had also cut several tendons. Initially fearful that he might be punished for his Yellowstone exploit, Rain-in-the-Face generally denied either killing Tom Custer or mutilating his body. But later one enterprising journalist managed to prime him with white man's "holy water" into claiming he had done both: "I leaped from my pony and cut out his heart and bit a piece out of it and spit it in his face."

As became a warrior, Rain-in-the-Face sought status and recognition. But his physical condition, and the end of Plains warfare, would not permit him to achieve renown among his own people through feats of arms. He would instead enjoy a strange celebrity among his conquerors as Tom Custer's slayer— typical of an era which would at

once subjugate and degrade the Indian, portray him as a vengeful savage, and make of him a curious combination of trophy and hero. The more "hostile" an Indian's past, the better, whether the red man was Sitting Bull touring with Buffalo Bill or Geronimo riding in Theodore Roosevelt's inaugural parade. His brother Shave Head, an Indian police sergeant, would die during the attempt to arrest Sitting Bull; but it was Rain-in-the-Face who would be remembered. And as with Sitting Bull, men were glad to shake the hand of one of Custer's conquerors—as though the terrible carnage had already dissolved into a nostalgic twilight of myth and dream.

Those who got to know the man found him decidedly unfiendish. "His features were very noble," wrote DeCost Smith, "and he had a pleasant smile and twinkle of the eye when pleased or animated." Smith concluded that his reputation had been "forced upon him by his admiring enemies, and probably was undeserved." This had its benefits, however, and as a "youthful, good-looking 'fiend incarnate,' it was inevitable that he should attract some white woman," though Smith declined to name the lady. Photographer D.F. Barry, acquainted with most of the more prominent Lakota warriors, wrote that "the savage, Rain-in-the-Face, we hear of nowadays in song and story," was "the truest friend I ever had, either red or white man."

When in 1887 Rain-in-the-Face expressed a wish to attend school in the east, poet John Greenleaf Whittier celebrated in verse this apparent evidence of his reformation. Standing Rock agent John McLaughlin, however, suspecting "Rain" of wishing to see the East's cities, noted that he had also pressed to be exhibited by a showman or museum, "as he is a little vain and somewhat inflated with his own importance." His rebuffed attempts at a more cosmopolitan life left Rain-in-the-Face depressed and confined to a dreary reservation.

Only when the death of Sitting Bull left him the most famous Little Bighorn survivor did Rain-in-the-Face manage to launch a show-business career, appearing at the Chicago's World's Fair in 1893 and touring with Buffalo Bill—where one man attempted to avenge Custer by murdering him. Years later, DeCost Smith found him at Coney Island selling his autograph, a transaction he had previously de-nounced when practiced by Sitting Bull. When a sightseer asked uncertainly, "Do you think that is really Rain-in-the-Face?", Smith could hardly blame him. "His hero, the 'fiend incarnate,' was disillusioned, apathetic. Having seen the wonders of the white man's world—or so he thought—and the ocean, there were no more worlds to conquer."

Rain-in-the-Face died in 1905, offering the deathbed comment, "Many lies have been told of me." He had been, wrote Barry, "a great Indian" and "grossly maligned in some respects." A number of men who had viewed Captain Custer's body would vainly labor to point out that, despite its evisceration, the heart had *not* been removed. But the mysteriously cherished legend would long endure in the minds— and hearts—of the perverse palefaces.

# CHAPTER VII

# An Army Humbled

## June-September 1876

$O$n the afternoon of 22 June 1876, the steamer *Far West* had begun its slow push against the Yellowstone's current, carrying General Terry, Colonel Gibbon and Major Brisbin on toward the Big Horn. That night the Montana column camped beside the river, the cavalry bivouacked a mile and a half above the doughboys.

Also on 22 June, the men of Crook's Wyoming column, possibly under the gaze of enemy scouts, continued to fish and expend ammunition in hunting while awaiting supplies and reinforcements from Fort Fetterman. What reporter Finerty termed "a kind of informal 'post'" was established, or declared established, "under the name of 'Camp Cloud Peak' (Goose Creek is not sufficiently heroic it would appear), so that our scouting parties can draw for supplies whenever they get run short which will be pretty often." Presumably Crook would move at some point, though the prospects for a quick victory seemed dimmed. As Finerty wrote, "Nobody expected that Crook was going to make an all-summer affair of this campaign, but it looks very like it now."

Others remained sanguine, Crook's aide Captain Bourke predicting that if the expected 5th Cavalry and other elements pitched in, "the Sioux will be crushed ere the summer solstice." Not that they were vital to success, of course, but it was "very desirable that all the cavalry and most of the

251

infantry of the Department of the Platte may have an opportunity to share in the glory...."

On 23 June General Sheridan, having returned to Chicago from his trips to Laramie and Fort Robinson, received the telegram from Cheyenne informing him of the Rosebud battle. To General Sherman he wrote that Terry's movements, as indicated in his dispatch of 12 June, led him "to believe that he is at or near the Rosebud about this time. He has formed a junction with Gibbon, and will, undoubtedly, take up the fight which Crook discontinued....I communicated to Gen. Crook by courier from Fort Fetterman the position and intentions of Gen. Terry." Sheridan also wired Fort Lincoln, so that Arikara couriers could ensure that Terry was equally well-informed of Crook's location and recent adventures.

That same day 1st Lieutenant Gustavus Doane, with an advance party of Company G, 2nd Cavalry, spotted buffalo and Sioux hunters along the Yellowstone's south bluffs. That afternoon, the 2nd camped about two miles above Fort Pease, the 7th Infantry and wagons a mile below it. The *Far West*, making slow progress, moored about 15 miles below the fort, while Colonel Gibbon took to his bed with what was thought to be "hepatic colic of the stomach and bowels" and Brisbin assumed temporary command.

On 24 June Terry ordered Captain Thaddeus Kirtland's Company B, 7th Infantry, to stay at the base camp to guard wagons and supplies. The rest of the command, ferried across the Yellowstone and supplied by mules for eight days, would march southward. Unsure whether the Sioux were to be found up the valley of the Tullock or along the Little Bighorn, Terry sent Crow scouts to explore the former, with orders, wrote diarist Bradley, to "proceed until they found a Sioux village or a recent trail." The Crows returned that night, having found a buffalo wounded by a Sioux arrow a mere six miles up the Tullock. Belittling the importance of this "momentous intelligence," since the beast might have been wounded far from any camp, Bradley commented, perhaps unfairly, that the Crows knew this, but "were glad of any subterfuge to return to the protection of the command."

*Custer Hill. An iron fence encloses the markers for the Custer broth-
ers and other men of the "Last Stand" group.*
**Photograph by Mary Minton.**

That morning Bradley sent six Crows up Tullock's Fork,
following with the other scouts and mounted infantry. Terry
was to follow, moving up the valley to a point a few miles
short of where Captain Ball's April scout had struck it on its
return ride. The command would then turn right, crossing the
divide to strike the Little Bighorn—which might have easily
have been reached during Custer's fight. But, apparently at

the suggestion of Brisbin and scout "Muggins" Taylor, the route was changed after three miles—resulting in an exhausting march west toward the Big Horn, into a "labyrinth" of hills and ravines. (The presence of officers from the April scout should have prevented this unexplained deviation, and it has even been suggested that Terry was *not* anxious to reach the suspected village *before* Custer struck it.) Returning to the column only to be dispatched to examine the Little Bighorn valley (from the wrong ridge), Bradley later learned that his six Crows had in fact seen the valley—and above it a disturbingly heavy smoke.

Terry now resolved upon a night march, though the infantry was "played out." When Brisbin proposed going on alone with the cavalry, Terry insisted on coming too. "We struggled on through the wet, mud and darkness," wrote Brisbin, "guided at times by the flashes of lightning." The Crows' guidance was not requested, and as the men stumbled due south across the badlands, the cry of "The battery is missing!" sparked a search which finally located Low's Gatlings rolling innocently onward a mile or so away. The soldiers climbed a narrow ridge only to find themselves on a bluff above the Big Horn too steep to descend, and the Crow scout Little Face was finally called upon to lead them back the way they had come.

The 7th Infantry set out at about 0400 on the 26th. Bradley, probing ahead with his scouts in the valley of the Little Bighorn, saw heavy smoke, and found the tracks of four unshod ponies. He sent men back to report, then took up the ponies' trail. Awakened by the messengers' arrival, Terry began the march without waiting for the infantry, visible some distance away. Upon finally gaining the ridge, Terry gazed out into the Little Bighorn Valley below. It was against this ridgeline that Lieutenant Bradley saw Terry and Gibbon, and galloped forward to meet them.

Finding bits of gear left by the men he had trailed, Bradley had been surprised to recognize the property of Crows who had gone with Custer. Three of them, after leaving the scene of what they were sure was Custer's final battle, had hastily crossed to the stream's left bank upon seeing Bradley's dust.

Noting the trio watching them from a safe distance, Bradley's scouts joined in an exchange of smoke signals. Finally Little Face and one or two others talked with the fugitives across the stream, the others waiting on the bluffs. Then Bradley's men turned back with loud cries—a song of mourning for the dead:

> Little Face in particular wept with a bitterness of anguish such as I have rarely seen. For awhile he could not speak, but at last composed himself and told his story in a choking voice, broken with frequent sobs. As he proceeded, the Crows one by one broke off from the group of listeners and going aside a little distance sat down alone, weeping and chanting that dreadful mourning song, and rocking their bodies to and fro. They were the first listeners to the horrid story of the Custer massacre, and, outside of the relatives and personal friends of the fallen, there were none in this whole horrified nation of forty millions of people to whom the tidings brought greater grief...

Part of their grief must have stemmed from the refugees' claim that Half-Yellow-Face and White Swan were among the slain, and that the missing Curley had probably also perished. Since the three had not lingered to witness the death struggle, they (like Trumpeter Martin) probably recounted what they thought *must* have happened. Yet Bradley believed. He could still hope that they had exaggerated: "But that there had been a disaster—a terrible disaster—I felt assured." He resolved to report personally to Terry.

The Crows' story was met with shock, then disbelief, and dense smoke far up the river was dismissed as evidence of triumphant troopers burning a village. Some on Terry's staff insisted, wrote Bradley, that the alleged disaster "was wholly improbable, nay, impossible; if a battle had been fought, which was condescendingly admitted might have happened, then Custer was victorious, and these three Crows were dastards who had fled without awaiting the result and told this story to excuse their cowardice. General Terry took no part in these criticisms, but sat on his horse silent and thoughtful, biting his lower lip...." Finally he ordered the advance.

Leaving behind the grief-stricken Crows (soon to gallop off

sans permission toward their agency, along with interpreter Bravo), Bradley and a party of 11 men took the advance, after sending 2 "citizens" by different routes in the hope of finding Custer. Coming across five stray Indian ponies, Bradley deployed his men as skirmishers after seeing three or four riders several miles to his front. Then one of Terry's messengers galloped back down the valley, announcing an encounter with numerous Indians.

With Terry and Gibbon riding to the front, the column advanced slowly, ready for battle. Bradley's men moved up the valley to the left, while Lieutenant Roe's cavalry company rode to their right. Single horsemen and small groups were visible, and Roe spotted, as if suddenly emerging from the earth, "a perfect skirmish line of mounted Indians." To its rear appeared some 300 or 400 Indians—and what was "from all appearances, a troop of cavalry," advancing by twos with guidon flying. A second troop joined the first on the ridge; then two men, "as though it might be the Captain and Lieutenant," joined the troops.

Dr. Paulding vainly protested that *all* of these horsemen were Indians. A more convincing argument arrived as bullets whizzed near three soldiers advancing with a white handkerchief on a carbine barrel. As the Indians broke up their line, uttering war-whoops and circling their horses, Roe turned and headed toward Terry.

Bradley, seeing Indians galloping into the timber at a narrow point in the valley, feared an ambuscade:

> ...in my whole career as a soldier never did anything call for so much nerve as the riding slowly up with eleven men, half a mile from the rest of the column, on this body of ambushed warriors. My men sat their saddles with pale faces but closed lips with stern determination, expecting in a few minutes more to be shot down, but resolved not to flinch though the cost were death.

Bradley's men were still nerving themselves "for the expected annihilation" when the column halted a quarter mile or so from the timber. Four ponies emerged from the woods, but the waiting Sioux refrained from firing as two civilians rode forth to capture them. Terry decided to form camp as

*Custer's dead cavalry, as depicted by Sioux participant Red Horse in 1881. "The Sioux took the clothing off the dead and dressed themselves in it, recalled the artist.*

dusk fell, forbidding fires and picketing his stock within a hollow square of men. They kept their clothing on, recalled 7th Infantry private George Berry. "Each man slept with rifle beside him, and each one had a belt full of cartridges." But, said 2nd Cavalry trooper William White, "The average hours of sleep per man were greatly diminished"—though no one actually thought Custer dead.

With morning, while Bradley's mounted doughboys scouted, Gibbon's men, inadvertently passing Custer's battlefield east of the river, stumbled across the first evidence of a great hostile camp. It seemed as though the villagers had fled hastily—leaving behind lodgepoles, buffalo robes, and kettles. But these were more likely items from households suffering men slain, abandoned along with their lodges. One tipi held the bodies of three warriors, another five, sacrificed ponies lying without. Other bodies lay on scaffolds.

Dr. Paulding picked up a pair of gloves marked "Yates, 7th Cav.," and a bloodied buckskin shirt bearing the name Porter, a bullet hole beneath its right shoulder. The feet of boots were found, their tops cut away, and even wounded horses bearing the 7th's brand. But there was more grisly evidence of disaster—including the severed heads of white men, and a human heart, still attached to the lariat used to drag it along the ground.

Gibbon, peering through field glasses, could see dark objects on a distant hill, which he thought might be animals or stubby trees, but which seemed to increase in number as they were observed. As Terry's men marched up the valley in two columns, Gibbon could see three horsemen, apparently watching. They descended to a lower hill, but there halted.

They were still visible when Lieutenant Bradley returned from his scout and, recounted Gibbon,

> rode up to where General Terry and I sat upon our horses, and his voice trembled as he said, "I have a very sad report to make. I have counted one hundred and ninety-seven bodies lying in the hills!" "White men?" was the first question asked. "Yes, white men." A look of horror was upon every face, and for a moment no one spoke. There could be no question now. The Crows were right, and Custer had met with a disaster, but the extent of it was still a matter of doubt...

The night of the 26th, Fred Gerard and Billy Jackson had succeeded in making their way to Reno Hill and safety, followed early that morning by Private O'Neill and Lieutenant DeRudio—who had also seen from the timber the light-hearted parade of guidon-bearing Indians dressed in dead soldiers' uniforms. With daylight, Reno's men looked out onto the valley and saw only a few abandoned ponies grazing in the distance. But Major Reno had his men hold their positions, fearing a trap.

Reno prepared a message for General Terry, writing that "I am very much crippled and cannot possibly pursue." He had heard or seen nothing of Custer since his orders to charge: "I have fought thousands and can still hold my own, but I cannot leave here on account of the wounded. Send me medical aid at once and rations." But Reno's Indian messengers soon returned, saying that there were still warriors in the area.

At about 0900 a column of dust, slowly advancing, inspired

new fears of an Indian assault. Buglers sounded assembly, troopers filled canteens and camp kettles with water. Wrote Godfrey: "An hour of suspense followed; but from the slow advance we concluded that they were our own troops....We looked in vain for a gray-horse troop. It could not be Custer; it must then be Crook, for if it were Custer, Terry would be with him. Cheer after cheer was given for Crook." Lieutenants Hare and Wallace were ordered to contact the troops, advising them on the best route to Reno Hill.

It was these officers—and an unknown man, perhaps Reno—who had been observed by Gibbon on the bluffs. As they finally rode forward, he dispatched an officer to meet them. Soon, wrote Gibbon, "Hands were grasped almost in silence, but we questioned eagerly with our eyes, and one of the first things they uttered was, 'Is General Custer with you?'"

Terry rode to Reno Hill, while in the black and smoking valley Gibbon attempted to select a bivouac with enough grass. He began to discover dead cavalry mounts, and near one of them a dead soldier—killed during Reno's retreat. Captain Walter Clifford, of Company E, 7th Infantry, wrote of a camp:

> surrounded with ghastly remains of the recent butchery. The days are scorching hot and still, and the air is thick with the stench of the festering bodies. We miss the laughing gaiety that usually attends a body of soldiery even on the battlefield. A brooding sorrow hangs like a pall over our every thought. It seems too horrible for belief—that we must wake and find it only a shuddering dream. Every sound comes to us in a muffled monotone, and a dull, dogged feeling of revenge seems to be the prevailing sentiment. The repulsive looking green flies that have been feasting on the swollen bodies of the dead...crawl over the neck and face, into eyes and ears, under the sleeves with a greedy eagerness and such clammy, sticky feet as to drive taste and inclination for food away... •
> Let us bury our dead and flee from this rotting atmosphere.

Arriving at Reno Hill, Bradley asked for his friend Godfrey, who recalled immediately asking about Custer's whereabouts: "He replied: 'I don't know, but I suppose he was killed, as we counted 197 dead bodies. I don't suppose any escaped.' We were simply dumfounded. This was the first intimation we had of his fate. It was hard to realize; it did seem impossible." Reno's men, unknowing, greeted Terry's arrival with prolonged cheering. But the "grave countenance of the General awed the men to silence...."

Reno's men numbly busied themselves in preparing to move, and in destroying whatever surplus property an Indian might salvage. Wounded men were transferred to the Montana column bivouac. Not until the morning of the 28th did they leave their position to bury Custer's men. Godfrey and other officers rode to a high vantage point from which the whole field was visible, and viewed the distant bodies. Horribly white they seemed; but some, at least, had blackened in the sun, or would do so before the day was over.

The remains of Custer's five companies, over 200 officers and men, lay scattered over a wide area. Most were stark naked, others wearing a few odd bits of clothing with the owner's name mysteriously sliced away. Some men still wore boot legs, the tops cut off. On the western slope of the northern end of Battle Ridge, on a high point later known as Custer or Last Stand Hill, Godfrey counted 42 bodies and 39 dead cavalry horses, some apparently shot to form a rude breastwork. Near the top of the hill lay Custer, his brother Tom, Captain Yates, Lieutenants Cooke, Smith and Reily, Dr. Lord, and Custer's personal guidon-bearer, Sergeant Hughes. Farther down the slope lay Boston Custer and Autie Reed. Lieutenant John Carland, 6th Infantry, told of Terry's reaction to the sight: "As he looked down upon the noble general the tears coursed down his face as he exclaimed: 'The flower of the army is gone at last.'"

At the highest point of the ridge two dead soldiers lay naked, one across the other. Custer's body, also naked, was found in a sitting position between and leaning against them, his upper right arm along and on the topmost soldier's body, his right forearm and hand supporting his head as though during one of his catnaps in the field. On this part of the field the Indians had apparently done their best to pick up spent cartridges. But Sergeant Ryan would find beneath the body four or five brass casings from his commander's Remington rifle, while Carland wrote that "we found 17 cartridge shells by his side, where he kept them off until the last moment."

Custer had been shot in the head and breast, though eyewitnesses apparently differed on the details when describing his wounds. "He looked as natural as if sleeping," testified Moylan. Asked why Custer had been spared mutilation, some Indians would later say it was out of respect for the great chief; but perhaps it was mere chance, especially given the widespread belief that they had again defeated Crook's command. Few, if any, would have recognized in that stripped, once-powerful body, with its short hair and receding hairline, the vigorous soldier-chief known to them as "Long Hair."

The condition of Custer's body was in striking contrast to many others. Thirty-year-old Lieutenant Cooke, doubtless Wooden Leg's victim, had had one of his great Dundreary whiskers skinned from his cheek, hideously exposing the teeth. Perhaps 20 feet from his brother lay the corpse of Tom Custer, face down, disemboweled, split down through the muscles of arms and thighs, and with features pressed out of shape—the head, in Ryan's description, "smashed as flat as the palm of one's hand." He was identified by the initials "T.W.C." tattooed on his arm. Captain Moylan, brother-in-law to Captain James Calhoun, felt obliged to explain in painful detail to Margaret Custer the condition in which he found her husband, three of her four brothers, and her nephew: "I think most of what you have heard of the mutilation of Tom's body, except perhaps cutting out his heart, was true." Perhaps Tom, the only man to win two Medals of Honor during the Civil War, was alive when the carving started; or perhaps he was the buckskin clad, tattooed soldier whom the Cheyenne White Shield saw being stripped. "He died," wrote George Grinnell, "with his pistol in his hand."

An effort was made to identify the slain officers. Keogh, lying in a slight depression among at least 18 dead of his Company I—who had apparently rallied about their chief in

what one witness termed a "hollow square"—was supposedly spared mutilation because of a Catholic medal about his
neck. Lieutenant Gibson, handed a gutta-percha sleeve but-
ton as a means of identifying McIntosh's remains, replied,
"Yes, I think it will—it is my brother-in-law." Lieutenant
Crittenden was ironically spared a nameless grave by an
arrow shot into his glass eye, its crystal fragments making
identification possible. Lieutenant Harrington and Dr. Lord
were never identified, nor was the body of Lieutenant Jack
Sturgis, son of the regiment's colonel—though his head was
supposedly found in the Indian village.

Mark Kellogg was one of those few bodies which lay fully
clothed, perhaps an early casualty overlooked after a warrior
briefly paused to remove his scalp and an ear. Others had
merely been scalped, or prodigally riddled with arrows, or
maimed incidentally—perhaps bashed in the head or
chopped across the brow or eyes during the slaughter of the
wounded. Still others had been elaborately butchered. Private
William D. Nugent, having heard that there had been little
mutilation of his comrades, countered:

> It would be very difficult to convince one of the burial details
> that there could have been much more mutilation perpetrated.
> Will give a description of the first we buried. First he was
> scalped; the skull was bare to the ears; the crown of the head was
> chopped out; his cap was put into the cavity. The body was nude
> between the waist and the throat. There were twelve or fifteen
> places where no doubt a spear or knife had been thrust to the
> hollow. Blunt arrows were driven in and left in the wounds. The
> bodies were hastily buried, or at any rate covered with dirt.

"In a great many instances," confessed Sergeant Ryan,
"their arms and legs protruded." Inverted cartridge cases,
each containing a name and fitted onto sticks, were placed
over officers' graves, of which Custer's, at perhaps 18 inches
deep, was the most elaborate.

Starting late that afternoon to escape the worst heat, Terry's
men marched downstream toward the Little Bighorn's mouth
and the *Far West*'s expected berth, the wounded in an assort-
ment of hand litters, mule litters and Indian-style travois.

When couriers finally located the *Far West* about a half mile above the river's mouth, they found that the scout Curley had reached the steamer on the 27th. Unable to speak English, he was forced to rely on groans, hair-pulling gestures and a rough drawing to convey his message of doom. His listeners, in so far as they understood his story, tended to discount it—until Terry's couriers arrived.

On the morning of the 28th, Terry dispatched Captain Ball's 2nd Cavalry company to determine the direction of the triumphant Indians. Following their trail directly south toward the Big Horn Mountains for some 12 to 15 miles, Ball found the trail dividing, one group forking to the southeast, the other to the southwest—both groups burning the grass behind them. Marching back, Ball found a heavy lodgepole trail, a few days old, leading down the Little Bighorn. To the whites, it seemed that at least three large bands of Indians had joined the great Sioux camp just before Custer struck.

Ending a hideously jumbled march over rough and cactus-studded country, the command began loading the wounded onto the *Far West* shortly before sunrise of the 30th, fires burning along the path to illuminate the ravine. The men camped along the bank and prepared to head for the base camp at the Big Horn's mouth.

Later that afternoon Captain Marsh, having arrived at the mouth of the stream, tied his boat up to the bank of the Yellowstone to await the arrival of Terry's combined forces and ferry them to the north bank. The column reached the rendezvous point on 2 July, to await supplies and reinforcements.

Along with fourteen slightly wounded men, the steamer landed Captain Baker's infantry company, who were replaced by seventeen 7th Cavalry troopers without mounts. On 3 July, the *Far West* steamed out for Bismarck, and the next morning Private William George, the first of five men to die of wounds, was buried at the Powder River base camp. There a number of Arikaras had already told their stories of the Custer disaster, and Major Moore received orders to move his men up to the mouth of the Big Horn.

At 2300 on 5 July—just 54 hours after starting its record-breaking journey of 710 miles—the *Far West*, flag at half-mast, derrick and jack staff draped in black, reached Bismarck. As crew members went ashore to tell citizens of the incredible catastrophe, Captain Marsh hurried to the telegraph office. And at Fort Abraham Lincoln, Captain William S. McCashey, 20th Infantry, requested his fellow officers' assistance in a grim duty: breaking the news to the many new widows at the post. At the Custer home, where the officers' wives had gathered, he requested that they assemble in the parlor.

By 3 July the Bozeman *Times* had already rushed into print the first newspaper account of the fight, for scout Muggins Taylor, dodging warriors on an exhausting ride from the Big Horn base camp, had helped relay the news to the Montana settlements. On 4 July it was telegraphed east from Helena, and Sheridan and Sherman, in Philadelphia on the 100th anniversary of American independence, found themselves dismissing an Associated Press wire story alleging Custer's destruction. "I don't believe it," proclaimed Sherman. "And I don't want to believe it, if I can help it."

Wiring Chicago, Sheridan found that no information on the supposed disaster had been sent in, for Terry's initial report, left at the Bozeman telegraph office on the 3rd, would inexplicably be sent by *mail* two days later. On the 5th, Chicago received and forwarded Terry's second report, dated 2 July and marked "Confidential;" Sheridan learned not only of his friend's death, but of the complete annihilation of five companies of soldiers at the hands of Indians. The thought of such a slaughter had seemed scarcely conceivable in this progressive year of 1876—a reversion to an earlier time, perhaps. Yet it had happened.

"I think I owe it to myself to put you more fully in possession of the facts of the late operation," began Terry's "confidential" report—which quickly found its way into newsprint. Yet the report seemed less concerned with recounting the details of the fight than with clearing Terry of responsibility for its results. Terry's plan now became a matter of the two columns troops cooperating in attacking any Indians on the Little Big-horn. It was, said Terry, the only plan "which promised to bring the infantry into action, and I desired to make sure of things by getting up every available man."

But, alas, Custer had force-marched his men in following the trail, then attacked on his own rather than making the "wide swoop" which would have permitted both commands to strike on the imaginary target date of 26 June. Ignoring the fact that, largely due to Terry's misguided detour into the badlands, he had not arrived until the 27th, he assured Sheridan: "I do not tell you this to cast any reflection upon Custer, for whatever errors he may have committed he has paid the penalty, and you cannot regret his loss more than I do, but I feel that our plan must have been successful had it been carried out, and I desire you to know the facts." Naturally, Terry also desired reinforcements.

Terry's 27 June report had mentioned no reliance on cooperation in any actual fight, and the hope expressed even earlier—that *one* of two columns might strike the village—had apparently been forgotten. But now Terry attempted to attribute Custer's defeat not merely to his "misapprehension that the Sioux were running," but to his alleged violation of the plan. Even Sheridan seems to have implicitly accepted this notion, commenting to Sherman on 7 July that "Terry's column was sufficiently strong to have handled the Indians, if Custer had waited for the junction."

Yet the evidence makes it clear not only that Custer was expected to attack, but that Montana column officers feared his success would leave them little to do. As for there being too many Indians, even Terry's second report stated that he shared Custer's confidence that the 7th alone would suffice. Sheridan himself endorsed the same notion indirectly even while blaming Custer's actual method of attack. He stated that if Custer had "waited until his regiment was closed up," the Indians could not have defeated him. "I do not attribute Col. Custer's action to either recklessness or to want of judgement, but to misapprehension and a super-abundance of courage." And while the *New York Times* reported that both Sherman and Sheridan thought Custer "rashly imprudent" in attacking, the former privately commented that once he found himself in the presence of the Indians, he could do nothing else.

Blame, in any event, could be shared. Sherman himself came to feel that Crook's withdrawal from the Rosebud and subsequent hibernation had contributed heavily to Custer's defeat. "Surely in Grand Strategy we ought not now to allow savages to beat us," he proclaimed, "but in this instance they did."

The situation was even more embarrassing than Sherman painted it, for in fact, the United States, which a little more than 10 years before had fielded the world's mightiest fighting force, had been bested by an enemy with literally no strategy at all—and no leaders capable of giving a tactical command in the confidence that it would be obeyed. The divisional commander was one of the Civil War's greatest heroes, and his field commanders had all won glory in its battles. Yet the Army had been humbled by men only a few generations removed from the Stone Age, whose chief assets were raw courage, skill as individual warriors, and a belief in their own power—and whose total fighting strength was quite likely inferior to that fielded by Sheridan. Ironically, as Sheridan's biographer Paul Andrew Hutton has written, "the Great Sioux War was the only conventional war the army ever fought against the trans-Mississippi Indians. It was the type of conflict these Civil war veterans were supposedly used to, where large, massed bodies of troops maneuvered for control of battlefields. Reynolds, Crook and Custer were simply outmaneuvered and defeated in quite conventional battles."

Why had Sheridan's campaign climaxed in the Custer disaster? Given the premise that the Army had to force a confrontation with warlike but wary tribesmen whose only strategic points were their families and portable villages, a strategy of converging columns seemed to offer the best hope of bringing them to battle. With persistence, as the Army had shown in 1868 and 1874, even the heavy columns of a conventional army could run these mobile targets to earth. But the premise was entwined with several popular fallacies, including the fallacy that what had seemed true in the past would still be true, or perhaps even more true, in 1876.

These assumptions were not wholly baseless. Whether defiantly hostile or simply declared as such by Washington, the Sioux and Cheyenne displayed no desire for a head-on confrontation with soldiers, and would indeed prove elusive. But the notion that they would invariably flee if not cornered did not hold up. At the Rosebud, it was the Indians who attacked the troops; at the Little Bighorn, they felt sufficiently unimpressed to ignore signs of troops in the area, and rallied quickly after being attacked.

Perhaps, if Crook or Custer had succeeded in launching a well-timed attack in full force, a large camp could have been captured and its warriors stampeded. But as events unfolded, traditional Plains war-making came to the soldiers' aid in other ways: had the warriors been more "conventionally minded," they might have annihilated the entire 7th Cavalry before Terry's appearance, or even prepared a warm reception for Terry himself.

While much of the warriors' confidence must have stemmed from awareness of their own numbers, the soldiers' knowledge of the "wild" population was obscured by several factors. Agents were tempted to overestimate those Indians actually on the reservations; while padding the rolls offered obvious opportunities for graft, extra rations might also help succor Indians left hungry by a stingy government. Sheridan's knowledge of the Indians' logistic needs had convinced him that any large force could not long cohere. But Custer had met them just when such a force did coalesce.

Yet Sheridan can hardly be blamed for delusions infecting an entire army. Even officers with extensive Plains experience were obsessed by the danger not of catching too many Indians, but of letting too many escape, and Terry himself, absorbing an early report of 3,000 hostile lodges, had expressed confidence. On the tactical level, this spelled disaster. Custer's dilemma may have been lain in reconciling what he thought he knew with what his scouts told him of enemy numbers—inducing, in Robert Church's recent analysis, an "intellectual vertigo," like that of a pilot whose senses refute his instrument panel.

Withal, Custer seems to have been more sensitive to the uses of intelligence than his colleagues. Gibbon received precise information, only to squander it, while Crook, convinced that his foes would fight less fiercely than his old Apache enemies, managed to adjust the evidence to fit preconceived notions; faced with hundreds of attacking warriors, he remained fixated on a village which simply *had* to be within easy reach.

As for Terry's plan, it seemed to display an odd faith in the Indians limiting their movements to suit Terry. But had the trail followed by Custer turned to the east, or even split, with some Indians moving east and others heading west or south, he might have fought a battle far from any possible assistance. Rather than launch long-range scouts to gather fresh data on Sioux movements, Terry preferred to rush the plan into motion, dispatch Custer, and hope for Indian cooperation. When this failed to materialize, Terry, and his defenders, began to revise events. Not only did they write as though a coordinated attack had been reserved for 26 June (and as though the idea of Custer striking alone had never occurred to them), but also as though the approximate location of the village had been known. Hindsight and disaster made it easy. As General James B. Fry gently suggested, it was "highly probable that the plan when Custer moved had neither the force nor importance which it subsequently acquired in Terry's mind."

Concerning Custer's conduct of the battle itself, President Grant's singularly graceless comment almost matched his spiteful treatment of the living man. "I regard Custer's massacre," remarked the hero of Cold Harbor, "as a sacrifice of troops, brought on by Custer himself, that was wholly unnecessary—wholly unnecessary." Perhaps. But surprisingly, and in contrast to the military and civilian investigations launched following the Fetterman disaster, the government held no formal inquiry into the causes of defeat. The closest even the Army came was the Reno court of inquiry in 1879, reluctantly convened at Reno's own request. Custer, in effect, was left as the prime suspect by default.

Yet the debate would rage on, the participants themselves divided. Writing in 1892, for example, then-Captain Edward Godfrey ascribed the defeat to "the overpowering numbers of the enemy and their unexpected cohesion," Reno's "panic rout from the valley," and (admittedly an unknown factor) the "defective extraction of the empty cartridge-shells from the carbines." But Reno would blame the defeat on Custer's "several great blunders," including disobedience of orders, while then-Captain Luther Hare believed that Custer had erred in dividing his command in the face of superior numbers. "With the results of that fight before him," he wrote privately, "how any one can seek to defend the tactics used is an enigma to me."

Whether or not he evaded his instructions—and the very fact that his command packed rations for 15 days confirms Terry's awareness that he might find "sufficient reason" to deviate from them—Custer's decision to pursue the trail was militarily sound. Nor does the evidence justify the charge that he rushed his men in an exhausting grab for glory; even 24 June's tiring night march was intended to precede a day of rest and regrouping. That the 7th met the enemy alone could have surprised no one. As Lieutenant Maguire wrote in his preliminary report: "Each one who could not accompany them envied their good luck and the chance they would have of breaking up the Sioux Nation. Not for one moment did the thought cross anyone's mind that aught but an easy victory awaited them."

That Custer would be outnumbered, if not to the degree actually encountered, was also expected. But like his fellow officers, Custer knew nothing of Crook's disillusionment on the Rosebud, and initially, at least, believed that a bold assault against undisciplined warriors would overcome any disparity. In launching Reno's attack, he mistakenly believed that he had been discovered. But all evidence before him led naturally to such a conclusion.

If we accept the premise that a unified 7th Cavalry could

have rolled up superior Sioux numbers (and this may sell Sioux tenacity short), Custer's division may appear a fatal error. But Colonel Miles, even after the Little Bighorn fight, would also divide his command in defeating the Sioux. Perhaps timing and a failure of the proverbial "Custer luck" made all the difference; if the 7th's four elements were too far-flung when the fight began, it can be explained by Custer's need to rapidly probe the terrain and his enemy's location. The resultant "reconnaissance in force" left him to develop his tactical method as circumstances and knowledge dictated.

Even sending Benteen to the left, seemingly too far from any likely action, can be justified as insurance against Indians on the upper reaches of the Little Bighorn escaping southward or falling upon Custer from behind. The sense of an isolated Benteen could only be reinforced by what many have considered his laggard pace in returning to the main trail and reacting to the sounds of battle. As for Custer's presumed intention of supporting Reno by attacking from a different direction, it was consistent with the concept of sparking panic and blocking at least one path of escape.

But such a two-pronged attack, against great odds, required Reno to maintain contact with the Indians, preferably attacking and keeping them off balance. Though it cost Reno the initiative, halting his charge might have been justified, especially given his fear of a trap. The retreat from the timber is less easily defended, and the manner of it was inexcusable; it not only freed swarms of warriors to engage Custer, but also cost Reno's battalion horrendous casualties, and might easily have ended in its annihilation. One trooper, defending the retreat, gave Reno perhaps the most left-handed compliment in American military history, claiming that if his men had not been commanded by a coward, all would have been killed!

Furthermore, after Benteen had joined Reno, it became the latter's responsibility to rejoin Custer as soon as possible, not so much to "rescue" Custer as simply to commit the bulk of the regiment to the fight. What Reno actually did was neither move resolutely toward Custer nor control his command, as the disorderly movements to and from Weir Point made clear. Of course, such a move toward Custer might well have been too late, or even suicidal. But as Nelson Miles would observe, "No commanding officer can win victories with seven-twelfths of his command remaining out of the engagement when within the sound of his rifle-shots." And as Edgerly recognized, the soldier's code was a demanding one:

> What would have happened if Reno had charged through the village as we found it is a matter of conjecture. I believe that we would have captured and destroyed the village and won a costly victory. I also firmly and positively believe that we should have gone "to the sound of the firing" after Reno and Benteen united, and further I believe that if we had tried to join Custer at that time we would have shared his fate.

Perhaps Custer himself erred not in trying to take on too many Indians, but in *failing* to press home a vigorous attack with his five companies once within sight of the enemy (as some Indian survivors suggested), or in mismanaging his own defense. His thoughts, motives, and final movements are of course still matters of speculation. We cannot even say precisely at what point in the fight he was killed or incapacitated, or whether he could have saved his five companies had he deployed them differently.

But perhaps Custer's worst error lay in failing to communicate his intentions. Whatever Reno's thoughts about Custer's support might have been, his promise's ambiguity allowed Reno to argue that Custer had abandoned him. The 7th was ultimately divided less by its physical fragmentation than by the inability of each of its three combat commanders to know what their counterparts were doing or intending to do. It was a breakdown in communication which might stand as a plausible symbol of the entire campaign.

Following the battle on the Greasy Grass, as the Sioux termed the Little Bighorn, the Indian victors had departed on the afternoon of 26 June, though Terry's troops seem to have inspired little anxiety as they approached from the north. "All of the young men wanted to fight them," according to Wooden Leg. But the leading men decided to avoid the

*Nelson A. Miles—"Bear-Coat"—was perhaps the most successful Indian-fighting soldier of his day. He would later rise to become commanding general of the United States Army.*

soldiers. Traveling south, the Indians spent the night of the 27th near present Lodge Grass, Montana, where two creeks joined the Little Bighorn from southwest and southeast. "All over the camp there were big fires and kill dances all night long," remembered Black Elk, whose cousin Black Wasichu died that night. He also recalled some killsongs which, if actually composed that night, would indicate at least some Sioux knowledge of their foe's identity:

> Long Hair has never returned,
> So his woman is crying, crying.
> Looking over here, she cries.

The Indians moved the next morning, taking one trail to the southeast up Owl Creek and one to the southwest up Lodge Grass Creek, and a third ascending the Little Bighorn. Almost immediately, the great village had begun to break up, with several parties of Cheyennes and Sioux splitting off, the former bound for the Black Hills region, some of the latter for the Rosebud. Some summer roamers turned themselves in at agencies before the end of July.

The main body seems to have gone up Lodge Grass, westward to the Big Horn Mountains, where successive camps were made. Hunting parties ranged far to supply the still-large camp, Wooden Leg going with one party as far as the present Sheridan, Wyoming—near the site of Crook's Goose Creek camp. Traveling southeast, the village reached the head of the Little Bighorn by 7 July. With food scarce, the village continued down the Rosebud in search of game, turning east to Tongue River and thence down to the mouth of Beaver Creek.

The village was finally forced to fragment, not by any pressure from white soldiers, but because no buffalo herds were to be found. One portion turned up Tongue River, the larger one downstream, where it lingered for several weeks. The smaller division finally reached the Powder River above the present Broadus, Montana. The Army still had plenty of free-roaming Indians to worry about.

Preparations to catch them had, of course, begun almost as soon as a stunned nation absorbed the news of the Custer tragedy. The same Congress which had skeletonized the Army passed a 24 July bill authorizing two forts on the Yellowstone (three years after Sheridan had requested them) and the recruiting of cavalry companies to 100 men. This permitted 2,500 additional enlistees—including the 7th's "Custer Avengers," who briefly received a public support denied the typical "Regular." Of greater immediate importance was the Secretary of the Interior's 26 July authorization of military control over all Sioux agencies. Now Sheridan would be able to dismount and disarm the hostiles (and the friendlies too, for that matter), and punish those he deemed ringleaders.

In the meantime, while Terry waited on the Yellowstone for reinforcements, General Crook continued to range from his various Big Horn mountain camps seeking fish and game, if not Sioux warriors. He as yet knew nothing of Custer's defeat, though Captain Mills had seen smoke to the north on 28 June as Terry burned the remains of the Indian camp. On 1 July, while Crook set out on a four-day hunting jaunt into the mountains, Frank Grouard and "Big Bat" Pourier scouted to the head of the Big Horn, hurrying back upon spying a Sioux war party. Informed of this upon his return, Crook ordered a more elaborate scout. On 6 July, the 2nd Cavalry's Lieutenant Frederick W. Sibley rode forth with 25 troopers, as well as Grouard, Pourier, packer Jim Traynor and reporter Finerty. They were to move along the base of the mountains as far as the canon of the Bighorn, inspecting the landscape to the north and west.

But in the foothills, a mere three miles above the main camp, a large band of Sioux and Cheyenne attempted an ambush, firing a heavy but ineffectual volley at the whites. Recognizing Grouard, an Indian cried out: "Do you think there are no men but yours in this country?" By his own account Grouard managed to kill two Cheyenne horsemen with one bullet. "I had often wondered," admitted Finerty, "how a man felt when he thought he saw inevitable, sudden doom upon him. I know it now..."

Led by Grouard from their hiding place among the timbered country at the mountains' fringe, the men of the Sibley Scout abandoned their animals and finally lost their pursuers after two days of unceasing flight through forests, over rocks and across streams. "When they reached camp," wrote Bourke, "the whole party looked more like dead men than soldiers of the army: their clothes were torn into rags, their strength completely gone, and they were faint with hunger and worn out with anxiety and stress."

Crook's command learned of Custer's death from courier Louis Richard on 10 July. Sheridan's dispatch, offering the 5th Cavalry in reinforcement and urging Crook to strike the hostiles hard, inspired Colonel Royall to send a battalion after Crook's overdue hunting party, which rode in that afternoon. Wrote Bourke:

> The same day the Sioux made their appearance, and tried to burn us out: they set fire to the grass near the infantry battalions; and for the next two weeks paid us their respects every night in some manner, trying to stampede stock, burn grass, annoy pickets, and devil the command generally. They did not escape scot-free from these encounters, because we saw in the rocks the

knife left by one wounded man, whose blood stained the soil near it; another night a pony was shot through the body and abandoned; and on still another occasion one of their warriors, killed by a bullet through the brain, was dragged to a ledge of rocks and there hidden, to be found a week or two later by our Shoshone scouts.

Sioux arson, leaving vast areas of grassland burnt black and a sky darkened by lung-filling soot, stopped only when the rains began.

On 11 July, Washakie arrived with 213 Shoshones and two Bannocks, though other Bannock and Ute allies were delayed. And on 12 July, after that morning's Indian raid, three ragged volunteers—7th Infantry privates William Evans, Benjamin F. Stewart and James Bell —rode into camp, each with an identical dispatch from Terry sewn into his blouse. Described as "cool, determined men, and good shots," they had set forth on 9 July and ridden nearly 125 miles through hostile country. All would receive the Medal of Honor.

Crook learned from Terry that the "wholly unexpected" Indian strength made it "important and indeed necessary that we should unite, or at least act in close cooperation." Confessing his ignorance of both Crook's and the enemy's positions, Terry offered to follow any plan Crook devised, and even assured him that should their forces unite, "even in my Department," he would assume "nothing by reason of my seniority, but shall be prepared to cooperate with you in the most cordial and hearty manner, leaving you entirely free to pursue your own course...." He also gave further grim details on Custer's defeat. "Grief, Revenge, Sorrow, and Fear stalked among us," wrote Bourke, who lamented that "when frost comes and not until then can we hope to strike a decisive blow."

On the 13th Colonel Chambers arrived with seven companies of infantry and a supply train. Letters from Sheridan informed Crook that Colonel Wesley Merritt, with 10 companies of the 5th Cavalry, had left Red Cloud Agency, and that as soon as he arrived Crook was to resume the campaign. Crook's replied that the Sioux likely had "three fighting men to my one" and, while denying any inability to whip them with the force at hand, suggested that such a victory would "likely be barren of results." He would therefore wait until Merritt's arrival, ending things with "one crushing blow." However, Crook was in no mood to crush anybody, and for three weeks made no move to either march toward Terry or seriously scout the region.

Sheridan had explained that Terry would command due to seniority, and Crook assured Terry on the 16th that he would "most sincerely" serve under him. Crook also suggested, that Sitting Bull's village was still on the Little Bighorn. But the main hostile body had already left the area, only a comparative handful of summer roamers lingering to harass their contemptible white foes.

Writing again on 23 June, Crook bizarrely proclaimed it "now a pretty well settled fact that the Sioux are in the Big Horn mountains." Crook had not bothered to look for them there, but Washakie had thought that this might be the case. Suggesting that the column first striking the Sioux should somehow hold them until joined by the other (a physical impossibility given the Indians' ability to break off contact at will), he wrote that he might have to "take the aggressive" to avoid being attacked or burnt out. He expressed no such boldness to Sheridan that same day, confessing himself "in constant dread of attack" and "at a loss what to do."

Crook believed that the Sioux would scatter in the face of strength, obliging their pursuers to divide as well. They would then exploit their mobility and knowledge of terrain to "concentrate on and destroy" these smaller forces. Crook seems to have been more worried about the destroying part of his scenario than about the Indians escaping. But after long neglect, he dispatched a scouting party of Shoshones on 25 July. These hastened back after encountering Sioux, but further probing revealed a Big Horn basin empty of Indians, with sign indicating movement toward the lower Tongue and Powder Rivers. Crook had been concerned with phantoms.

Sheridan responded to Crook's fearful missive on the 28th advising that if he felt too weak to attack, he should at once unite with Terry. Noting that he had sent "every available man that can be spared in the Division," he informed Crook that his actions had been approved by both himself and Sherman, the latter directing him to "inform you that you need not mind the newspapers."

Whatever his assurances to the beleaguered Three Stars, Sheridan managed to strike a stout blow to another seasoned campaigner when Lieutenant Colonel Eugene A. Carr found himself replaced as 5th Cavalry commander by Wesley Merritt, who arrived in camp on 1 July, the very day his promotion to full colonel became effective. The promotion itself was quite orthodox. But no rule required Sheridan to switch commanders in mid-Indian war, and he chose the most awkward moment possible to strip Carr of his field command.

However, since his old Civil War comrade had enjoyed few opportunities for frontier glory, Sheridan would now let him try his hand against the Sioux, despite Carr's greater experience. "It is, of course, a humiliation to me to have him come in and take command," commented the old Indian-fighter. "It seems curious that the Government should find it necessary to spend large amounts of money and some blood to teach Terry, Crook and Merritt how to fight these Prairie Indians when there are others who know better how to do it." Carr was reduced to second in command.

On 3 July, two 5th Cavalry companies led by guide William F. "Buffalo Bill" Cody galloped in a 30-mile pursuit of Indians seen coming up the South Cheyenne valley. Two horses dropped dead under the strain, but the red men rode unhindered toward the Powder River country, abandoning pack animals laden with agency rations. Since the alerted Indians would probably not use the Powder River trail again, Merritt marched toward the stockade, garrisoned by a single infantry company, guarding Sage Creek. On the 7th, a messenger from Laramie brought news of Custer's destruction.

Orders received that night from Sheridan directed Merritt to head for Red Cloud Agency or Fort Laramie, whichever he thought best. Merritt decided to stay on Sage Creek, reacting from this central location to events at either agency as circumstances warranted. On 12 July he received new orders to report to Laramie and refit, then start north to join Crook.

But on the 15th Merritt delayed joining Crook after learning that an estimated 800 Cheyenne warriors were leaving Red Cloud Agency for the Powder River country, using the very route Merritt had been blocking. (The Indians apparently thought he was still blocking it, but had confidently decided to elude him.) The command was obliged to backtrack over the trail just used, then turn east. But as Lieutenant Charles King wrote, "If Merritt hesitated ten minutes, his most intimate associates, his staff, did not know it."

He made a forced march, his men gnawing their hardtack in the saddle, then paused at the infantry stockade guarding the road to Custer City. There he loaded his company of 9th Infantry and part of the 23rd Infantry garrison into wagons as a train escort. By 2000 on 16 July, Merritt had the 5th positioned astride the main trail at Hat, or War Bonnet, Creek, having marched 85 miles in 31 hours.

At about 0415, Cheyenne scouts from Little Wolf's band were seen to the southeast. Hiding in a ravine, other Indians eyed the tardy supply wagons struggling to join Merritt. Then a dozen warriors rode to cut off two horsemen—troopers bearing dispatches—drawing ahead of the train. "Savage warfare was never more beautiful than in you," wrote Lieutenant King years later. From his hilltop lookout point, he waited until the Cheyennes were within 90 yards of the creek, then shouted: "*Now*, lads, in with you!"

Buffalo Bill had suggested that a small party intercept the eager warriors. Now he, his friend "Buffalo Chips" White and six troopers galloped forth—with Cody and a splendidly warbonneted Indian leader riding straight at each other. King recalled: "It is the work of a minute; the Indian has fired and missed. Cody's bullet tears through the rider's leg, into his pony's heart, and they tumble in a confused heap on the prairie. The Cheyenne struggles to his feet for another shot, but Cody's second bullet crashes through his brain, and the young chief, Yellow Hand, drops lifeless in his tracks."

Another eyewitness noted that the meeting seemed to

surprise troopers as well as Indians: "Cody and the leading Indian appeared to be the only ones who did not become excited..."

Scalping the Cheyenne (actually named Hay-o-wei or Yellow Hair), Cody proclaimed the gory trophy "The first scalp for Custer!"—later noting, with a showman's ear, that "the cheer that went up when he fell was deafening." Meanwhile three troops of the 5th had chased considerably fewer than 800 Cheyennes for almost 3 miles. Taking up the pursuit for almost 30, Merritt found four lodges and considerable food left by the flight of Little Wolf's village. With his foes apparently headed towards Spotted Tail Agency, a satisfied Merritt made camp at Red Cloud—where many of the Cheyennes he had chased visited with the bemused bluecoats as they prepared rations.

From Laramie, Merritt's command marched to the forks of Goose Creek, where Crook, marching southeast, met them on 3 August. "Tomorrow morning," he wrote to Sheridan, he would "cut loose from the wagons," but added that if he met the Indians "in too strong force" he would unite with Terry; he knowledge that Plains Indians could not sustain such force had somehow been forgotten. On 5 August Crook sent his wagons back to Fort Fetterman and marched out for the head of the Rosebud. With him were 25 companies of the 2nd, 3rd and 5th Cavalry under Merritt, 10 infantry companies from the 4th, 9th and 14th Infantry under Major Chambers, and Washakie's warriors. The pack train carried 15 days' rations for the swollen force of 2,300 men, but lacked the mule power to haul an equivalent supply of forage.

Let us return to Terry. On 4 July he made his first effort to contact Crook, but the teamster, accepting the offered $500 bonus, was obliged to turn back. On 6 July, Terry ordered Captain Ball on a five-day scout upriver to the monumental rock formation called Pompey's Pillar, which still bore the carved signature of Jeffersonian explorer William Clark. But little was discovered. On the 7th Crow couriers appeared with news of the Rosebud fight, and on the 9th Lieutenant Bradley left for his post at Fort Shaw.

George Herendeen, sent to the Crow village upriver for reinforcements, returned with Bradley's missing Crows and 23 others, and on the 16th Terry, having decided to consolidate his Powder River camp with that on the Big Horn, went downriver in the *Josephine* with Company A of the 7th Cavalry in the hope of meeting the *Far West*. During his absence, Gibbon again managed to ignore whatever intelligence came in concerning the hostiles. On the 20th, Crows arrived to report no signs of Indians on the Little Bighorn, while a party of 30 braves attempted to make off with the cavalry's horses. On the 27th, fires were seen toward the Rosebud.

At the Powder River camp, Terry had the *Far West* and *Josephine* ferry supplies and fighting men to the north bank, then steamed toward the Big Horn camp, his column setting forth on the 21st. However, the low water not only delayed the completion of the 164-mile journey until 26 July, but further complicated the supply question; he could no longer use the wagon route up the Big Horn's left bank since nothing could be ferried to the other side.

But by the 30th men had reached the new base opposite the mouth of the Rosebud, fortified it with earthworks and, perhaps since they already had Forts Rice and Pease, named it Fort Beans. The command began absorbing reinforcements disembarking from steamers. On 1 August, six 22nd Infantry companies under Lieutenant Colonel Elwell S. Otis arrived, plus a dispatch from Sheridan.

He had, Terry read, "made arrangements for the construction of the two new posts on the Yellowstone," each to be manned by six cavalry and five infantry companies. Thus it was necessary to strike the Sioux simply to free soldiers to guard the workmen. Sheridan could send no more, and Terry was advised to form a junction with Crook. But Terry recognized that the river was not sufficiently navigable to permit construction until next spring. On 2 August the *Durfee* brought six 5th Infantry companies under the young, ambitious Colonel Nelson A. Miles, who could not recall ever having seen a command "so completely stampeded as this—

either in the volunteer or regular service." Miles condemned not his slain friend, but the demoralized souls left behind. "The more I see of movements here the more admiration I have for Custer," he wrote home, "and I am satisfied his like will not be found very soon again."

Certainly no effective attempt was made to actually locate the hostiles, though some novel skirmishing between steamboats and Indians hinted at their whereabouts. On 2 August Major Moore, landing infantry from the *Far West* to rescue forage left at the Powder River camp, even managed to toss artillery shells among forage-lifting Indians retreating into nearby timber; a white scout was slain from ambush, an Indian scalp taken, and 75 tons of forage recaptured. But rather than heed entreaties to attack these actual Sioux, Terry set forth against the phantom warriors on the Big Horn. On 8 August, leaving his depot garrisoned by artillery and an infantry company, he finally marched out with roughly 75 Indian and non-Indian scouts, 83 officers and 1,611 enlisted men, including light artillery pieces, Brisbin's command of 2nd and 7th Cavalry, and 4 infantry battalions brigaded under Colonel Gibbon, composed of 21 companies of the 5th, 6th, 7th, and 22nd regiments.

On the 7th Crook camped just below the scene of his 17 June fight, though a village site mistaken for the camp of that date had actually been abandoned a week earlier; down the fire-blackened Rosebud valley could be seen other old camps. The next morning, with scouts reporting a huge Indian force moving up the valley, Crook's men prepared for action before noticing the telltale wagon train. The Indians had been Terry's Crows, who in turn had taken Crook's Indians for Sioux, the 7th Cavalry deploying boldly to the front before a lone horseman riding ahead was recognized. Reported the *Chicago Daily Tribune*, "Major [*sic*] Benteen rose in his stirrups, waved his hat, and gave the rather unusual military command, 'three cheers for Buffalo Bill!'" Having bizarrely met head-on in that vast theater of war, at a point where a hostile trail turned eastward, they would now combine their mighty columns and pursue.

Comparing the two commanders, Bourke contrasted Crook's "bull-dog tenacity" with the "faint traces of indecision and weakness" he thought he detected in Terry's face. The opinions of the two departmental commanders also presented a dramatic contrast. Crook seemed indifferent to all but those Sioux who ranged south of the Yellowstone to menace the white settlements in the Department of the Platte, while Terry worried that Sitting Bull's northern following might escape over the "Medicine Line" to Canada.

After supplying some of Crook's wants, Terry sent his wagons back toward the Yellowstone; now both commands would travel light, fast, and together. But at the suggestion of Colonel Miles, yearning for an independent command, General Terry ordered the 5th Infantry back to the Yellowstone to hold the main fords and patrol the river in steamers, thus—or so it was hoped—blocking any escape north. The great march began at 1100 on the morning of 11 August. In the scorched valley of the Tongue, the soldiers found an old campsite and a divided Indian trail, one branch heading up the Tongue, another downstream, and still others to the east, toward the Powder. Rain hit the bivouacked troops and lasted well into the next day as scouts attempted to find the main Indian route and argued over its age. They decided that the downstream trail had been made by the main body.

The massive combined forces marched eastward for a week, through cold rains and thick mud, with mounts breaking down from lack of grazing. Then, at their sodden bivouacs above and below the mouth of the Powder, Crook's and Terry's men waited impatiently for boat-borne supplies from the Rosebud depot. By now none of the staff officers, according to Godfrey, were speaking to each other, and the weary troops had begun falling prey to scurvy, rheumatism and dysentery.

It had become apparent, at least to some, that even if the trail were fresh, there was little hope of a successful pursuit. The anxiety to be prepared for vast Sioux hordes was crippling; if Custer had had too few men, Terry and Crook—as Crook himself complained—had too many. The vast blue host was not only too clumsy to catch any Indians, but too large even to keep supplied. "It has reached beyond a joke that we should be kept out and exposed because two fools do not know their business," observed Colonel Carr sourly. "I would leave the expedition today, if I could."

Many who could leave did, including most of the journalists and the Indian auxiliaries, who saw little prospect of any action. While lingering for a time at Terry's request, Buffalo Bill departed, to continue his interrupted work of transmuting frontier strife into myth on Eastern stages. His next extravaganza, "a succession of scenes in the late Indian war" entitled *The Red Right Hand; or, Buffalo Bill's First Scalp for Custer*, was in the words of its star "a five-act play, without head or tail, and it made no difference at which act we commenced the performance...." Despite this description, Cody had not intended to dramatize the command failures of the campaign.

While Crook complained that supplies arriving by boat were inadequate for their combined forces, it was Terry who proved more tenacious, offering to share his supplies and suggesting that they push on—even if they had to live on horsemeat. He agreed to delay movement until the *Far West* delivered forage, rations and shoes for Crook's footsore infantry. When it arrived on August 19, Miles and his infantry, save for one company, disembarked, establishing a camp on the north bank. Terry ordered the evacuation of Fort Beans and the transfer of stores and men to the Powder's mouth. On the 20th, the Shoshones and Crows rode out of the campaign.

Terry wrote to Sheridan explaining his plan to march up the Powder "until we strike the trail again and then pursue it. It will lead, as I think, to the Little Missouri." Due to the systematic grass fires, he would await the arrival of forage. With the arrival of supply steamers, Terry came to Crook's camp to tell him that he could now fulfill all his needs—only to find him gone! Crook's Wyoming column had commenced marching up the Powder without so much as a word to the commanding officer. Terry marched up the same route on August 25, but Crook made no effort to wait for him.

By this time Crook's vaunted Spartan ways had become a bit tiresome, *New York Times* scribe Cuthbert Mills asserting that the heavy rains had "at last washed the enthusiasm out of the staff officers. I hope I do these gentlemen no injustice, but it had seemed to me there had been just a little tinge of ostentation in the extreme primitiveness of their style of living. It would have been as easy to carry half a dozen tin plates, forks and spoons, as to carry one solitary specimen of each of them, and pass it around the mess....The solitary fork was from choice. The continuous rain was not."

Reports of Indians seen on the lower river by steamboat personnel and the Glendive garrison moved Terry to ride with Cody and a cavalry escort to Crook's camp. The two brigadiers agreed to go their separate ways, with Crook following the Indian trail and keeping Terry informed of any change in plan. For his part, Terry would return to the Yellowstone and accumulate supplies, which Crook could draw upon should the trail lead him near Glendive. On 26 August Terry learned from Sheridan that a temporary cantonment was to be constructed at or near the mouth of the Tongue, where Miles would winter with 1,500 men, including the 5th and part of the 22nd Infantry, as well as a full regiment of cavalry.

With all boats needed to stockpile supplies for Miles, Terry marched overland to Glendive, swinging to the north toward the Missouri-Yellowstone divide and, on 29 August, unwittingly frightening Long Dog's village of Hunkpapas into abandoning its lodges. Finally making camp near the Glendive post, Terry soon learned that, with the river fallen and three steamers already run aground, the upper Yellowstone was closed to navigation; since every available wagon (requiring escort troops) would be needed to sustain Miles through the winter, maintaining his own force in the field would simply eat up supplies needed by the winter garrison. Only good news from Crook could justify holding out.

But on 3 September Terry learned from Crook, then camped on a tributary of the Missouri known as Beaver Creek, that the Indian trail had disappeared. He formally disbanded his force

*Proud warriors such as Wooden Leg faced new challenges with the end of the free life and its opportunities for heroism— and even peace itself had its drawbacks. "It is pleasant to be situated where I can sleep soundly every night," he commented in 1930. "But I like to think about the old times, when every man had to be brave."*

on 5 September, the battered 7th leaving for Fort Lincoln, Gibbon's and Brisbin's men for Forts Ellis and Shaw, and Moore for Fort Buford. While Surgeon Paulding declared the expedition to have "died a natural death," Miles had already bid a relieved adieu to Terry's demoralized command and started toward his new Tongue River cantonment.

The cantonment was a key element of Sheridan's revised strategy; since Congressional permission had come too late to beat the Yellowstone's falling waters, he would have to wait until spring to begin work on two permanent forts. His distaste for a fair-weather campaign justified, Sheridan would now return to first principles—a grinding war of material attrition, fought and marched to the limit of the weaker side. "I have never looked on any decisive battles with these Indians as a settlement of the trouble," he assured Sherman. "Indians do not fight such battles; they only fight boldly when they have the advantage, as in the Custer case, or to cover the movement of their women and children as in the case of Crook...but Indians have scarcely ever been severely punished unless by their own mode of warfare or tactics and stealing on them."

It was clear, however, that Sheridan had put too much trust in a strategy of convergence, and that his officers had imagined that such decisive battles were indeed possible. Henceforth the hunting grounds of the Yellowstone would be occupied, the agencies controlled by troops. Fear of soldiers and the inability to harvest game would thus force the harried Indians to surrender at these agencies, where all would be disarmed and, even more drastically, dismounted. He had already instructed that Indians would not be allowed to return without "unconditional surrender of their persons, ponies, guns and ammunition."

While the dismounting and disarming were to be delayed until late autumn so that Indians learning of his scheme could not easily scatter, Sheridan ordered Colonel Ranald Mackenzie and six companies of his 4th Cavalry north from the Indian Territory, giving Mackenzie command of the District of the Black Hills. Mackenzie reached Camp Robinson, Nebraska, on 17 August. On 16 September, Sheridan himself (bringing with him two Japanese army officers who, despite their lack of English or an interpreter, desired to observe the U.S. Army's methods of subduing the red men) reached Fort Laramie to confer with both Mackenzie and Crook, the latter arriving on the 21st. Sheridan, vetoing Crook's proposal to use the Black Hills as his winter base, told him instead to establish a cantonment near old Fort Reno, dominating the region between the Black Hills and the Big Horn Mountains. The Big Horn and Yellowstone Expedition was clearly over.

But before meeting Sheridan, Crook, in his eastward march across Montana and Dakota, had already won the campaign's greatest combat victory. He had entered the Little Missouri Valley and proceeded to the head of the Heart River, inexplicably following the trail made by Terry's column that spring. Traveling slowly and thus using up more provisions per mile, Crook's column marched over the fire-scorched plain, men and beasts slogging through mud and rain as their commander blindly sought an enemy. Wrote reporter Mills: "We are stripped down to less baggage than the *enemy carry*, but it is hard catching an Indian in his own country when he does not want to be caught....The questions which everyone appears to be asking now are: '*Where are the Indians?*' and '*Where are we going?*'"

Here and there, small groups of warriors could be seen, and reasonably fresh trails were finally found heading south toward the Black Hills. But despite his discouraging dispatch to Terry on the 3rd, Crook would go on. Two days later he ordered the command on half-rations. By this time cavalrymen walked, for their mounts were starving. An officer wrote of men "so exhausted they were actually insane....I saw men who were very plucky sit down and cry like children because they could not hold out."

Crook had rations for two and a half days. Either Fort Lincoln or the Glendive depot could be reached in four or five. But Crook decided to go south, into the unknown, with the Black Hills at least seven days' march away. Never had his taciturn habits inflicted more anxiety upon even his most faithful followers. The consequent "Starvation" or "Horse-meat March," with men living on two crackers a day and meat from horses and mules, came close to destroying the command. "I am a hippophagist!" wrote Carr.

On 7 September Crook sent Captain Mills, with scout Grouard and 15 picked men from each 3rd Cavalry troop, to push on with 61 mules toward Deadwood City, or any other mining town where food could be had. But the next day Grouard spied a small Indian village tucked into the eastern edge of the lofty Slim Buttes.

Mills quickly concealed his force. Despite the argument that other villages might be nearby, and the fact that his men had brought only 50 carbine rounds each, he decided to attack at dawn after positioning his men. Two 50-man groups advanced on foot, stretching skirmish lines on the left and right sides of the camp, while 25 mounted cavalrymen were to charge straight through it before regrouping on its far side.

At the first shot, 25 horseholders with the pack train would rush forth to complete the "surround."

But as they made their final approach, the frightened pony herd thundered toward the village. Lieutenant Frederick Schwatka's mounted men improvised by charging with drawn pistols behind the ponies, taking almost 200 with them through the village. The dismounted men, taking up positions on the camp's eastern side, fired volleys into fleeing figures.

The surprised Indians seized their weapons. As women and children fled to the bluffs on the left, their menfolk returned fire from nearby bluffs and ravines. Despite the crash of musketry, Lieutenant John Bubb's horseholders were sheltered too far back to hear it; Mills sent word to Bubb to summon help from Crook and to advance himself. The horseholders dug in on the east side of the village, fending off repeated attempts to snatch back the captured ponies.

Lieutenant Emmett Crawford led his left-hand group in charges to force the warriors back to the southwestern bluffs. Then he entrenched, leaving the Sioux to dominate the heights beyond. Once again white troops had captured a village and found themselves surrounded—by perhaps only half their number of Indians, since the village contained only 37 lodges.

A new phase opened when Private John Wenzel was shot dead from a brush-filled ravine near the edge of the camp; three more men fell wounded trying to flush the marksman until Mills forbade any forward movement. Crook, met by Mills' couriers 17 miles from the village, had hastily assembled a flying column of well-mounted men and medical personnel under Colonel Carr. It reached the village before noon; Crook and the remaining cavalrymen were next, with even the weary infantry in by 1400.

While Crook (angry that Mills had not summoned him instantly) had the village searched for food, calls for the ravine's holdouts to surrender were met with bullets; two men were wounded, one fatally, while three would earn Medals of Honor for this phase of action. Ascending a bluff to get a better line of fire, Buffalo Bill's faithful follower "Buffalo Chips" was shot through the heart and with a piteous cry plummeted to the ground. The scout Big Bat shot a warrior rising above the brush to take aim, then plunged with Sioux-like daring into the ravine to take his scalp. Even after a few women were helped out, firing continued. But Crook persisted, calling, wrote Finerty, "upon the dusky heroes to surrender."

The warriors finally gave in. First came the broad-chested Oglala chief Iron Plume, generally termed American Horse by the whites. He surrendered his rifle to Crook and was helped out, clutching a wound from which his intestines protruded. "Some of the soldiers," wrote Finerty, "who had lost comrades in the skirmish, shouted, 'No quarter!' but not a man was base enough to attempt shooting down the disabled chief." Only two other men emerged; a total of four Sioux warriors had managed to slay three bluecoats and wound at least four. There were 23 survivors in all, recorded Bourke, with 1 warrior, 3 women and 1 infant taken out dead—1 wounded child soon dying, according to Cuthbert Mills, who wrote that talk of a white renegade found in the ravine led to cries for vengeance:

> There was no white man, however. When the body was dragged into light, it proved to be that of a squaw, whitened by death. She was frightfully shot. Bullets had torn half her neck away, three had gone through her breast and shoulder, and two through each limb. Her body and clothing were one mass of mud and coagulated blood. The woman seemed to have been killed instantly, for her face wore a smile of perfect peace. Another squaw was dragged out, scarcely less shot up than the other. Both were quite pretty, for Indians. Then followed the half-naked body of the old Indian "Big Bat" had killed. It was very unceremoniously hauled up by what hair remained, and the leather belt around the middle....The body had stiffened in death in the posture of a man holding a gun...He was an old man, and his features wore a look of rigid determination....

The dead were laid out, and Nicaagat, or "Ute John," who had remained when other Indians had abandoned Crook, calmly scalped the women—abetted by several soldiers. Leaving the slain Indians, the soldiers looked to their own

*Captain Mills carried off a buckskin lodge as a trophy of Slim Buttes, later using it as a backdrop for photographs with military personnel and Indian prisoners. Captain Mills is seated second from right.*

dead. Sergeant Van Moll helped bear Private Wenzel's body toward its burial place, wrenching the cocked carbine from its stiff fingers after picking the unfired cartridge from the chamber. The soldiers raked over the astonishingly rich array of plunder from this mixed village of Miniconjous, Oglalas, Brules and Cheyennes, including thousands of pounds of badly-needed food. Slits in tipi walls showed that the speed of the attack had prevented the Sioux from untying their doorways. Also found were trophies of the 7th Cavalry, including Company I's guidon, Keogh's bloody gauntlets wrapped inside.

Despite warnings that reinforcements were on their way from Crazy Horse's larger camp near the Little Missouri, Crook did little or nothing to prepare for a counterattack, and the men were devouring Indian provisions or sleeping. But late that afternoon warriors—perhaps no more than 200—appeared to fire from the commanding bluffs into the natural amphitheater sheltering the village. They yielded when charged only to circle and advance at another point. But with over 2,000 men, there seemed little danger of being overrun.

The Army's dead were buried and the graves obliterated—
a futile gesture in the presence of prisoners and watching
warriors.

Lieutenant von Leuttwitz, his knee shattered as he led the
left-hand skirmishers, survived amputation, though Private
Edward Kennedy did not. "Tell him he will die before next
morning," said a surgeon treating Iron Plume, and that night
the chief, refusing chloroform and suppressing any cry of
pain, expired with barely a sound. He was spared scalping,
even by Ute John.

Lieutenant King noted proudly that "the big white chief
Crook has managed to gain all this with starving men and
skeleton horses." Yet he had so exhausted his command that
any pursuit of Crazy Horse's greater village was now impossible. The next morning, Crook simply departed, leaving most
of his prisoners to care for their dead and take a message of
peace to their friends. Warriors attempted to drive in his
pickets and engaged Carr's 5th Cavalry rear guard as it
burned the village. After a careful withdrawal of several
miles under fire, Carr set out after the main column.

Even the captured food proved inadequate, and on 11
September Crook ordered a party under Mills to drive on
toward Deadwood. The next day over half the infantry
dropped out on the march, and cavalrymen who had carried
their saddles now dropped them into the mud. Precious
ammunition, now too heavy, was cached. Finally the men
simply stopped. But when a courier brought the galvanizing
news that a provision train was approaching the Belle
Fourche River, the hungry troops arose. Fording the river,
they waited for 13 wagonloads of food purchased at the
mining settlement of Crook City, plus a herd of 50 beeves. On
the 14th Crook received orders to meet Sheridan at Fort
Laramie; turning his command over to Colonel Merritt the
next day, he rode with his staff to Deadwood.

"The fact of the case is," wrote Sheridan to Sherman early
in 1877, "the operations of Generals Terry and Crook will not
bear criticism, and my only thought has been to let them
sleep. I approved what was done, for the sake of the troops,

*Cavalry troop at Deadwood City*

but in doing so, I was not approving much, as you know." Sheridan himself could hardly be blamed for the post-Custer timidity of his department commanders, and particularly Crook's persistent wrongheadedness. But he might have attempted to exert firmer control over their operations, instead of deeming it "the best judgement to give no positive orders." And his was the strategy, punishing enough when employed on the Southern Plains, which had in this theater produced an insoluble logistical nightmare. In attempting to run the Indians to earth, the troops had instead run themselves into the ground.

Crook's victory at Slim Buttes, however small, had given Army morale a badly needed lift, and provided a measure of revenge for Custer's dead. But it could not redeem Crook's earlier failures, nor disguise the one-sided nature of the combat. One suspects that for some white participants, it was not the triumph over an outnumbered foe which provided the day's most enduring memory. Rather it was the bloodstained figure of Iron Plume, clutching his death-wound as he stood before the soldier-chief, later to die in stoic silence—a grim symbol of the still unconquered Sioux.

# Warriors No More

The old ways ended with stunning speed. With authority for military rule, General Sheridan stripped the agency Indians—many of whom had not roamed with Sitting Bull—of their ponies and weapons. (Most Lakota calendars or "winter counts," representing each year with a significant event, would recall it not as the year Long Hair was killed, but as the year the Sioux lost their horses.) With indecent haste, a government commission arrived at the agencies that September to demand the sale of the Black Hills. Threatened with a ration cut-off, the chiefs "touched the pen."

With winter, both Crook and Colonel Miles embarked on new expeditions—Crook's nearly 2,200 men including 11 troops of cavalry under Ranald Mackenzie. Fighting a two-day battle against Sitting Bull's warriors that October, Miles, using fewer than 500 infantrymen and judiciously employed artillery, finally drove them toward the Yellowstone before hounding Sitting Bull across much of Montana. On 25 November, in a canyon of the Red Fork of the Powder River, Mackenzie and 1,100 cavalrymen thundered into the Cheyenne village of Morning Star (Dull Knife) and Little Wolf, dispossessing some 400 warriors and their families. On 7 January 1877, Miles met Crazy Horse at the battle of Tongue River; seemingly indecisive, it proved demoralizing for the Sioux.

More crippling than battle was the constant military pressure on these hunting bands. By 5 April, almost all the hostiles had agreed to come in, and on 6 May Crazy Horse himself surrendered at Red Cloud Agency, though Sitting Bull had already left for Canada. By September, the last harried bands had arrived at the agencies, and soon the two forts long requested by Sheridan were at last built—to be named Keogh and Custer. Arriving at the Fort Keogh site near the Tongue River Cantonment that July, Sherman declared: "The Sioux Indians can never again regain this country." The war was over.

There would be other troubles on the reservations, and the Northern Cheyennes, deported to the Indian Territory, would begin in 1878 a tragic exodus toward their homeland, pursued by troops; after much bloodshed, the survivors were eventually allowed to settle in their old Montana homeland. By 1881 even Sitting Bull himself had surrendered. A last Sioux "war" broke out in 1890, when the Ghost Dance promised the buffalo's return and the end of the white man.

It was a lie. The warrior was taught to farm like a woman, his sons, their hair cut short, taught to despise the old ways at the schools they were forced to attend. "The Indian is like a prisoner on his reservation," said the Arapaho Left Hand in 1920. "The buffalo are all gone, the antelope are gone, and now we old men can only sit by the fire, sing our war-songs and dream of the past." One of the old men, Dewey Beard, had fought Custer at age 14, and lost almost his entire family at Wounded Knee. He died in 1955—the last survivor of the Battle of the Little Bighorn.

*Even after the military's successful efforts of 1876-77, thousands of Sioux remained defiant. The bloody inroads of white hide-hunters against the buffalo herds finally destroyed what Sheridan termed the "Indian's commissary." Famine accomplished what the United States Army could not.*

# Little Bighorn Battlefield National Monument

While many Indian Wars sites remain private property, and the Rosebud field only became a Montana state park in 1978, the burial of so many U.S. soldiers at the Custer battlefield demanded government interest from the start. In 1877 the remains of 12 officers and 2 civilians were exhumed for reinterment elsewhere; though some have questioned their identity, those deemed to be Custer's now lie at West Point. But scandalous reports of unburied bones led to an 1879 cleanup, each grave being marked by a stake. That same year the site was formally designated a national cemetery. In 1881 a truncated obelisk of granite, engraved with the names of the slain, was erected atop Custer Hill, and the remains reinterred in a mass grave around its base. In 1890 white marble slabs replaced the wooden stakes to mark where each soldier fell—a feature unique to the Custer battlefield.

Unfortunately, the War Department mishandled this potential boon to future military analysts. Custer Hill had been landscaped and leveled to accommodate the monument, and an officer supplied with extra stones disposed of them by marking phantom graves. Later, apparently to fit an iron fence around the "Last Stand" area, all stones on this location were removed and reset farther down the slope. (Custer's body was actually found within six feet of the present monument and buried some 25 feet below it.) A subsequent road made the site more accessible to motorists, but further altered the character of the ground.

Yet most of the sprawling battlefield, in the heart of the Crow Indian reservation, still looks much as it did in 1876, though the Little Bighorn River has changed course dramatically. The government, securing small areas encompassing the Custer companies' final positions and the Reno-Benteen defensive position, left much of the land in private hands, but thus far there has been virtually no development.

In 1940 Custer Battlefield National Cemetery was transferred from the War Department to the National Park Service, and in 1946 was renamed Custer Battlefield National Monument. In 1952 a Visitor Center was established, housing a museum and a depository for documents and other historical materials, including the Elizabeth B. Custer Collection. While this is generally the first stop for most tourists, the unfolding fight is better understood by securing interpretive materials and then starting the tour four-and-a-half miles away, at the Reno-Benteen Battlefield. Here stands a modest stone erected in 1929; at the urging of General Edward Godfrey, it bears no names of individual survivors and thus avoids honoring Major Reno. Aside from a wooden sign indicating the general area where Lame White Man fell, the only Indian monuments are old stone cairns; several of these near the Reno-Benteen site mark the deaths of individual braves.

The military cemetery located behind the Visitor Center contains the graves of almost 5,000 servicemen and dependents from the Indian Wars and subsequent conflicts; the remains of many black, white, and red Army veterans were moved here from abandoned post cemeteries. Notable Sioux War participants buried here include Lieutenant Crittenden, Curley, Major Reno, and White Swan.

If museum exhibits and interpretation initially tended to overemphasize Custer's doomed companies at the expense of the Indians (and even the Reno-Benteen men), since the early 1970s the National Park Service has exhibited an alarming eagerness to appease so-called "Indian activists"—even permitting some to disrupt the battle's centennial observance and, in 1988, to desecrate the mass grave with impunity. In 1991, political correctness, if not history, was served when Congress renamed the park Little Bighorn Battlefield National Monument, on the quite spurious grounds that battlefields must not be named after participants.

Given such an atmosphere, even the movement to erect a monument to the Indian fallen has aroused fears that—through a misguided attempt to compete for attention by placing it on Battle Ridge—the grim beauty of the current grave marker may be destroyed. But for now, it still exerts its somber power. Dominating the hill and the pitifully small group of white markers below, the weathered shaft is starkly impressive, evocative not of martial glory or magnificently caparisoned warriors, but of lonely death.

# The Bones of Their Dead

It all started with a fire. In August, 1983, a prairie blaze—perhaps sparked by a carelessly tossed cigarette—swept over almost 600 acres of the 640-acre Custer Battlefield reservation before it could be contained. Superintendent James V. Court sought Park Service authorization for archeological research, seizing the opportunity to explore terrain now stripped of vegetation—and already revealing spent cartridge casings and other artifacts lying exposed on its surface. Since there were no National Park Service (NPS) funds for a "dig," archaeologists Richard A. Fox, Douglas D. Scott, and Melissa Connor supervised eager volunteers, their expenses borne by the Custer Battlefield Historical and Museum Association. Work began in May, 1984, involving some 100 volunteers over a five-week period, and in 1985 the team returned to the sight.

Over 4,000 artifacts were uncovered, from brass buttons and the odd arrow head to unfired cartridges and leaden slugs. The quantities of expended shells tended to confirm accounts of Indians largely armed with breechloaders and repeaters; firing positions below Calhoun Hill and northeast of Custer Hill were dubbed "Henryville" and "Henry Hill" due to the numerous .44 casings uncovered. Scientifically matching spent shells bearing the firing-pin and/or extractor marks of individual weapons, investiga-

tors could attempt to trace the movements of their users—and offer a new reconstruction of the fight.

Objecting to the "dig" as a desecration of a hallowed site, novelist A.B. Guthrie, Jr. urged in verse, "Let the bones lie." Instead, the remains of slain troopers would provide not only stark reminders of violent death, but also lessons in "osteobiography." Some bore the scars of knives, confirming accounts of mutilation, while fragments of skulls broken while the bone was still "green" indicated to forensic anthropologist Clyde Snow "perimortem blunt instrument trauma." One almost intact skeleton, labeled "Trooper Mike," still had its right foot in a boot with the top cut away. The soldier was between 19 and 22 at the time of his death, had been 5 feet 8 inches tall, with a defect in the fifth lumbar vertebra that would have made riding painful. Shot twice in the chest and with a bullet fragment in his left wrist, he had had his teeth knocked away by a massive blow, and his thighbones hacked as though with a hatchet.

Skeletal evidence failed to support claims of mass suicide, though the locations of some bones seemed to confirm theories of a "south skirmish line." And while evidence of burials was often found near marble markers, it supported suspicions that each of about 38 *pairs* of slabs had been placed on the field to mark the grave of a single soldier.

The greatest disappointment came with the failure to locate a group of "missing" men. Eyewitnesses had told of men from Company E—several counted 28 bodies—found in a deep coulee, where they had supposedly been trapped and killed. Most of these troops had presumably been buried in the ravine itself, their comrades kicking or tossing earth and brush down upon them. But in subsequent clean-ups and reburials, no markers were placed for these forgotten men—and despite digging 11 backhoe trenches along the ravine's length, archaeologists could find no trace of them. (One student has suggested that they died in a different ravine.)

The bones uncovered would be studied, then reburied. In 1986, mostly fragmentary remains of some 34 men—including a pipe-smoking, part-Indian individual believed to be Mitch Boyer—were solemnly interred in Custer Battlefield National Cemetery, with an honor guard of 7th Cavalry troopers and Indian veterans. In 1989, a volunteer taking a break from a dig at the disappointing Reno-Benteen "dumpsite"—where the 7th's survivors had burned or wrecked items of potential value to the enemy before departing—discovered a human skull imbedded upside down in the riverbank, staring at him with hollow eye sockets. The jawless skull, a humerus, and a clavicle were all that remained of a soldier whose grave had been bared by the Little Bighorn's changing course.

Judging by their location and survivors' accounts, the bones apparently belonged to either Sergeant Edward Botzer of Company G or Private William Moodie of Company A. But while no photographs were available of either man, a forensic sculptor's bust built up from the skull strongly resembled a photograph of Botzer's brother Rudolph, convincing relatives that the skull belonged to the sergeant. On 23 June 1991, as hundreds watched under a clouded sky, the bones were committed to the ground

# Guide for the Interested Reader

## Recommended Reading

### Non-Fiction

The late John S. Gray's *Centennial Campaign: The Sioux War of 1876* (Fort Collins, CO, 1976) is considered the best critique of the three columns' activities—concise, nasty and opinionated. Edgar I. Stewart's *Custer's Luck* (Norman, OK, 1955) is a useful narrative of the campaign, but ends with the Little Bighorn fight. Colorful first-hand accounts include John F. Finerty's *War-path and Bivouac; or, The Conquest of the Sioux* (Norman, 1961) and John G. Bourke's *On the Border With Crook* (Lincoln, NB, 1971). Robert M. Utley's *Frontier Regulars: The U.S. Army and the Indian, 1866-1890* (New York, 1973) provides an overview of the "miserable skeleton," while Paul Andrew Hutton presents a "view from the top" with his exquisitely fair-minded *Phil Sheridan and His Army* (Lincoln, 1985). George Bird Grinnell's *The Fighting Cheyennes* (New York, 1915) remains perhaps the fullest account of a Plains tribes' wars and conquests as gathered from Indian informants. J. W. Vaughn's *With Crook at the Rosebud* (Harrisburg, 1956), the standard on the fight of 17 June, has recently been supplemented by Neil C. Mangum's *Battle of the Rosebud* (El

Segundo, CA, 1991). Vaughn also wrote *The Reynold's Campaign on Powder River* (Norman, 1961) and *Indian Fights: New Facts on Seven Encounters* (Norman, 1966).

The incredible literature of the Custer fight cannot be adequately dealt with here. W.A. Graham's *The Story of the Little Bighorn* (Harrisburg, 1926; slightly revised 1941) was the first book devoted solely to the battle; it is badly dated, despite Colonel Graham's skepticism concerning the likelihood of any important future discoveries. Robert Utley's 1988 official National Park Handbook, *Custer Battlefield*, is both a well-written introduction and a useful guide for the visitor. Reconstructions of the battle include Charles Kuhlman's groundbreaking *Legend into History* (Harrisburg, 1951; revised 1952) and John Gray's *Custer's Last Campaign: Mitch Boyer and the Little Bighorn Reconstructed* (Lincoln, 1991). Amid the embarrassment of rich primary material, some basic "makings" of the saga appear in W.A. Graham's *The Custer Myth: A Source Book of Custeriana* (Harrisburg, 1953). *Custer in '76: Walter Camp's Notes on the Custer Fight* (Provo, UT, 1976), edited by Kenneth M. Hammer, presents interviews with participants by a dedicated amateur. Among Indian accounts, the most useful (despite its mass suicide story) is perhaps Thomas Marquis's *Wooden Leg* (Lincoln, n.d.), originally published in 1931 as *A Warrior Who Fought Custer*. Another diligent interviewer of "old-time" Indians, Stanley Vestal (Walter S. Campbell) numbers among his works the biographies *Sitting Bull, Champion of the Sioux* (Norman, 1956) and *Warpath: The True Story of the Fighting Sioux Told in a Biography of Chief White Bull* (Lincoln, 1984). Frank Linderman presents a Crow viewpoint in his *Plenty-coups* (Lincoln, 1962). While one may differ with such writers' conclusions or approach, their work is invaluable and must not be confused with that of latter-day mountebanks who have attempted to cash in on a supposedly suppressed "Indian side" of the story—sometimes with considerable financial success.

A guide to the first 90-plus years of vast Custer literature is Tal Luther's *Custer High Spots* (Fort Collins, CO, 1972), which also points out a few low spots. The best biography is Robert

Utley's *Cavalier in Buckskin: George Armstrong Custer and the Western Military Frontier* (Norman, 1988), while his *Custer and the Great Controversy* (Pasadena, 1962) traces the initial evolution of the Little Bighorn legend, a subject pursued by Brian W. Dippie's *Custer's Last Stand: The Anatomy of an American Myth* (Missoula, 1976) and Bruce A. Rosenberg's *Custer and the Epic of Defeat* (University Park, PA, 1974).

Books to avoid taking seriously include Dee Brown's mendacious *Bury My Heart at Wounded Knee: An Indian History of the American West* (New York, 1970), Mari Sandoz's novelistic *The Battle of the Little Bighorn* (New York, 1966) and David Humphreys Miller's absurd *Custer's Fall: The Indian Side of the Story* (New York, 1957). Evan S. Connell's bestselling *Son of the Morning Star: Custer and the Little Bighorn* (San Francisco, 1984) may rank as the most incoherent book on either subject.

**Fiction**

Most novels dealing with the campaign of 1876 are routine Western melodramas and/or rely on stock elements such as white renegades among the hostiles. "Lone survivors" flourish. But Thomas Berger's *Little Big Man* (New York, 1964) lampoons the theme while exhibiting a canny knowledge of the Last Stand mystique, and the caddish anti-hero of George MacDonald Fraser's *Flashman and the Redskins* (London, 1982) can claim to have survived both the Charge of the Light Brigade and Custer's Last Stand. Charles K. Mills' *A Mighty Afternoon* (Garden City, 1980), a novelized reconstruction of the battle, is the work of a diligent Custer scholar. Science fiction has repeatedly embraced Custerian themes, though the Steve Utley-Howard Waldrop story "Custer's Last Jump" (*Universe 6*, 1976) is perhaps the only attempt to envision Long Hair dying in aerial combat against an Indian air force.

**Journals**

Aside from those issued by specialist organizations mentioned below, scholarly articles on the 1876 campaign and related topics appear most frequently in *Montana: The Maga-zine of Western History.*

## Interest Groups

Founded in 1952, the Custer Battlefield Historical and Museum Association (P.0. Box 129, Crow Agency, MT 59022) is a non-profit organization cooperating with the National Park Service in programs of interpretation, research and general historical work, subsidizing the well-known archeo-logical work of the 1980s with both money and volunteer labor. Besides its yearly journal *Greasy Grass*, it has published each year since 1987 a collection of addresses delivered at its annual Hardin symposium. The Custer Battlefield Preserva-tion Committee (P.O. Box 7, Hardin, Montana 59034) is devoted to purchasing privately owned battlefield land in order to prevent unsightly development.

The Little Big Horn Associates (P.O. Box 14708, Fort Worth, TX 76117), founded in 1967, strives "to seek the truth" about Custer, the 7th Cavalry, "and all of Custeriana"; it enlisted its thousandth member in 1991. Less exclusively oriented to-ward "The Battle," it holds an annual conference at locations related to Custer's life and times, publishing a newsletter and a semi-annual *Research Review.*

The Order of the Indian Wars (P.O. Box 7401, Little Rock, AK 72216), named for the old organization of former frontier officers, issues a bi-monthly *Communique* offering the latest news on Indian Wars-related events and sites.

## Film, Documentaries and Videotapes

Nonfiction videotapes on the Custer fight include the mediocre *Red Sunday* (formerly shown at the park itself) and the disappointing *A Good Day To Die*. The best such video is the 1989 Old Army Press production *Touring Custer Battlefield*. Bill Armstrong's *Custer's Last Trooper* centers on bones un-earthed at the battlefield in 1989 and an attempt to establish the trooper's identity. The most unfocused documentary is the 1987 *Dreams Along the Little Bighorn,* which detours into an inanely irrelevant discussion of Montana's Rocky Boy Indians.

While filmmakers dramatized the Custer battle as early as 1909, the earliest film available on videotape is the 1912 *Custer's Last Fight.* The heroic portrayal of Custer reached its zenith with the lavish *They Died With Their Boots On* (1941)—innocent of history, but so epitomizing the legend that, as Brian Dippie commented, "after Errol Flynn's Last Stand there was really nothing more to say on the subject." Custer was reincarnated after World War II primarily as an Indian-bashing villain, the climax being Arthur Penn's self-hating 1970 travesty of *Little Big Man;* faced with an evil but loony Custer, the audience cheered his destruction—shot on portions of the actual battlefield. The 1991 miniseries *Son of the Morning Star* is more accurate, though still hampered by gross errors and a remarkably pointless script apparently rewritten lest Custer "look good;" star Gary Cole, though unable to ride a horse, delivers a suitably annoying performance. Films treating of the last stand theme sans the Custer name include John Ford's 1948 *Fort Apache* (which reveals the best understanding of the "myth") and the 1965 *The Glory Guys.*

# Orders of Battle

## Battle of the Rosebud, 17 June 1876

### *Big Horn and Yellowstone Expedition*
Brig. Gen. George Crook

**Staff:**

Captain A.H. Nickerson, 23rd Infantry, A.D.C. ADG
Lieutenant John G. Bourke, 3rd Cavalry, A.D.C.
Captain George M. Randall, 23rd Infantry, Chief of Scouts
Captain W.S. Stanton, Eng. Corps, Chief Eng. Officer
Captain J.V. Furey, AGM, Chief Quartermaster
Lieutenant J.W. Bubb, 4th Infantry, Acting Commissary of
    Subsistence
Asst. Surgeon Albert Hartsuff, Medical Director

**Expedition Cavalry:** Lieutenant-Colonel W.B. Royall, 3rd Cavalry
**3rd U.S. Cavalry**, Major Andrew W. Evans
1st Battalion, Captain Anson Mills:
    Company A, Lieutenant Charles Morton
    Company E, Captain Alexander Sutorius
    Company I, Captain William Andrews, Lieutenant Foster,
        Lieutenant A. King
    Company M, Captain Anson Mills, Lieutenant A.C. Paul,
        Lieutenant Schwatka
2nd Battalion, Captain Guy V. Henry
    Company B, Captain Charles Meinhold, Lieutenant Simpson
    Company D, Captain Guy V. Henry, Lieutenant Robinson
    Company F, Lieutenant Bainbridge Reynolds
    Company L, Captain Peter Vroom, Lieutenant Chase
Van Vliet's Squadron, Captain Frederick Van Vliet

Company C, (Captain Van Vliet, Lieutenant Adolphus Von Leuttwitz)

Company G, (Lieutenant Emmet Crawford)

**2nd U.S. Cavalry Battalion,** Captain Henry E. Noyes, 2nd Cavalry

Company A, Captain Thomas B. Dewees, Lt. Peirson

Company B, Lieutenant William Rawolle

Company D, Lieutenant Samuel M. Swigert, Lieutenant Huntington

Company E, Captain Elizah R. Wells, Lieutenant Sibley

Company I, Lieutenant Fred W. Kingsbury—commanding Noyes' company

**Mounted Infantry Battalion:** Major Alex Chambers, 4th Infantry

4th U.S. Infantry

Company D, Captain A.B. Cain, 1st Lieutenant Seton

Company F, Captain Gerhard Luhn

9th U.S. Infantry

Company C, Captain Sam Munson, 1st Lieutenant Capron

Company H, Captain A.S. Burt, Lieutenant Robertson

Company G, Captain T.B. Burrowes, 1st Lieutenant Carpenter

Packers, Tom Moore, Chief Packer

"Montana Miners" (65)

Crow and Shoshone Auxiliaries, Captain Randall

Others: 4 surgeons, citizen guides Frank Grouard, Louis Richard and Baptiste "Big Bat" Pourier.

# Sioux-Cheyenne Village—
# Before the Battle of the Rosebud

Northern Cheyennes—100 Lodges
Oglala Sioux—70 Lodges
Blackfoot Sioux—12 Lodges
Brule Sioux—?
Sans Arc—55 Lodges
Miniconjou—55 Lodges
Hunkpapa—154 Lodges
Santee—15 Lodges
Total: 461 Lodges

Estimated lodge counts from John S. Gray, *Centennial Campaign.*
Possibly two warriors per lodge if older boys fought. But youngsters and
older men (among the Cheyennes "retirement" age was roughly 37)
would normally fight only in an emergency or a strictly defensive
situation. Accepting Gray's (unusually low) lodge count, the attacking
Sioux-Cheyenne force of 17 June may thus be put at roughly 750 warriors—or about half of Crook's defending force.

# Battle of the Little Bighorn, 25 June 1876

## *7th U.S. Cavalry*

### Headquarters and HQ Detachment

Lieutenant Colonel (Brevet Major General) George A. Custer
1st Lieutenant (Brevet Lieutenant Colonel) William W. Cooke, adjutant

### Custer Battalion(s)

Company C, Captain (Brevet Colonel) Thomas W. Custer, 2nd Lieutenant Henry M. Harrington
Company E, 1st Lieutenant (Brevet Captain) Algernon E. Smith, 2nd Lieutenant James G. Sturgis
Company F, Captain George W. Yates
Company I, Captain (Brevet Lieutenant Colonel) Myles W. Keogh
Company L, 1st Lieutenant James Calhoun, 2nd Lieutenant John J. Crittenden (20th Infantry)
2nd Lieutenant William Van W. Reily, supernumerary
Dr. G.E. Lord, Assistant Surgeon
Mitch Bouyer, Citizen Guide (and acting Crow interpreter)
Armstrong Reed, Herder
Crow Scouts: Curley, Goes Ahead, White Man Runs Him, Hairy Moccasin

Custer evidently divided his command into two smaller battalions, Captain Keogh probably commanding C and I, Yates with E, F and L. Captain Thomas Custer probably served as aide to his brother, leaving command of Company C to Lieutenant Harrington.

### Reno Battalion

Major (Brevet Colonel) Marcus A. Reno
2nd Lieutenant Benjamin H. Hodgson (Co. B), Adjutant
Company A, Captain Myles Moylan, 1st Lieutenant Charles DeRudio
Company G, 1st Lieutenant Donald McIntosh, 1st Lieutenant George D. Wallace
Company M, Captain Thomas B. French

H.R. Porter, Surgeon
J.M. DeWolf, Acting Surgeon
Indian Scouts, 2nd Lieutenant Charles Varnum (Co. A), 2nd Lt.
Luther R. Hare (Co. K), Sergeant Bobtail Bull
Civilians: George Herendeen, Courier; Fred Gerard, Arikara
Interpreter; Isaiah Dorman, Sioux Interpreter; Charley
Reynolds and Bloody Knife, Guide

## Benteen Battalion
Captain (Brevet Colonel) Frederick W. Benteen
Company D, Captain (Brevet Lieutenant Colonel) Thomas B. Weir,
2nd Lieutenant Winfield S. Edgerly
Company H, Captain F.W. Benteen, 1st Lieutenant Francis M.
Gibson
Company K, 1st Lieutenant Edward S. Godfrey

## Pack Train
Captain Thomas M. McDougall (Co. B), 1st Lieutenant Edward G.
McDougall (Co. M)
Company B, Captain T.M. Mathey
Reinforced by one NCO and six privates from each company, plus
civilian packers.
Boston Custer, Forage Master.

U.S. fatalities numbered 268, including five dying of wounds.

Surviving wounded included 42 soldiers, two officers (Varnum in
both legs, and Benteen, very slightly, in the right thumb), and two Indian
scouts.

# Indian Village —25 June 1876
## (with known Chiefs and War Leaders)

### Northern Cheyennes—120 Lodges
Brave Bear, Charcoal Bear, Comes in Sight, Crazy Head, Dirty
Moccasins (Black Moccasins), Ice Bear, Lame White Man
(White Man Cripple), Last Bull, Little Hawk, Maple Tree, Old
Bear, Old Man Coyote, Two Moon, White Bull (Thin Ice)

### Oglala Sioux—240 Lodges
Big Man, Big Road, Black Twin, Crazy Horse, He Dog

### Combined Blackfoot Sioux, Brule Sioux and Two Kettle—120 Lodges
Blackfoot Leaders: Kill Eagle, Scabby Head (Scabby Face)
Brule Leaders: Crow Dog
Two Kettle Leaders: Runs the Enemy

### Sans Arc Sioux—110 Lodges
Fast Bear, High Elk, Red Bear, Spotted Eagle

### Miniconjous—150 Lodges
Iron Plume (American Horse), Fast Bull, Hump (High Backbone)

### Hunkpapa Sioux—260 Lodges (including 25 of Yanktonnais and Santee Sioux)
Hunkpapa Leaders: Black Moon, Buffalo Calf Pipe, Crow King,
Gall, Knife Chief, Sitting Bull
Santee Leaders: Inkpaduta (Red Point or Red Top)

Estimated lodge counts from Gray's *Centennial Campaign.*

Though it is currently possible to compile 38 Sioux and 18 Cheyenne
battle dead, no such list can be considered comprehensive—not only
because some names might be absent, but because some individuals
bearing two names might unwittingly be listed more than once.

# Index